Walking on Air

TREVOR JONES

Walking on Air

The inspirational story of a true British hero

HEINEMANN : LONDON

Published in the United Kingdom in 1997 by William Heinemann

1 3 5 7 9 10 8 6 4 2

First published in the United Kingdom in 1997 by
William Heinemann
Random House UK Ltd
20 Vauxhall Bridge Road, London, SW1V 2SA

Random House Australia (Pty) Limited
20 Alfred Street, Milsons Point, Sydney,
New South Wales 2061, Australia

Random House New Zealand Limited
18 Poland Road, Glenfield
Auckland 10, New Zealand

Random House South Africa (Pty) Limited
Endulini, 5a Jubilee Road, Parktown 2193, South Africa

Random House UK Limited Reg. No. 954009

A CIP catalogue record for this book is available
from the British Library

Typeset by Deltatype Limited, Birkenhead, Merseyside
in 12 on 14.25 point Baskerville
Printed and bound by Clays Ltd, St Ives plc

ISBN 0434 00279 8

This book is dedicated to my mum

Acknowledgements

'You should write a book' is the sort of compliment friends pay from time to time, it is rather a nice way to flatter one's ego. Knowing that the only time I have willingly lifted a pen, other than for necessary exams, was to write home news from my ship and only then to secure a reply, a book was always going to be an unlikely event in my life. So it remained until friend Jonathan Shalit uttered those words and within a week had introduced me to five professionals all willing to take on the task. So *Walking on Air* was born.

My story is similar to those of thousands who every year damage their spines and one way or another set about the task of rebuilding their lives. I take no credit for this book, but thank the great skill of my writer Jim Parton for telling it and all the fantastic, wonderful and amazing people who have surrounded me all my life, egged me on, set me up and watch me fly or fall.

My accident made me realise how much I loved my brothers; I already knew what a very special mum we had and how Dad inspired me. My experience – our experience has brought us all closer together. I had no idea however how lucky I was – am – with my friends. This book is a tribute to all of them: their every act of kindness, the time spent with me, thinking of me and doing whatever it was for or because of me. They helped me not only to rebuild my life but also to have a great life, a fun life, the life you will read about, and enjoy. For the sake of narrative only a few are mentioned in the book; with any luck those who are not have been saved the embarrassment but they know who they are and I thank them.

Again without mentioning any names I would like to give a special thanks to everyone who put their hands into their pockets, or someone else's pockets, in support both of me and of the Trevor Jones Trust, some in a very big way. Your funds bought wheelchairs and adapted cars, microlights and, in the case of one very special friend, a flat. You helped equip me on the road to greater independence, to build confidence and self-esteem. Gradually more people benefited in a similar way. Today the Trevor Jones Trust no longer exists; from it were born REGAIN and APT (Aviation for Paraplegics and Tetraplegics), two new charities to continue the work. I am grateful and very proud and I thank you.

There is much work still to do. Young men and women will continue to break their necks and have great needs both on an individual basis and as a group. In the nine years since my accident, much progress has been made to integrate disabled people in our society on more equal terms and to reduce prejudice and discrimination. My thanks to all those who have campaigned and continue to campaign, lobby and demonstrate on my/our behalf. The campaign goes on and I hope this book will in some subtle way stimulate debate on the many issues which continue to affect us as a group so deeply.

Special thanks to my solicitor John Cahill at Stewarts for all his hard work and successes for me, both on and off the case. I cannot recommend his services highly enough.

A final word of thanks to my publishers for the hard work of some great people and finally to you, whoever you are, for buying it. I hope you both enjoy it and gain something from it.

Prologue

I was collapsing with fatigue so I asked the hotel proprietor, 'Kann Sie in die bed helfen?'

'Ja, ja, ein Moment, Ich something or other will den Chef something machen.' I was a bit worried he was going to send for another Wiener Schnitzel, but I'd got that wrong. The chef was merely the beefiest man about the place. Together they took me upstairs, dumped me on the bed and put the TV on, which I didn't want (but I couldn't explain) until I saw that it was World Cup footy.

Since I broke my neck I've been a light sleeper, well, except when microlighting, when I get bloody exhausted. I was just about asleep when the footy ended leaving me with the signal tone. At midnight the proprietor came back, but I was worrying about the whereabouts of Emma, my carer.

He turned the telly off and I dozed fitfully until the morning. When I woke to the noise of hoovering in the corridor there was still no sign of Emma and my leg bag was full to bursting. I yelled at the top of my voice 'help', 'Helfen' and 'Achtung', hoping the cleaning Frau would hear me over the noise of her hoover. I was sure she must have heard me but every time I started shouting the hoover would start up again. I was becoming very agitated.

It felt like half an hour at least before she got the proprietor. Still no sign of Emma. I dozed for another hour or so in a mood of helpless frustration, then finally the door opened and Emma came in.

'I told you I'd never find this bloody hotel,' she said and, without pausing, seeing me still fully clothed and clearly uncomfortable on the bed, added, 'Well, I found a good hotel and had a good night's sleep, breakfast and a shower and I'm well rested.'

I thought, You bitch, you absolute cow, but just said, 'Well that's good, do you think you could get me into my wheelchair?'

She said, 'I'm fed up with you, I've had it. You're such a bastard and I don't know how anyone works with you. You're just incredible and I'm going. I'm leaving.'

Care assistant abandons paralysed man in the middle of Germany with only his microlight aircraft for company. She had to be calling my bluff. Perhaps I should immediately have become contrite; I was feeling a mixture of relief and disbelief so I just said, 'Good riddance. On your way out just tell the bloke you're leaving me here.'

She stormed out. I was left on the bed for another hour. At that point I seriously hoped I would never see her again. The relief of tension was huge. But when she came back in with the electric wheelchair and the proprietor, I thought to myself, Thank God for that. At least in the chair I had some independence.

She said, 'We're going to have to have a chat, because you clearly can't fly down to your meeting without me,' which to all intents and purposes appeared true. I held my tongue and said to myself, wait until you're in the chair, then tell her. I was scared she might just leave me.

Then I spoke my mind. 'You're wrong, Emma, I don't need you. It's just that you need me and the only reason you came back is to get your money and I'm not paying you. You can't expect me to pay for you to walk out, then come back when you feel like it. Just go. Get lost, get out of my life.'

And I drove the electric chair past her into the restaurant where I began at long last to have some breakfast. I would have been quivering with rage, except that tetraplegics don't quiver, although we do get extra spasms in moments of stress or tiredness, so my legs were shooting all over the place.

By this time we had exchanged a few more words and she had started crying and was becoming hysterical. Fearful that she might just drive off, I removed the keys from the car and gave them to the bemused proprietor for safe keeping. I was half-way through my boiled egg, wondering how I was going to get anyone to take it out of its shell for me, when she came in, grabbed my wallet and took my credit card out of it.

'If you don't pay me I'm going to keep this.'

'You can bloody well get lost. Give it back, or I'll call the police.' And I carried on eating my breakfast.

She took my address list to the phone booth, eventually got my brother Stuart on the line and persuaded me to speak to him. He tried to calm me down a bit. 'Listen, Trev,' said Stu, 'you can't leave the poor girl in the middle of Germany with nothing.'

Me leave her? It was advice which had its ironies.

It made me more determined that that was precisely what I was going to do, but the main thing holding me back was that she had parked the microlight's trailer in the village and I didn't know where. Once I'd left it safely at the airfield, my plan was to take her to Frankfurt airport, buy her a ticket, pay her and send her packing. If I hadn't needed to get some cash on my credit card I would have put her in a taxi straight away.

'I'm going to put you on a plane and I never want to see or hear from you again,' I said. She just looked at me incredulously.

When we went to get the trailer she refused to get out and hook it up. I lowered my window just in time to catch a passer-by on a bicycle and he did it for me instead. Then once I'd left the trailer at the airfield I drove her the fifty kilometres to Frankfurt airport, bought her a ticket to London and got her some cash. That wasn't easy; I had to drive my chair from one bank to another, queuing at each until one would take Visa. I gave her the money and ticket, and then departed. We hadn't exchanged a single word since leaving the trailer.

By the time I arrived at the airfield there were only three hours to go until sunset. The flight would have taken two hours, but it takes at least an hour to refuel, get me into the aircraft, draw a line on the map and load the wheelchair into the back seat. Unfortunately I got lost on the way back to Egglesbach and wasted a vital half-hour.

So there I was, the world's most paralysed pilot, stuck in the middle of Germany, with nowhere to stay, no one to help me to bed.

One

I was born on 20 March 1960 in former Rhodesia (now Zimbabwe). My father had been sent out by a firm called Ferro to see if there was a market for non-stick saucepans on the Dark Continent and to assess the desirability of building a factory to make them. Electricity and running water for the African villagers were for some undefined date in the future, but it was hoped that non-stick saucepans were for now. For whatever reason – Rhodesia's Unilateral Declaration of Independence came a few years afterwards – the plan was not carried through and we returned to England, with me still a babe in arms.

Mum was, still is, a physiotherapist and mad on sports. After another six years she had produced three more boys and we all lived in a large house in Chalfont St Giles, Buckinghamshire, complete with kidney-shaped swimming pool which Dad and Mum built themselves. Dad had left Ferro and started a wallpaper business with his brother and mother. It began as a shop, and later became a thriving distribution business called Hopson's Wallpapers, with a fleet of lorries and vans which for me, the boss's son, were a little boy's dream.

Mum used to drag us round every sporting activity going. I say 'drag' as if we were reluctant, but we loved it. Every evening we did something different: soccer, swimming, diving, judo, mini rugby, tennis, cricket. Rod, the brother below me (where I like to keep him), is only seventeen months younger, and we were fiercely competitive. There is a two-year gap down to Stuart. Then three years after that there's Angus, all keen sportsmen.

I love nearly all sports but since the very first magical touch on the helm of a big boat when I was about four, my biggest love has been the sea. The boat was my grandfather's classic and revolutionary racing yacht *Kiff*, one of the first great cruiser racers, along with her sister ship *Finisterre*. Yachties will know what I am on about.

Dad too was mad keen on boats – I wonder if that is the real reason why land-locked Rhodesia never got its non-stick saucepan factory. As soon as we were old enough all our weekends and summer holidays revolved around sailing. He'd sail *Kiff* to St Peter Port in Guernsey or Cherbourg while we crossed on the ferry with Mum or the au pair and met him there.

Until the age of eight I went to Russel primary school in Chorleywood, and then Rod and I were despatched, blue-capped and blue-blazered, to a prep school called Gayhurst in Gerrards Cross, a few miles from home. Hopson's Wallpapers went well for a while, but I wasn't really aware of the transition when the company quietly went bust. Somehow my parents managed to keep us at Gayhurst and then my father got a job setting up the UK subsidiary for a German wallpaper manufacturer, Pickart & Siebert.

At first we were day boys, but when Dad's business with the Germans started to take him overseas we began to board during the week and only come home at weekends. Boarding might be unfashionable now but all I can say is that Gayhurst was a very happy school and I loved it.

There was only one teacher whom I hated, Mr Langrish the Latin teacher. He was the second master, a disciplinarian and an active sadist as far as I was concerned. It probably didn't help me that I was useless at Latin and couldn't see the point of it. I was really good at sport but rotten at my lessons, although I hasten to say that I am not thick, even though I failed my eleven-plus. I was usually, but not always at the

6

bottom of the class and could never work out what it was I'd done differently when I came near the top.

My problem was that I threw myself into things I liked – and I mean really threw myself into them – and neglected things I didn't like, such as Latin, or indeed all my school work. I would sit in class because I had to, but my mind was always on the sports field. I even hollowed out my bible to accommodate a radio so that I could listen to the Test Match commentary during class.

We all liked the headmaster, Mr Stafford, enormously. He had a slight smell to him and his hands used to shake a little when he taught. He used to spank us with a cricket bat if we were caught up to no good but we got the feeling that his heart wasn't in it. It was more a pat than a spank, and he never noticed if you'd stuffed your trousers with exercise books, or more accurately, I suspect he chose not to notice. He was a real Mr Chips (the 1930s film was shot at Gayhurst).

Shortly after I left, Mr Stafford left too. I know now that the smell and the shaking were caused by gin. It was very sad. He had been very well respected by the boys, loved even, but when it was discovered he had a drink problem it was felt he had to go. I think his departure was regretted by everyone, boys, parents, the teachers who worked with him.

I loved cricket and would spend hours practising with other boys on the slip catching cradle. I mean hours, until it was too dark for us to see. In the winter, during the fifteen-minute mid-morning breaks between lessons, those of us really keen on football or rugby would change into full kit, play for ten minutes, then change back again. I am sure I was the kind of boy who always had dirty knees and a grubby face. None the less I was shy and it was only sport which gave me any confidence. I got into the rugby XV two years early, and in my final year was made captain, and won the Victor Ludorum prize for best all-round athlete.

In the school holidays it was sailing – we had our own Mirror dinghy – or boating on the Thames in a small motor boat called *Chuggerbug* at nearby Henley. Accustomed to command, I was dictatorial, especially towards my brothers. It was great being the eldest.

Aged ten or so, I joined the Sea Scouts and then when I was about twelve, my father bought a fourteen-foot Merlin Rocket, a beautiful mahogany boat. It had a lot more sail than the Mirror and was far more difficult, and therefore exciting, to manage. She was so speedy you could feel her planing on windy days as she breasted the waves like a porpoise on full throttle.

One of my greatest friends from Gayhurst days featured large in my life after I broke my neck. Marc Koska was an only child.

His mother worked in a casino and she had a partner called Martin who dealt in cars, nice ones too. Marc would be picked up in a Lamborghini one week, a Bentley the next.

It is unthinkable these days, but when we were thirteen or so Marc's mother would dump us off during the summer holidays at their caravan at Stand Lake near Oxford, where Martin kept a powerful speedboat. We'd take it in turns to drive the boat and got pretty good at water-skiing, progressing from mono-ski to bare feet. The only limit on our activity was the amount of petrol Martin left us with. For food we went to the clubhouse and ran up a tab. The water-ski club had a bar as well which in the evenings was left open for members. Pernod was the tipple, for which Marc had developed a taste on an exchange trip to France. Two sub-teenagers drunk in charge of a speedboat.

Rod was the first to take up the other kind of skiing. At the age of nine my parents encouraged him to join the Kandahar Club which coached him every Christmas and Easter and summer holiday. I was twelve when I decided it wouldn't do for my brother to be better than me at anything, so they arranged for me to spend a week over Christmas in the Cairngorms, where I learnt the basics. I never did quite catch Rod up but joined him during the holidays for training; later on, he turned down a place on the British Olympic squad for Lake Placid. He was beating Martin Bell who at that time also trained with us. I'd have killed to have been on that. I was once invited to ski for the Welsh juniors – not quite the same thing – but I never did.

By that Christmas a distinct chill had begun to creep into my parents' relationship, so I was relieved when they said they would join me in Scotland for a few days over the New Year, but it was while we were there that my mother met a gentleman in his mid-thirties called Frank Coleman. In fact I introduced them; I found myself stuck at the bottom of the ski slope with no means of getting home and he lent me a pound, which my mother insisted on returning to my benefactor personally.

In my final year at Gayhurst I developed a first awareness of girls. There was a girls' school nearby, but the only way of getting anywhere near it was to join the choir, which I attempted to do. My voice must have been exceptionally bad; I was the only applicant to be turned down.

This left me with no choice but to get on to the chess team; chess is a game involving the brain, but I was good at it because it also involved competition. We had a match against the girls' school, Maltmans Green. The match itself was a bit of a let-down. I played against a skinny, red-haired, freckled girl who was not at all pretty or good at chess and I beat her quickly, but later there was a dance where I met another girl and fell in love. I was a shy boy and never actually saw her again, but we exchanged letters for at least a couple of weeks.

Academically I was nowhere and had no favourite subject; lessons were a tiresome interlude between games. I seldom listened to teachers, preferring to watch the sparrows on the window-sill while dreaming of being on the sports field.

I don't remember doing any work but having failed the eleven-plus I must have knuckled down a bit because I passed the Common Entrance exam to go to Gordonstoun. Mr

Stafford had recommended Gordonstoun as the ideal school for a boy with a passion for the outdoors and for sport.

Gordonstoun is situated on the southern side of the Moray Firth in spectacular countryside. In the late summer my parents took me for an interview with the headmaster, Mr Kemp, followed by a tour of the buildings and manicured lawns. There was a weed-covered, pike-filled lake, an obstacle course and splendid playing fields. We saw Gordonstoun House, a magnificent old stone building with an eighteenth-century façade masking a much more ancient stone-built castle inside.

Afterwards my parents and I went for a long walk in the surrounding hills and along the banks of the fast-flowing burn. The sheer beauty of the place, the bracing air, the friendliness of all we met and the sense of freedom made me feel instantly at home.

Two

I was keen, not nervous at all, excited and certain I was going to love Gordonstoun. All enthusiasm, I helped the other new students with their heavy trunks into the new boys' house. On one such errand I knocked a chap flying. It turned out to be Prince Andrew who'd joined the school a year before in the footsteps of his brother, Prince Charles, and of his father, the Duke of Edinburgh, who had been one of the first pupils when the charismatic founder of the place, Kurt Hahn, moved from Germany during the Nazi ascendancy before the last war.

After the first term I was put into Bruce House (the one I wanted to be in because the housemaster ran the school rugby side). As a third-former I slept in a ten-man dormitory and shared a study with six, one of whom was Bill Carrington, who, like many Gordonstoun people, has featured large in my life post accident.

He was a bit of a weedy town boy from Kensington who liked his creature comforts. He was a good sportsman – he became Scottish schoolboys squash champion – but he was the type who embraced the outdoor parts of the Gordonstoun ethos with the kind of reluctance that typified, well, Gordonstoun boys. (NB: all old Gordonstonians – apart from William Boyd – will swear with hindsight that it was the most valuable part of their education and that they wouldn't have missed it for the world.)

Bill's Singaporean mother used to get the local delicatessen – a traditional, up-market food wholesaler called Gordon and

MacPhail – to prepare food parcels for him. He would eat the whole lot himself and only share if blackmailed or bribed.

'I'll bet you your Camembert that you can't eat your Philadelphia in one go,' I said one day.

'I can,' he said, and ate the whole slab. He looked quite ill afterwards, but I never got any of the Camembert.

There was a certain arrogance about him; he had a sense of humour that was often sharp at others' expense, but without malice if only you knew it. A similarity with my own personality would be a degree of arrogant self-belief which makes us both highly competitive, but which masks an underlying lack of self-confidence. Given his own mixed-race background he had a surprisingly White-supremacist world view. You take him as he is or you leave him, but he has remained one of my best friends.

A short time before my accident, when I was on leave from the Navy, I caught him when he was quite unfit and beat him at squash for the first and only time.

He often says, 'If I could just give you your body back for half an hour, Trevor, I'd thrash you,' and I get great pleasure from reminding him, 'Bill, you are only as good as your last game.'

My first year was also the first that the school had gone fully coeducational. I certainly meant no harm, but at the end of my first term my parents got a letter from my housemaster, Llewellyn Davies, saying that some of the girls' parents had been complaining that I bullied them and that unless I bucked up my ways I would have to leave.

Blimey. I thought I had been quite good friends with some of these fragile creatures; I hadn't been aware that I had been upsetting them but obviously I had. It would have been all chat, not meant to hurt, but women . . . honestly.

In fact I did become good friends with one of them, a girl in the year above me called Suzie Huntingdon, who took a bit of a shine to me and even led me astray in a thirteen-year-old sort of way, taking me into one of the squash courts, turning the lights off and initiating me in the joys of snogging (no more than that). For a while after that we were inseparable and did a lot of walking around the grounds together holding hands in the darkness (which in the Scottish winter starts at about half three).

I never got on well with Llewellyn Davies. I was much stronger and fitter than my contemporaries. If I got the rugby ball, for example, I could plough through the other players, and I think he may have felt I should be kept in my place. The letter about being mean to the girls really shook me up, made me far less cocky and did have the effect of making me much more considerate to them, indeed to everyone.

Not quite everyone. I do remember that a small gang of us used to torment our form teacher, a lovely and blameless Scottish lady. One day after a mounting campaign of paper pellets and silly things written on the blackboard, she could take it no more and ran out of the classroom in floods of tears.

I still think that Llewellyn Davies exaggerated the evil in me and so I was delighted about a year later when he left, in circumstances that were never fully explained to us.

The outsider's image of Gordonstoun is often of a regime of cold showers and murderously bracing cross-country runs. Not surprisingly, they are two aspects of the education blown up out of proportion and context. Gordonstoun was certainly different from other schools, but in many positive ways which since its birth have had a profound influence on other schools and educators around the world.

One of Kurt Hahn's more obscure, but none the less well founded, ideas was something called the Training Plan under which you were supposed to have done a list of things by the end of each day. This included a short run every morning on waking, and after a hot shower a cold shower, and some proper exercise – which could have been a bracing cross-country run. You also had to say whether you had eaten between meals or brushed your teeth.

At bedtime seniors checked the juniors' lists. As you got

older the list diminished and it also became something you filled in every day yourself. Hahn's idea was that you shouldn't be checked up on all the time. You would gradually develop self-discipline and could be trusted. The development of Trust is a major pillar of the theory. Also the crumbliest bit of it; in practice you never filled in the form until you got wind of the fact that the housemaster wanted to see it.

Much to the disappointment of a lot of former pupils, recent headmasters have abandoned the Training Plan along with many of the other systems.

Trust was, and remains, a big part of Hahn's Development of the Whole Man. Rather than traditional public-school punishments, one of his favourites was to send a miscreant on a long walk to think things over. No one checked up on you, that was part of the trust system.

Hahn's Whole Man had Knowledge, Character and Compassion.

His ideas were revolutionary at the time he started his first school at Salem in Germany in 1918. The school set out not to overemphasise any one part of education, for example academic results, at the expense of physical achievement.

The boys in the new school were undernourished because of the Allied naval blockade of Germany, so a three-week burst of physical training for the annual sports day was abandoned in favour of fifty minutes a day throughout the school year. Thereby Hahn stumbled on one of the big secrets of sports science. What now seems to us a common-sense approach to training was, in its day, radical. A little exercise often is the most effective way of keeping fit. The boys at Salem were not allowed to compete in their training either, only to better their own personal performances. The same theory was applied to study.

Hahn had died some years before I got to Gordonstoun but there were still teachers there who remembered and revered him. One of the things about him that made the biggest impression on us was the stance he took against the Nazis.

When Nazi thugs trampled a Communist to death in front of the man's mother in 1932, he circulated a letter to all Salem old boys condemning the action. He risked his own life to stand up for what he believed in and to warn of the threat to freedom.

Imprisoned for his opposition to Hitler, he was released when Ramsey Macdonald remonstrated on his behalf, and came to live in exile first in England, then in Scotland, founding Gordonstoun in 1934.

The Knowledge bit of Hahn's Whole Man doesn't need defining. I couldn't say that Gordonstoun was overwhelmingly successful with me in this department. Graham Broad, my tutor, had the tough responsibility of fostering my intellect. His final report is a masterpiece of sensitivity:

> Trevor has reached a plateau academically. He did well to achieve eight passes at O-level. He worked hard and deserved his passes. In the last two years he has taken on more and more extra-curricular activities and responsibilities within the school and house which has meant less and less time for his A-levels. No doubt in the future he may move from this plateau to a higher level but a change of environment and motivation are required.

The Character bit is fostered by all the expeditions and activities, and there my teachers rated me more highly. If I had been an academic kind of child they could have got me into Oxford, but as I wasn't they took whatever other qualities I had and helped me develop those. They even made me Guardian (or head boy), somewhat controversially passing over Prince Andrew, who some felt should be given some practice just in case he became king. The new headmaster Michael Mavor wrote:

> Trevor demands and gives everything of himself and this rubs off on to other people. In addition to being firm Trevor is entirely fair, though at times he had to strain a little to see one or two situations from a girl's point of

view. When one considers his appetite and physique this is perhaps understandable. I could not have asked for a better Guardian in my first two terms at Gordonstoun.

The third strand of the Hahnian ethic was Compassion, represented by many local community service projects, everything from visiting local centres and old people's homes to running a fire station with a teacher driving the engine – not just for fun, but actually putting out real fires in Lossiemouth and the surrounding countryside.

The activity I chose was the Surf Life-saving Service where we learnt rescue and resuscitation techniques plus sea canoeing and surfing, going out even when there was snow on the surrounding hills, a sort of Moray Firth version of *Baywatch* (but we had better bodies).

We were called out to perform rescues for real a couple of times, once when a raft fell apart during the Findhorn raft race. We were waiting in our canoes at the bottom of a waterfall. The raft disintegrated; three crew members popped up but the fourth was clearly in some difficulty. We dragged him ashore and noticed a bone sticking out through his leg. Ben Goss, the master in charge, and now one of my best friends, asked me to splint his leg up so that we could carry him, something we'd all practised many times, but never performed 'in anger'.

I was overcome with nerves, but saved when by complete fluke a search-and-rescue helicopter happened to fly over. We waved it down and the man was flown off to hospital in the capable hands of proper paramedics, so I was never fully tested.

And then of course there was sport of every kind. My three main sports were rugby, hockey and cricket and I was also the school tennis champion. A letter to my parents said 'I could write a book on each rugby match alone.' Fear not, dear reader.

Another said, 'I am determined and so is everyone else to

devote everything to our work for exams this summer . . .'
Only a white lie; I am not by nature dishonest.

Every day was packed full of activity, rarely would we go to bed less than exhausted. Apart from sport, the highlights were the cruises on the school yacht *Sea Spirit*, drinking when we should not have been and the expeditions, some serious challenges like climbing Munroes or ice flows, others less so like fishing on the Spey.

Once Jimmy Sutherland, who ran the local garage and taxi firm, dropped us off at Craigellachie with tents and rucksacks. Jimmy did all the school's official ferrying hither and thither and the unofficial stuff too. He treated us like adults and was the slightly irresponsible father we'd all like to have had. On this occasion, however, he was unlikely to have known that our rucksacks contained several bottles of port, wet suits and a thirty-foot drift net.

The plan was for us to run the salmon we caught into Aberdeen market and make a fortune. Fortunately the port got the better of us and we woke up having missed the cover of darkness and had to get back to school. A lucky escape, because if we'd been caught poaching salmon, expulsion, criminal record, we'd have got the lot.

In the holidays before my final term and A-level exams I went to stay in Cambridge with my new girlfriend, Sarah Slight, who had left the year before and was acquiring words per minute at a secretarial college. By now my parents were divorced. Dad lived in America and Mum lived in an isolated cottage in Wales with Frank Coleman, with whom I could find little in common.

So rather than stay with Mum and Frank I stayed with Sarah, my excuse being that I would get more study done for my A-levels. She'd go off to work and I'd go off to the library. Probably I did study more, but it was too little, too late and I failed all my A-levels.

I had one massively formative experience at Cambridge, not an academic one (and not losing my virginity). One weekend George Milford-Haven, who had also left Gordon-stoun the year before, took me up in a Cessna that he had learnt to fly at the Cambridge Flying Club. The thrill was immediate and lasting.

George said, 'You know you really should think about joining the Fleet Air Arm, Trevor, I think you would be very well suited to the life – not only do you learn to fly but you get paid for it.' George had tried but failed the aptitude test but he seemed to think that I'd stand a better chance.

Above all, I value the friendships I made at Gordonstoun and the relationships which will last for ever. The press write dollops of fiction about the place because of the royal connection and the cold showers. There is no denying, of course, that a good royal story will help book sales, so here goes.

It was when I had been made Guardian of Gordonstoun that Prince Andrew invited me to dinner with his mother, the Queen.

Even Andrew called her 'the Queen', never 'Mum'. Apart from being a parent she had come up to Gordonstoun to open the new technology block. Andrew invited me and a girl called Sue Barnard. Sue was a big, tall, self-confident Canadian who had represented Canada in the Olympics at swimming and was a fellow Surf life-saver. I was a little worried about having dinner with Her Majesty, even though she was just the mum of one of my mates and the dinner was not supposed to be that formal.

Prince Andrew had a detective, called Steve Burgess, whom we all knew and liked; in those days the security risk was considerably less than now and he did not need to spend all his time with his shades on scanning the bushes (in a sinister way) for terrorists or paparazzi. Bill Carrington tells how he did once come across Steve scanning bushes in a mysterious sort of way and concluded that Andrew might be in them with someone, Sue Barnard perhaps.

I asked Steve how I would be expected to behave. 'Don't worry,' he said, 'just look at what everyone else does and do the same.'

The evening came and I spruced myself up, even shaved the hairs off my neck for the first time – Steve advised that the Duke of Edinburgh had a thing about it. School uniform was all I had, a blue blazer and grey slacks. The detective was to drive us to the house of Captain Ian and Lady Margaret Tennant where the Queen and the Duke of Edinburgh were staying. Captain Tennant was the Lord Lieutenant of Morayshire.

Try as he might Steve couldn't find the strong, self-confident Canadian swimmer. We searched high and low, but then it began to get a bit late and we had to go without her.

I was shown into the living-room and introduced to the Duke of Edinburgh. He offered to get me a drink and I asked for something sophisticated, a beer. I also noticed lots of pictures of the Queen and the Duke dotted around and I wondered if they had just come out for the visit.

I was struck by how the Duke also referred to his own wife as 'the Queen'. We were made to wait a bit for dinner – apparently the Queen was anxious about the health of one of her horses – but when she made her entrance it was truly regal. She looked, well, she looked like the Queen – a million dollars.

When it came to taking our places at dinner, I was horrified, or rather deeply honoured, to find myself sitting next to Her Majesty. I might have been the Guardian of Gordonstoun, held in some awe by one or two juniors, but sitting next to the Queen of Great Britain and Northern Ireland and various obscure dependent territories like Hong Kong, Bermuda and the Falkland Islands, I was just another gawky teenager.

She sat down; then, as the detective had advised, I copied everyone else and did so too. The first thing the Queen did took me a little by surprise. She opened a small handbag and started fishing around inside. Of course many would like to know what the Queen keeps inside her handbag – a crumpled handkerchief? Some 'coral pink blush' lipstick by Estée Lauder? Compact, mirror, mini-cab number, an M & S debit card? A bit of loose change along with the odd feminine accessory of the kind which would make an eighteen-year-old boy blush?

She held the bag open on her lap and I tried not to look until, finding my eyes drawn, I was unable not to. I saw this massive jewel come out, half the size, say, of a squash ball, the largest jewel I'd ever seen outside the Crown Jewels.

She took it out of the handbag and put it on the table next to her (as one does, if one has a large jewel in one's handbag at dinner time). Naturally this object excited my curiosity, but I wasn't going to say anything daft like 'That's a nice jewel, what's it for?' or 'Where did you get it?' I just assumed it must be some symbol of state which comes on to the table at supper time.

But the jewel had a purpose; it had a hook on it on to which was to be hung the royal handbag, that is, would have been hung had it not fallen on the floor.

Instinct took over; I was at the zenith of an expensive Gordonstoun education; A-levels I wasn't going to manage, but good manners I had a-plenty. Before I'd had time to think about it, I found myself down on the floor under the table, scrabbling around at the Queen's ankles, trying to find where the wretched thing had rolled. I found it and appeared, bauble first, in some triumph, saying nothing, slightly dishevelled, with every eye around the table boring into me. I wondered if I had done the right thing.

The dinner proceeded smoothly. I made a policy decision to sit there and say nothing. Only once did I open my mouth and I immediately wished I hadn't. A pause in the conversation arose which I tried to fill. 'Oh do tell us more about your trip to Saudi Arabia,' I said. What a prat.

For dessert the butler came round with fruit. The Queen chose a banana and so did I. After everyone had chosen their fruit he came around with a plate of tools. The Queen chose a device the like of which I'd never seen before. I watched her use it to peel her banana. I had had no idea that a special implement existed for peeling bananas.

As it was the only one, I sat there looking at my plate wondering what to do. Then I noticed Captain Tennant – and I'm sure he did it for my benefit – pick up his banana and eat it with his hands. He was a perfect host and I shall never forget how he tried to involve everyone in the conversation and put the awkward teenager at his ease.

When the dinner came to an end Steve Burgess, the detective, drove me back. I did wonder what had become of Sue and the next morning at breakfast I sought her out to discover why she had made no appearance, what it was that had resulted in this lapse in protocol. 'Where were you, why didn't you come, the chance of a lifetime, what were you up to?'

She said she had been so terrified at the thought of dinner with the Queen that she had gone for a long reflective Hahnian walk and hidden in the woods.

Three

My final summer term ended and I eased gently out towards, but not exactly into, the real world.

I went off on a hockey tour to Canada with a team called the Dragons and from there travelled to see Dad in Marblehead, Massachusetts from where I was to help him sail his boat *Quest*, a 41-foot ketch, down to Bermuda for the winter. There was one other male crew member called David and a Gordonstoun friend of mine called Mona Leonard.

The voyage passed reasonably uneventfully until we reached warmer tropical climes and were caught in a storm system in the Gulf Stream. In fact it was a hurricane, with 100-mph winds, the seas dumping themselves on deck. After a while we were exhausted and decided to hove to and ride out the storm. Leaving just a stroboscopic light on the top of the mast so that passing ships wouldn't run us down, we battened down the hatches and went below where we stayed for twenty-four hours. The noise was horrendous, David spent the time quietly throwing up and Mona spent it in tears.

When the storm abated we went down below and slept solidly for another twelve hours. Our sails had been ripped, the boom taken out of its track and much of what had been stowed on deck washed overboard.

We repaired as best we could but it was only about a day before we hit another severe weather system.

The effects of this were more serious. We lost our engine when water got into the fuel system, and hence our generator and electric power. Our sails were ripped again. Dad had bought the latest in electronic position-finding equipment, a Loran 'C', but without any power it was useless. Without any sun, so was a sextant.

We sailed past Bermuda without noticing it. Meanwhile, food supplies were running short and then Mona left the fresh-water tap running after brushing her teeth, so we were without water.

My test of a good woman, one I might want to marry is: Would she be any good on a boat? Mona would probably have failed the test at that time (although she had done fantastic work sewing the sails back together).

Using the emergency battery we managed to contact Bermuda by radio, and they gave us a bearing to steer down.

By this time we were no longer under threat from the enormity of the seas or the wind, which had died down, but we were all tired, hungry, thirsty, and near the end of our tether. I had a barney with Dad about the navigation which was supposed to have been my job. 'You can bloody well navigate now, Dad,' I said and stormed out on to the deck.

We were trying to get through a reef towards St George's Harbour in the middle of the night. Dad dropped down into the cabin and stood on the parallel ruler whilst trying to get orientated on the chart. I sulked on deck until he emerged looking genuinely upset and threw the ruler overboard, when I pulled myself together. We threaded through the reef with waves crashing around us. The lasting memory I have is that while David, Mona and I went through various stages of fear, panic or delusion, Dad remained calm and reassuring throughout.

By the time we came upon St George's Harbour the wind had dropped considerably and was alternately calm or blowing in squalls. St George's is a difficult harbour approached between two high crags and as we got between them we suddenly found ourselves utterly becalmed, with no motor, drifting towards the rocks. We were too tired to panic, but just as we were about to hit them we were rescued by a gust of wind. We cleared the lee of the rocks and made for a jetty to tie up against.

We did not see the sign on it which said 'DANGER', and sailed alongside. It was two in the morning, and there were people on the jetty to whom we shouted to take a line, not realising there was nowhere to secure the boat. They were all half-cut and clearly on their way back from the pub. Fortunately they hung on to the line we'd thrown them. There was a nasty moment when the the halyard became knotted so we couldn't lower the sails.

Simultaneously we were hit by another squall which threatened to take us out to sea again trailing the half-dozen drunkards behind us on a rope in the water. If they'd been sober they would have let go. That certainly was a nasty moment. I succeeded in hacking through the rope, the sails fell to deck and the boat was made secure, but not before a little damage had been sustained.

After so much misfortune it was then that our luck turned. One of the men was a restaurant owner, and he opened his shop for us. That first beer was to die for (we very nearly had).

Like father like son, my father perhaps hoped. I'd passed the good-on-a-boat test going down to Bermuda. Dad is an entrepreneur, and until the day he dies he will be starting and running new businesses. Later that year, when we had sailed *Quest* down to St Thomas's in the British Virgin Islands, the thought of this yacht lying idle made him think that he should be getting the thing chartered out – after all, the going rate was something like $2,000 a week. I'd finished a temporary job as a bus-boy in a Florida hotel and had nothing better to do, so he left me on the boat with $1,000 to see if the yachtsman in me wouldn't be matched by the entrepreneur.

He flew back to Marblehead, Mass., leaving me, an eighteen-year-old boy, in charge of a beautiful 41-foot ketch with eight berths and of proven seaworthiness, to drum up charter business.

First I needed to get her up to scratch after her long voyage from Marblehead via Bermuda and the storm, which involved a large amount of sanding and varnishing. I worked hard until she looked beautiful again, but once that was finished I got bored, and got into the habit of sailing the boat round the coast and anchoring it next to the airfield to watch light aircraft landing and taking off. In the back of my mind was that experience in George Milford-Haven's Cessna.

I'd swim over to the beach by the airfield holding my shoes and shirt over my head. If I'd gone in the dinghy it might have got nicked. After a while I met the owner of the flying school, an absolutely delightful Trinidadian man, as charming as only Trinidadians can be. Before long he'd offered me this can't-say-no deal to learn how to fly. Once I'd explained my business and financial constraints – namely that I only had $1,000 given to me by Dad to start the charter business – he offered this fantastic deal for twelve hours of instruction for the especially cheap price of $1,000.

I'd turn up at the airfield each day, then I'd wait. My instructor, a tall Black man with a heavy West Indian accent and bloodshot eyes, was always late, usually by several hours. He had the same excuse every time: 'Me so sorry, me met this lovely lady last night . . .'

Then we'd take off and he'd throw the Cessna around the sky, doing dummy landings over beaches, buzzing yachts. It was fun but he barely let me get my hands near the controls; mostly I sat there effectively paying for him to have a jolly time.

Sometimes I'd turn up and there would be no aircraft for me to fly in. 'Forgot to tell you,' the Trinidadian said, 'that one crashed into the sea yesterday,' or 'The usual Cessna ran out of fuel and is stuck down South,' or 'That one we had the other day has gone off to the States.' A fat load of flying I learnt. But the man was very nice and he had my $1,000, a situation about which he was charm itself. I never did get any money back.

I had a few charters but the business never really took off. I should have been out chatting up wealthy-looking tourists in the smarter hotels, but I just wasn't brass-necked enough.

I got a bit bored sitting on the boat waiting for clients to approach me and say 'Have you a boat for charter?' which of course they never did, so one day I telephoned Sarah Slight and persuaded her to come out and join me. She chucked in the secretarial job she'd got in Cambridge and soon I found myself, aged nineteen, with a nice boat, a nice girl and loads of sun.

It should have been a kind of paradise but I had little money and felt no direction. In retrospect it was one of the most difficult times of my life; I was quite self-conscious about being this young kid with a nice yacht and not really justifying my existence.

I was not good company for Sarah either. I remember once it was a choice of spending our last five dollars on food or a chart. We bought a chicken. Sarah was roasting it while I rowed across to another yacht to borrow an ingredient. They offered me a drink, I forgot the purpose of my errand and stayed the whole evening there while Sarah slaved over a hot stove minus the ingredient and with no one to feed it to.

One day I got a cable from Dad saying that he was going to be marrying his girlfriend Polly in Bermuda; could I get the boat back across there and come to the wedding?

The invitation came at a good time. I needed something to do. He also cabled me another $1,000 to pay for some repairs. As crew I would have Sarah and an American friend called William Crugar who was to fly out with a friend. Sarah and I went to the airport to pick them up, but Bill was alone. His friend had gone missing at their graduation party, which was a bit of a crisis; I needed a fourth crew member.

Worse, I discovered that the new $1,000 had fallen out of my pocket, not frittered this time on flying lessons. I'd had this bundle of folded notes in my pocket and it had simply fallen out. I hadn't even been pickpocketed.

We searched all night for it without success. When we finally returned to the boat she had dragged her anchor, her stern had smashed against the wall and needed making good. Hatches were open and tropical rain had flooded the cabin and engine.

Fortunately the boat was just about seaworthy, but to make the wedding we really needed to leave that day and with a crew of four.

After I'd drawn a complete blank asking around English Harbour, my washer-lady spotted me looking disconsolate on the jetty, the weight of the world on my shoulders. I explained what was wrong.

'Don't worry, skip,' she said in that lovely, lilting West Indian way. Within half an hour she returned with a youth about my age complete with a small bundle of belongings. Her son.

We set sail within the hour. To start with Bill was horribly sick but he soon settled in. Sarah is good on a boat.

My washer-woman's son had never been to sea before. He smoked dope the whole way (except when he was asleep from having smoked too much) – his 'wee pleasure' he called it. He steered a good course but was not that keen on doing anything else, like cook or clean or any of the other jobs needed to keep a boat going. Not that hard work was my forte either, except on a playing field, or in a squash court or on a boat.

We sailed hard, it was touch and go as to whether or not we would get to the wedding on time. We reached Bermuda the evening before the ceremony.

Dad had hired a tuxedo for me but he had not thought about shoes. Eventually the cook at the yacht-club found some leather ones in a sail locker, which were green with mould and slightly too small.

Polly had not been keen that Sarah come to the wedding. She was not family. I thought this showed a lack of generosity of spirit, but it wasn't the moment to stand up to my future stepmother. Or perhaps I should have. We'd sailed bloody miles to be there and without her it would not have been possible. I also hadn't realised that Sarah was quite important to me. By the time the shoes were polished up I was late for the wedding and Dad and Poll were already standing by the altar, and had been waiting for me. Poll was convinced I was boycotting it.

A long-standing dream of mine had been to sail the Atlantic so when I was offered a passage as crew I couldn't say no. Especially as the boat was a Swan 45, in my view the world's most beautiful production boat and possibly the fastest. On it were to be the skipper, three girls and me.

I left Bermuda without a thought for Sarah or for my father. I had succeeded in making the wedding, but my father found himself in Bermuda on his second honeymoon in circumstances less than ideal.

To his care I'd abandoned one mightily disgruntled girlfriend nursing not one but two grudges: firstly, being rather rudely left out of the wedding (I should have insisted); secondly, being abandoned by her boyfriend while he jaunted across the Atlantic with three birds.

Dad also had care of a smashed-up yacht with a sick engine, almost a thousand miles from where he would have liked it to be. In addition he had responsibility for a West Indian boy, who had set off from Antigua with a bundle containing all his worldly belongings. In the lad's head was the idea that he had escaped a life of poverty on Antigua and was going to find his fortune and a good position in the rich man's playground, Bermuda.

I had simply left the whole caboodle behind me. What it is to be young, fit, spoilt and irresponsible. Breathtakingly bad behaviour, looking back on it. Dad wanted to give me opportunities and responsibilities he'd never had, but somehow I wasn't up to them. I'd felt out of my depth failing to charter the yacht and wanted to achieve something for myself. The passage on the Swan was the perfect escape.

The crossing itself was amazing; at one point we had the spinnaker up for five solid days and nights without taking it down as we swept via the Azores passage. They were two exhilarating weeks; the wind was a constant force six, sometimes seven, the seas huge. The sensation of power has stayed with me always. One of my fondest memories was of wrestling with the helm at night with the spinnaker lit up as we surfed down huge rollers, listening to 'This is the Moody Blues' at full volume on the cockpit sound system.

We eventually pitched up in Palma Majorca, our destination. From there I found another yacht which took me to Corfu.

The month was August, the height of the European summer, so having nourished a desire for travel I took my kitbag and got the ferry across to Italy. There, Dad (bless him) had cabled some more money to help me on my way on the standard school-leaver's adventure across Europe. I was absolutely skint and while I was waiting for the money to be cabled over I had to sleep rough.

I'd been warned that Naples was a dangerous place for tourists but I wanted to find out why and if it was true. A personality trait of mine is that I've never really been good at listening to sensible advice. I arrived at the station late and asked for directions to a camp-site, somehow getting lost and finding myself in the middle of the docks.

I spoke not a word of Italian but eventually found myself being guided by a kindly but extremely drunk stevedore. He took me off between piles of containers, over fences, through clanging metal gates to what I thought was going to be a camp-site.

We would have to pause every so often, because the guy was so drunk that from time to time he'd fall over. Eventually we came into a lorry park and he gestured me into the back of one.

I thought I was going to be abducted and have my ear sent

to my father with a ransom demand at the very least, but he mimed sleep, then left me.

Once my money arrived I did all the usual things – Pompeii, Rome and Florence – eking out my limited cash (Dad hadn't entrusted me with $1,000 this time) by having a roll for breakfast, fruit for lunch, a bowl of pasta in the evening, sleeping rough to save money wherever I went. I was joined by my brother Rod who had just left Gordonstoun and together we made our way up through Yugoslavia, Hungary, Germany and Austria back to the UK.

Four

Back home in Wales I went to the local Royal Navy recruiting office, more or less the day I arrived. My love of the sea had been confirmed by the trip across the Atlantic, and of flying by the $1,000 squandered on my Trinidadian instructor's joy-riding.

The recruiting officer gave me forms to fill in and send off to Admiralty House. He asked me if I had any friends flying in the Navy.

'Two,' I replied.

'If you really think the Navy is for you, then get one of them to show you around,' he advised.

I rang up HMS *Culdrose*, and asked for – who else – a student pilot called Sub Lieutenant HRH The Prince Andrew who invited me down for a couple of days. The weather was awful and there was virtually no flying going on, but Andrew's instructor, Phil Shaw, offered to take me up in the Gazelle helicopter. He said, 'I can usually tell within minutes whether someone has the makings for a pilot.'

There were two defining moments for me. The first was when the aircraft broke through cloud into brilliant sunlight; the second when we were nearer the ground and the instructor demonstrated to me how to hover, then handed me the controls. For a moment the Gazelle held in the hover, then it began to drift backwards, then gently to spin. It was impossible to hold steady. But there had been a second when I thought I'd had control and I was hooked.

Back on the ground I was anxious to find out what the

instructor had discovered about my potential for further training but he was non-committal. 'You might have the ability,' was all he would say.

During the evening in the bar Andrew introduced me to the Big Wheels on the Station and all the people on the training course with him. By the end of the two days any doubts I may have had were gone. My heart was set on becoming a Navy pilot.

At the Admiralty interview board at HMS *Salton* I discovered I had forgotten my socks and had to borrow some off the Chief Petty Officer in charge. Later I was asked the standard question about whether I had any friends in the Navy, but was too embarrassed to mention HRH, so just said, 'Yes, I managed to spend a bit of time at *Culdrose* with one.'

After six months at Britannia Royal Naval College, Dartmouth, those recruits aiming for the Fleet Air Arm were sent for flying grading at Roborough near Plymouth in the old Chipmunk trainer.

This took place under the supervision of some very experienced pilots, men now in their sixties retired from the Navy or Air Force proper. They assess a recruit's potential for further flying training. Many fail this stage.

My first flight was in the company of a tremendous old character by the name of Greenhow. He took me up in the Chipmunk, giving me a running commentary about the role of the Navy pilot. Once up, he started throwing it around the sky in the most stomach-churning aerobatics, all the time keeping up this lecture.

'You will be part of an élite,' he said as the aircraft turned upside down, 'trained to fly to the very limits, to your own and those of your aircraft' – we were now screaming towards the ground in a spin – 'and if you ever once step beyond those limits' – my mouth was in my stomach, or the other way round – 'you're dead, and worse than that you will have wasted valuable property' – as we levelled out (briefly).

After twelve hours I was sent solo. I don't know why my instructor, Mr Pugh, singled me out for this – only two or three others went solo at flying grading. Maybe it was a psychological trick to try and boost my confidence; I had been having difficulty keeping the aircraft straight after landing.

We did just two or three circuits together when he unexpectedly climbed out. 'One circuit, Trevor please, on your own.'

Without his weight the plane leapt into the air quicker than I had expected and climbed. I did my circuit and then came in for a relatively smooth landing. When I applied the brakes the Chipmunk suddenly started weaving. If I corrected one way the plane ended up turning too much and so I'd have to correct the other.

The plane thundered off the runway and careered towards some old Portakabins where everyone was congregated watching. There were fuel pumps there too, and in as much as I had time to think of anything, I realised disaster was impending. Still weaving from side to side, I finally came to rest feet, if not inches, away from the pumps. I sat there in my straps, shaking, and thinking about how my flying career had just shot off the runway.

My instructor, who was a bit lame, came hobbling out, pulled back the canopy and just said those immortal words for any pilot, 'Any landing you can walk away from is a good landing. Don't worry about it . . .'

At the end of the fortnight came the decision as to whether we had passed or failed. I sat in the corridor with the others. It was like waiting for a baby to be born (I imagine). Quite a few came out of the little room having failed. And then there was just me. I had to wait the longest of anyone, there was clearly quite a debate going on. I was called in and told I'd passed. I was also told that it had been a very close-run thing.

The next phase was eleven weeks at RAF Leeming in Yorkshire learning how to fly a Bulldog, a trainer more powerful but easier to fly than a Chipmunk. My instructor was energetic and inspirational, a naval officer called Andy Barnwell, only five or six years older than me.

He looked after me and seemed determined that I would pass.

Each flight was assessed, each sortie written up. On my first night sortie Andy said to me, 'Don't ever tell anyone what you are about to see,' and put the Bulldog through an eight-point roll around the full moon, an illegal manoeuvre, but beautifully executed. Aerobatics were not allowed at night, for fear that the pilot would become disorientated, crash and burn.

There was a lot to study and I compensated for a past marked by a lack of academic discipline by working harder than anyone. Many of the other participants on the course were graduates or out of the world of work, accustomed to graft. I was one of the youngest. It was a struggle and I had to work especially hard to stay off the bottom of the class.

I was the only one without a car so I put in the hours when the others were off jaunting.

My own jaunts were at weekends when I hitch-hiked down the A1 to Dishforth to go gliding. It was a club affair sponsored by the RAF, the idea being that everyone helped everyone else and the flying was strictly by rotation. At that stage an extra ten minutes in the air was worth a lot to me.

I enjoyed the aerobatics best, but we also covered all aspects of elementary flying training: circuits, stalling and spinning, navigation, formation and instrument flying.

On a land away to RAF Leuchars, when we were half-way across the Firth of Forth, I noticed that the oil gauge pressure was reading zero. An instructor called Chris Slade had the controls at the time, as I took out my flight reference cards ponderously to read the actions to be taken. Chris had already taken them. This was no practice. First he'd throttled right back on the engine and checked the circuit breakers, then he had picked a landing site and issued a Mayday call to Edinburgh.

Fortunately we were high enough to glide to East Fortuneswell, an abandoned airfield where he made a perfect landing.

From RAF Leeming we progressed to RNAS *Culdrose* in Cornwall to learn to fly helicopters. It was a relief to be back amongst one's own kind. The trouble with RAF stations is that they are full of RAF (or Crabs as we call them). There is a fundamental difference between the type that joins the RAF and the Fleet Air Arm, summed up by the phrase 'boring Crabs'.

We were learning on Gazelles. The Gazelle is a French machine with a single engine. For a military helicopter it is small and manoeuvrable, you could call it a sports helicopter.

It is beautifully engineered, with a powerful gas turbine engine that drives the rotors through gearboxes, and has an impressive safety record. My dream car was, and remains, a Jaguar XJS, but give me a Gazelle any day.

From the airmanship point of view the job was the same as on the Bulldog, the same use of the runway except we hovered along it rather than rolled. There were the same airspace regulations, the same radio calls so the course concentrated on the handling of the aircraft.

When someone repeatedly struggled with some aspect of the course they would get either an Air Warning or a Ground Warning. I never got a warning, although I continually felt under threat of failure – I think we all did. Three warnings and you 'met Sooty'. Our CO, Trevor Lockwood, would never tell pilots they were chopped. He put on his glove puppet, Sooty, who would tell them. We had lost several student pilots on the Bulldog course but our Gazelle course was almost unique in that no one got chopped.

Initially, flying a helicopter requires a lot of co-ordination. On a fixed-wing aircraft you essentially have two flying controls: a joystick and rudder pedals. As a straight comparison a helicopter is more difficult, certainly to begin with. For a start you have three flying controls, not two.

There is the 'cyclic', a joystick between the legs which

controls pitch and roll by tipping the main rotor blades forward, backwards or to one side.

At your feet there are the 'yaw pedals' which control the amount of power to the tail rotor, which counteracts the natural tendency for a helicopter to spin because of the torque of the main blades.

Then there is the 'collective', positioned to one side of you like the handbrake on a car; this controls the pitch of the rotor blades. You increase the pitch of the blades so that air is forced over the top and bottom at different speeds (the same principle as a wing), giving lift.

It sounds easy; pull on the collective and the pitch on the blades increases giving you more lift, and up you go. The trouble is that steeper blades resist the air more, so the engine struggles; a governor senses this and gives it more power. When that happens the tendency to spin is increased with the extra torque and you have to compensate for that with the yaw pedals.

Also, there is a tendency for one side to drop, which you have to compensate for with the cyclic.

Understand all that? If not, imagine what it is like learning to fly one.

In my spare time, as ever, I threw myself into my sport. I'd given up serious rugby (too risky for a student helicopter pilot) and concentrated on hockey. Pretty soon I had the honour of being selected to play for the Navy, which I did for a whole season, travelling up from Cornwall to London sometimes twice a week. We played sides like Oxford University and the British Police.

The really big match, though, was against the Army during the Inter-services Championship at Aldershot. I ran out as left back and five minutes into the game limped off the pitch having done my knee in.

I'd damaged a cartilage and it was a hospital job, just about my first trip to hospital since being born. I was absolutely terrified, fearing that I would never play sport again, and life would not be worth living.

The op was done at RNH Stonehouse in Plymouth. After a couple of days in a wheelchair, I started to hobble around and learn how to walk again and was out in less than a week.

I was told that the rest was up to me. In a letter to my mum I wrote, 'Since I've been up and met a few of the patients who are permanently crippled and terminally diseased, it's made me see how insignificant my own grumbles are.'

When it came to my first Gazelle solo I was far more confident than I had been when I had careered off the runway in the Chipmunk. I was apprehensive and excited, but once I had lifted off, done my circuit and returned the aircraft safely to the spot, I had a great sense of achievement.

At the end of the course came our wings parade. We were now qualified pilots; there was still scope for failure on conversion to operational aircraft, in my case the Sea King; others went off to fly small ship's helicopters, the Lynx or Wasp; some the Wessex in support of the Royal Marines; and one to fly the Sea Harrier, but whatever happened we had our wings.

Wearing that badge made me feel very proud. There was an admiral flown down from the MoD to present them, a marine band, parents, wives, girlfriends. I had no girlfriend at the time – Sarah Slight had sensibly given me the boot – but my brothers came, and it was the first time I'd seen my parents together since they divorced.

The Sea King is very different from the Gazelle. It is large and powerful, designed to operate in all weathers. The flying controls are no different from those on a Gazelle, but much of our time was spent flying on instruments. Part of the role of a Sea King is to dunk a sonar buoy to search for enemy submarines, so there was a lot of coming down to the hover at forty feet over the sea.

Unlike on the Gazelle there is a type of autopilot which,

when engaged (usually at night), can take you from forward flight into the hover automatically. The pilot's job is to monitor it, keeping an eye on his instruments, especially during the descent.

To start with the workload on you is high with so many different things to pay attention to. On one occasion during a night dunking sortie my instructor pulled a circuit breaker to simulate an emergency, which I should have picked up on my instruments, but completely missed. Suddenly he yelled, 'I've got control.' When an instructor unexpectedly says 'I've got control' you know you have just ballsed up in a major way. He said, 'You've just killed us both.' We immediately flew back to base.

I was shaken and upset by the experience. I'd been caught out in a second of inattention and it instantly made me a better pilot. It was the most profound moment of my learning career.

After the Sea King conversion at 706 I took time out to do a mountain leadership course in Norway, then was posted to 810 Squadron for operational flying training, at which point the whole previous eighteen months' work came into perspective.

We teamed up with the observers, whom since Dartmouth had been off on their own separate training, and were introduced to the aircrewmen who also had completed their specialist training. Together we became a crew.

Flying in the Navy is, in the jargon, a 'whole ship evolution'. In plain English this means that everyone on the entire ship is involved. For example, on HMS *Argonaut* where I flew the Lynx a few years later there are ten people involved on the flight deck. The captain has his team on the bridge, doors and hatches are closed. The radio room and the ops room are manned, the engineers, stokers and tankies are all involved too. Then there are weapons specialists, look-outs, the met officer, the medics, the firemen. Even the cook and stewards are involved as they may have to feed the aircrew at a different time from everyone else.

You are the centre of attention. The flight deck crew like to judge the skill of a pilot by how close he gets to finding the centre hole in the grid with his harpoon to secure the aircraft when he lands. Strictly for poseurs only (i.e. me).

Between July 1982 and 24 January 1984 the Plaintiff was based at RNAS *Culdrose* where he received basic training in Gazelle helicopters, advanced training in Sea King helicopters and operational flying training. He earned his flying badge on 25 May 1983 and promotion to Sub-Lieutenant on 1 November 1983.

After our operational training it was back to *Culdrose* to await posting to an operational squadron. I applied for 820 Squadron because they were about to set off on deployment to Australia, but instead I was sent to 826 which was on Falkland Islands protection duties, which sounded less appealing.

The posting was to be a two-and-a-half-year one and over that period I did three tours. The Squadron was divided into three flights of five helicopters, with one flight always on station in the South Atlantic, another in transit or on leave and the third at *Culdrose*. Each flight consisted of fifteen pilots, seven observers, and about a hundred maintainers.

Following the stress of training, to be doing a job at last was exhilarating yet I was not quite off the hook; I still needed to win the confidence of colleagues and seniors and to be awarded my Certificate of Confidence. I continued to have the feeling that I was being assessed (I was) and that until then I would always be the junior pilot on the aircraft, never in command of it.

The trip down from Ascension to the Falklands on SS *Uganda*, taking ten days accompanied by flying fish and sunshine, was a scream. We only had to abandon our shorts a day and a half before arrival. Mornings we took quite seriously and gave one another lectures on various need-to-know professional subjects. I hate lecturing; talking for forty-five minutes on hydraulic systems is not something anyone would volunteer to do.

The afternoons were dedicated to sport and lying in, on and around the pool. As our flight was a major entity, providing 120 of the 500 personnel on the boat, we were asked to organise the ship's routine. Naturally, for sports, everyone turned to me. I made it compulsory for everyone, much to the distaste of some of the more elderly and plump officers and senior rates.

They played football, hockey, deck quoits, table tennis. We had kite-flying competitions and, after I had the pool filled, *jeux sans frontières*.

The SS *Uganda* was a glorious old ship with soft leather chairs, delicate wood panelling, brass chandeliers, beautiful murals. She took you right back to the last days of Empire. There was even a pair of elephant's tusks in the smoking-room. She was the last of her kind – a luxury liner requisitioned by the Navy as a troop-ship – and the tragedy was that she was destined for the scrap-yard. Unfortunately she was so old at the seams that she might have taken matters into her own hands and sunk pre-emptively, but the real reason was that they were opening a runway down to the Falklands, which meant that in future we would fly in and out on Crab DC–10s. Pity.

Five

The Falkland Islands were far more beautiful than I had expected. Granted, I was seeing them from the air and the warmth of a cockpit, from where you could get the whole landscape. The light was amazing, constantly changing; every time you looked it had changed to a different shade or colour. The weather totally dominated the place. One hour the landscape might be covered in snow, the next it would all be gone. The temperature remained as a sort of mild cold, not that different from winter in Britain.

It was easily as bleak as Dartmoor, similar in places to remote parts of Scotland. There were vast open expanses of flatland, hills, rocky crags, steep cliffs and sandy beaches, even a couple of largish rivers, stocked full with trout and salmon. But it struck me that since the war those I had spoken to, and the press, had highlighted the hardness and loneliness of the place and completely omitted to mention its beauty.

Port Stanley was something of a shanty town with a slow, even lazy, pace of life which reminded me to some extent of the places I had visited in the Caribbean on Dad's boat *Quest*.

It was just a couple of years after the war and British forces were still there in a big way. The Army, Navy and RAF had camps on the islands including a few large radar stations and rapier missile batteries. The RAF had Phantoms, Harriers and Herculeses at the old Port Stanley airport, and Chinook and Sea King helicopters based elsewhere.

The Navy had a frigate, a destroyer and sometimes a sub. The Royal Fleet Auxiliary (RFA) had an oiler, a stores support ship and RFA *Diligence*, the repair ship, plus a few ships taken up from trade.

The bases were formed almost entirely of Portakabins, hundreds if not thousands. Dining cabins, wash cabins, latrine cabins, multi-gym cabins, video cabins; it was amazing what could be achieved with a Portakabin and the facilities were excellent. It was also evident that we could move everything out as quickly as we had brought it in, and almost without leaving a trace.

My first trip into Stanley was on a beautifully clear, cloudless day, with the sun slanting low and everything I saw was worth a picture. I shot off a whole film, some of the best shots I've ever taken. The tragedy was that the film didn't wind on, for which I was roundly mocked in the ship's magazine *Buzz*: 'Anyone requiring photos of the sunset at Port Stanley contact Sub-Lieutenant (Scoop) Jones of the Flight.'

I enjoyed the flying on this, my first job. At least the trips had some purpose beyond pure training. Most of the tasking was surface search, so the trips were quite long. More than likely a four-hour surface search spent logging fishing boats. We'd often come to an end only to be hit with another job, like picking up passengers for the fleet from Port Stanley or distributing mail.

The islands are sparsely inhabited (apart from sheep), so the obvious opportunity presented itself for some very low flying. Strictly speaking we were not supposed to fly below five hundred feet without clearance. On the other hand it was not as if anyone was going to report us, least of all the recently liberated and thus grateful inhabitants, or the sheep or the penguins.

On my very first flight we followed the course of the San Carlos river, not once rising above the banks – unnerving at first but it made us into much better pilots and there were no accidents. In a conflict you'd be expected to fly like that and yet there is little opportunity to practise in Britain, where noise-abatement rules are getting stricter and stricter.

Somehow I seemed to have become identified with leisure so, as on SS *Uganda*, I was given the role of organising recreation for the flight and ship's company, being made sports and expeditions officer and secretary to the welfare fund.

I led many adventure-training expeditions including taking a team of sailors on a sixty-mile walk from San Carlos to Port Stanley – the original yomp. We complied with military regulations more or less and had a fascinating trip, the last day especially, going through minefields and the debris of war.

These remains were virtually the only evidence of human activity apart from the odd fence, sheep, cow or goose. More aircraft flew over than birds, a constant reminder of why we were there.

I am also very proud of having led the first-ever descent by canoe of the San Carlos river. I was never happier than when under my own power in a remote place and there are few places more remote than the San Carlos river, in the middle of the Falkland Islands.

I had three four-month tours of the Falklands during my two-and-a-half year stint with 826 Squadron. One notable event occurred towards the end of my second tour, when I was involved with what was then the longest distance helicopter rescue ever. A new Task Force was on its way down to the South Atlantic to replace us; there was a frigate, a destroyer and an oiler and they ran into a big storm. A freak wave hit the oiler, causing severe damage and even washing an Exocet missile overboard. An Exocet is a bloody big missile, which implies a bloody enormous wave.

A group of men were detailed to go forward and inspect the damage when another rogue wave knocked them flying across the fo'c's'le. One man was killed and three severely injured. Their lives being in danger it was decided to cas-evac them to the Falklands.

Our flight was tasked with this and our oiler, RFA *Olna*, was immediately sent north to act as a staging post. I was second pilot to Mark Walker. Jerry Awenat and Kev Weller were in the back as observer and aircrewman respectively. We took off, caught *Olna* up and spent the night on board so that by morning we were within range to take off again and meet the ship as she steamed south towards us.

I wish I could report that we flew grittily into the teeth of a fierce South Atlantic gale, fighting for our own survival, but the main characteristic of the trip was that it was bloody long and very sore-bum inducing and the weather was fine.

We arrived on the ship where the accident had happened, refuelled, picked up the two stretcher cases, one walking wounded and two doctors and headed back.

As I say, the flight was only slightly more than routine. If we had had to put down for any reason we would have been quite lonely but the real drama was occurring in the back of the helicopter.

'I hope this man doesn't do what I think he is going to do,' said the doctor, about half an hour into the flight.

'You mean he's only hanging on in there?'

'Let's just say I'm not confident.'

Fortunately he survived as far as Port Stanley where he made a full recovery . . . as did my bum.

In another of the interludes from the Falklands, in August 1985, I made the first operational deck landing on the new HMS *Ark Royal*. We embarked with two aircraft and three crews to help work up the ship for her initial trials off Portland.

She was brand spanking new, and beautifully constructed, probably the Navy's most prestigious (and expensive) ship. However, the crew were very green, unsure and a bit jumpy. Because of this, and with the number of senior officers around there was a fair amount of tension on board; not for the first time I felt glad to be aircrew, avoiding the not inconsiderable amount of flak being dished out. In true naval tradition the blame got passed down the chain of command, an attitude we didn't share on our flight.

The time was of particular significance to me as it was the

first chance I'd had to fly regularly as captain of the aircraft and first pilot and was learning a lot from the added responsibility. It was a very busy time, what with the ship's work-up programme, flying twice a day and again at night. I was only getting the regulation eight hours of sleep a night – most of what I got during the day was extra. (Navy pilots are embarked to sleep, eat and fly and are good at it.)

While alongside in Portland I invited Prince Andrew, based at the air station, on board for dinner. Unknown to me the ship had a major bomb exercise planned. Not everyone was on duty and about for hundred crew members were on shore. When the alarm went I decided the best thing to do was to hot-leg it off the ship and cancel the dinner, but on my way to the gangway I was arrested.

I said, 'Hang on a moment, I'm just waiting for Prince Andrew.'

With a story like that they immediately assumed I was the bloke in their exercise delegated to plant the bomb and so I was led straight into custody. I protested in vain.

'Likely story, Sir.'

It wasn't until Geoff, the bodyguard, turned up in the middle of the bomb-alert mayhem asking for 'Sub-Lieutenant Jones' that they finally believed me and let me go. Shortly afterwards the exercise ended, and it was just amazing how many senior officers suddenly popped out of hidden recesses of the ship wanting to join us for dinner.

Prince Andrew invited me to be an usher at his wedding to Sarah Ferguson, an honour which must be put in perspective. I was one of quite a number (this was not a small wedding), all of them naval officers but still, I was given one of the best spots by the Great West Door (the front door) of Westminster Abbey, the one through which the bride and top guests were to come, and at which the world's press would be directing their cameras. I was with my CO at 826 Squadron, Keith Dudley, Phil Shaw (Andrew's instructor, the one who first took me up in a Gazelle) and a captain. I was the most junior officer there by far.

It was the first time I had had to wear a sword since Dartmouth. The prescribed Navy way of handling your sword is to throw it in front of you and catch it as you walk into your stride. If you were standing you were supposed to place it on the ground. I spent the first ten minutes falling over it until I saw the captain just carrying his, so I copied him.

My main job was to look out for the Speaker of the House of Commons, Bernard Weatherill, and show him to his seat, but I had no idea what he looked like. The captain, more versed in current affairs than I, said he'd look out for him on my behalf.

Gordonstoun friends began to arrive. George Milford-Haven, complete with beautiful girlfriend, I hadn't seen since he took me up for that formative flight in a Cessna. We had a bit of a reunion in the middle of the porch, forgetting the queue of guests waiting to be shown to their seats.

While we were talking, Mr Weatherill arrived and was past me before I had had my chance to perform the one big duty assigned me. I gave chase but the Speaker knew exactly where his seat was and had no need to be shown to it by a whipper-snapper of a young officer trying to make polite conversation, and he dismissed me. This dismissal was compounded when I was given a discrete bollocking for inattentiveness to my duty by the crusty old gentleman from the Queen's Honour Guard who seemed to be in charge.

During the service I was stuck behind a pillar and couldn't see the action – I watched it on telly like the rest of the British public. Or not quite. I was seated immediately behind Elton John.

I spent the time spotting famous faces and nodding greetings to old school friends. I saw Fergie walk past with her dad, then come back with Prince Andrew, and that was about it.

Most of all, though, I remember thinking how surreal the

whole occasion was. I mean here was a bloke who used to sit at the back of the English class, coming down the Mall in an open carriage, being waved at by half a million people, then getting married in front of a television audience of several hundred million.

Weird.

After my last Falklands tour I took my leave period on board HMS *Endurance* on a work patrol in the Antarctic. I had no real duties and was free to roam the ship, watch, listen and learn. I spent a lot of time on the bridge but most of the time I was with the flight.

I shall never forget the first landfall, or rather snow fall. A vast white expanse grew out of the cold sea, and as we approached it turned into vertical mountains, white-capped and crawling with glaciers, the ends of which extended into the sea in great ice cliffs. As if called to create an appropriate atmosphere, humpback whales broke the surface near the ship and schools of penguins leapt past like tiny dolphins.

Endurance carried two Wasp helicopters. I shared a cabin with Pete Griffiths, one of my greatest friends; the observer; and Guy Solleveld, one of the two pilots and someone who has since become a great friend.

I did a lot of flying on the Wasp as a sort of acting aircrewman, helping with their work surveying uncharted waters, flying hydrographers hither and thither, setting up trig points. You'd be put ashore with a drill, a stick of dynamite and some cement to make a permanent site for the trig point. Shooing the penguins away was a problem; they were utterly unafraid of us or our dynamite.

I have a great photo of Peter posing with a penguin on his lap. Although friendly, it shat big time all over his flying suit. This was nothing like the conventional bird dropping for good luck. These particular faeces were fish-derived and very smelly.

We saw just one rare Emperor penguin. The captain was so

pleased he stopped the ship and the whole ship's company watched this three- or four-foot-tall creature for a couple of hours strutting around an iceberg. He is probably the most photographed penguin in the Antarctic. Albatrosses, on the other hand, were an overrated spectacle, like large seagulls.

The wilderness landscape was constantly changing. Sometimes there was a howling gale, at others it was completely still. There were small rocky islands, big mountains, ice shelves, narrow passes and the light was never the same from one moment to the next. You would never believe how many colours ice can have.

Icebergs would come and go, all shapes and sizes, from little growlers barely above the surface, to huge ones many times bigger than the ship. One had a huge arching hole; the ship's boat was launched for the men to get some good photos and Pete and Guy flew the helicopter through it. Once the ship became stuck as the whole sea froze all around us.

Then there were the whales. You understand and feel sympathy for their vulnerability when you visit the old whaling stations in places like South Georgia. They are like time capsules, unchanged from when they were abandoned twenty or thirty years ago. Old books and unopened cans of meat and vegetables sit where they were left, and everywhere about lie piles of whale bones.

When I wasn't either flying or required by the navigation officer my time was my own, so I threw myself into accounts of Scott and Shackleton (his ship, lost when crushed by the ice, was called *Endurance*) in the wardroom library, every twenty minutes or so leaping to my feet to look out of a porthole for fear of missing what we were passing.

In addition to the longest ever rescue I can claim another record of sorts. We flew further south than any Navy helicopter had before. It was on our way back from this that a drama almost occurred; the Wasp tipped on to its side and Pete fell on top of me, disconnecting my helmet. When I reconnected, we were descending and Guy was putting out a

Mayday. 'Mayday, Mayday, engine failure, ten miles south-east landing.'

I hurriedly checked my harness as we autorotated down towards a flat bit of iceberg. Then, just as we neared it, the helicopter regained power and we pulled away. Guy and Pete roared with laughter. They'd been having me on, disconnecting the radio so that I was the only one who heard the Mayday call. Arseholes.

Once my Falklands tours ended I applied for a course to convert from Sea Kings to the Lynx. I'd developed a been-there-done-that feeling about Sea Kings, the work had become a bit routine. I needed new challenges and it had always been my ambition to fly the Lynx, like the one in the recruitment brochure I'd stared at every night before joining.

The Lynx is a small ship's helicopter, belonging to a frigate or destroyer, usually with just one pilot and one observer. You become much more a part of a ship's company than when part of a Sea King squadron. I felt I would learn more about warships and the seaman's Navy, perhaps even learn to drive one.

For the final part of the Lynx conversion course we set sail on RFA *Engadine* for ten days and nights of intensive flying training, stopping for a break at Gibraltar. I was over the side and on to the quay with my squash racquet before the first rope was hooked up to a bollard.

Having been thrashed by the Navy squash captain, our course officer and great friend Bill Johnson, I was soon back on board and dressed up for an RPC (Request the Pleasure of your Company) at which a normal amount of drinking took place. By 11 p.m. we were ashore again to check out the night-life.

We settled at the bar of an establishment called Penelope's and got in a first round of drinks. The manager came across and said to one of us wearing jeans, 'You'll have to leave, we don't allow jeans in here.'

Our drinks had arrived and we'd paid an entry fee so I said, 'Why let us pay to come in just to chuck us out again?' We decided to stay until we had finished our drinks.

The guy then said, 'If you don't leave, I will call the police.'

We took no notice, but before we knew it three policemen had arrived. I was just saying to one of them 'This is all a bit off isn't it . . .' when another jumped me from behind and pinned me to the ground.

Naturally I resisted this. They were physically small and when I stood up they spun around the room. I anchored myself to the beer pump with both hands, while they rained blows on me with their torches and fists.

Eventually I was overpowered and dragged off through the kitchen yelling 'Police brutality'. Unfortunately no one from Amnesty International was there that evening. Behind the closed door of the kitchen I was dropped painfully on the floor and clubbed some more. As I fell I grabbed at a jacket and could feel the guy's uniform ripping pleasingly. There was a worryingly long kitchen knife and a cleaver available for my quick despatch but fortunately they only handcuffed me painfully behind my back, stood me up and marched me out.

I was hurled head first into the back of a van and left on the floor. With my hands bound behind me there was not much I could do but enjoy the company of a large pile of heavy chain which slewed around the place with me as we careered off, sirens blaring. One of the policemen drove while the other sat watching me slide around the floor with the chain, all the time insulting me, spitting at me and hitting me around the head – always above the hairline.

The only way to fight back was to laugh at him and it worked very well. He became incensed.

At the police station I was strip-searched, and the handcuffs were taken off my wrists, which were bleeding from the pressure. Then my clothes were given back to me, shoes minus shoelaces.

I was taken down to the cells, which I hope are not a

testimony to standards in all British colonies. Mine was positively mediaeval: dark, damp, with a pool of urine in the middle and mould and shit all down the walls. As the bed was soiled I decided that there was no way I would sleep on it, so I stood and leaned against the wall. I was feeling groggy, though, and soon gave in, falling asleep on the bed.

It took until about three-thirty before the military police came to pay bail and get me out. Back on ship the doctor examined me.

The terms of my bail were that I should appear in court at 1400 hrs Monday afternoon to be charged. The problem with this was that the ship was due to leave at 0800 hrs. Ships in the Royal Navy wait for nobody, ever.

I spent the rest of the weekend shitting bricks about this. I would miss the rest of the Lynx course and have to wait six months for the next one, marking time in a non-progressive job. That is if the Navy took an understanding attitude to my story and didn't cashier me.

The ship duly departed, leaving me forlornly in the custody of the naval provost, my career in tatters. He got me a barrister at the magistrate's court and I was charged with assault on two police officers and failing to leave licensed premises. The barrister successfully got me freed on bail until a trial some time in the future.

I was rushed to the airfield where I was told that either the ship's flight would pick me up, or I'd be placed on the next flight home to the UK, depending on my luck.

The waiting was tense, I can tell you, as I saw my entire Navy career disappear in a brawl in a second-rate bar in Gibraltar. Then I heard the distinctive sound of a Lynx approaching and, recognising our aircraft, could have wept with relief. Our ship was by now well out into the Atlantic so the Lynx had been equipped with long-range fuel tanks, the first and only time I saw such tanks installed in all my time in the Navy. A lot of people had gone to a lot of trouble to get me back.

The helicopter had been given the radio call sign 'Jailbird one'. When we landed on Engadine the flight deck was apparently deserted. I walked to the hangar and suddenly the door opened and the entire flight was there, all chanting 'Jailbird, jailbird, jailbird'. I felt as if I'd just walked on to a film set.

I finished the Lynx conversion course and was posted to HMS *Argonaut*. At the end of my joining interview with the captain of the ship, Commander Tim Barton, I was asked, 'Have you any questions or is there anything you want to tell me, Trevor?'

I had to explain rather sheepishly that I was on bail for a criminal assault charge in Gibraltar; I thought this might not go down too well but he took the news with far more understanding than I could have expected.

Much later – well after my accident – I discovered that Captain Woodard, the Captain of Portland, had been asked to appear before a very angry admiral to explain how one of his officers had been charged with assault in Gibraltar. He wanted my head on a plate, an example made; there'd been a run of incidents, something must be done.

One of the great things about Captain Woodard is his sense of humour, another that he too had once been arrested on a run ashore, so he said, 'That's fine, but I have already punished Sub-Lieutenant Jones,' which was not strictly true. In the Navy the principle is that you cannot be punished twice, which is as it should be. All through my Navy career I was very lucky with the captains I served under.

Just before being posted on to the Lynx course at Portland I had done something I had always dreamt of. I took out a mortgage, sold the beautiful Merlin dinghy for £2,000 and my car and lashed out £25,000 on a yacht called *Yoldia*. I'd tried to put together a syndicate to buy it but had failed. Some of the money was in the form of a loan from Simon Kemp with whom I had learnt to fly.

As the only two midshipmen we had stuck together so much that we often competed to avoid bottom place in our ground school exams.

Yoldia was a Chance 37, a cruiser racer designed by Brittan Chance, built in France by Henri Wauquier in 1972 of fibreglass with a fin keel, skeg rudder and beautiful teak cabin.

A further act of good will by Captain Woodard had been to help me get a mooring. This was a major kindness; the only way to get a mooring at the sailing centre at Weymouth is to hope that someone dies or his boat sinks (or both).

About an hour after my joining interview with him I got a call from Wilf Westlake, Master at Arms at the sailing centre and a man I'd had no luck with before. He was offering me the mooring used by the captain's barge. The next day the chief diver rang saying, 'I understand you want a mooring put down, sir.' Before I knew it, all was arranged.

I lived on *Yoldia* and would come ashore using my old Mirror dinghy. At first I had no oars and used to borrow someone's from the sailing club, my theory being that I got them back so early their owner would never miss them. I was wrong. The someone took the trouble to row out and nick them back when I was asleep, with the result that I missed my first shareholders' meeting. This is the regular morning meeting at which the briefings for the day's activities take place. In the Navy, just as a ship never waits for late-comers, you are *never* late for a shareholder's meeting.

Fortunately Splot (the senior pilot) was so amused by my story that he let me off. I became known as the chap who missed his first shareholders' because he lost his rowlocks.

Happy times. Very soon afterwards I met the captain's daughter Melissa Woodard, and indeed his wife. A tradition at Portland was a summer party on the dummy deck half a mile off shore on which we practised landings. A rule was that you had to get there under your own steam, by swimming, wind-surfer, dinghy, canoe or, in my case, yacht.

After the party Mrs Woodard made it clear that she and her daughter wanted to catch a ride back on my yacht rather than with the captain on his barge. I was flattered, honoured, puzzled. Protocol insisted that the captain's wife should go on the captain's barge, but she was absolutely insistent that she and Melissa come with me, a decision doubtless influenced by the fact that the punch had been rather strong.

I was out of it. I remember putting up the mainsail to return to my mooring, then waking up at my mooring, wondering how my boat could possibly have got there without me in command.

Melissa, Mrs Woodard and assorted drunken people started to disembark and head off to the wardroom for dinner. I stayed back with the drunken idea of cleaning the boat up a bit. I doubt I achieved much beyond rearranging the untidiness before rowing for shore in the Mirror dinghy.

Melissa's mum had said she'd send the captain's car back for me. Half-way to the wardroom in the car I began to feel very unwell. There was no time to say 'Stop the car', so I opened the door as we swept through the dockyard and chundered all over the road without the car stopping.

I never made it to the party; after half an hour hugging the porcelain in the wardroom heads, I went back. Instead of rowing out to *Yoldia* I decided to put the Mirror's sails up but got in such a muddle I capsized. The sight of the oars going off in one direction and my naval cap in the other sobered me up sufficiently to focus my mind and get to the boat.

The next day I met the captain's secretary at his office. He said to me conspiratorially, 'You at the dummy deck party last night? This funny thing happened. I was finishing my rounds in the dockyard when I saw the captain's car, came to attention and saluted. Just as it got to me a head appeared out of the open door and was sick on the road.'

'What a funny story,' I said. 'How very odd. The captain must have eaten something off.'

HMS *Argonaut* was a towed array Leander class frigate. I was to operate as part of a ten-man flight, led by a flight commander, in this instance the observer, with a ground crew consisting of a team of maintenance ratings, with specialisations in mechanics, weapons and electrics and radio.

On 24 January 1984 the Plaintiff joined 826 Squadron as a pilot and attended the Lynx Conversion Course at Portsmouth between May and December 1986. He was promoted to Lieutenant on 16 July 1986, ahead of the due date of 1 October 1986, embarking with HMS *Argonaut* as a Lynx Flight pilot.

While I was a pilot aboard HMS *Argonaut* we did a port call to a Swedish town called Gavle.

I had actually been banned from shore visits by the first lieutenant, Andy Underwood, for missing procedure Alpha (when the ship's company stands to attention as you come into port). This hadn't worked because I was sports officer, so an exception was made for sports events – and I had arranged a fixture of some kind every day and most evenings too. On the only fixtureless day the captain, Tim Barton, invited me to play golf, thereby (unwittingly) undermining the authority of his first lieutenant.

Andy became more determined to see me punished and insisted I climb into full mess kit for dinner which pissed me off so much that I informed him I would sit in my cabin rather than eat. He made it clear that if I dressed up he might relent. So I did and then he said, 'You can go ashore now, Trevor.' Prat.

As was the custom on all port visits, the captain hosted a cocktail party on board for a guest list of local people. A chap introduced himself as Anders Schlyter and said, 'I hear that you are the helicopter pilot.'

'Yes.'

'I've got a helicopter at home which I've never flown. Can you show me how to fly it?'

I hedged. 'Well, they aren't all exactly the same you know; it might not be all that easy. I'm not sure that I could, or even that I'd be allowed, or that it would be safe.'

'I am sure you could manage it; why don't you come out for dinner anyway?'

A couple of nights later I took a taxi to his address, expecting it to be a big house in the country with a hangar, and was surprised when we pulled up in a quiet suburban cul-de-sac.

After a drink Anders disappeared, emerging a few moments later proudly carrying a four-foot model helicopter.

'I have the instructions, but they are in Japanese, perhaps you can work out what to do.' He explained he'd been given it as a leaving present from his last job.

We got the engine running. Holding it at arm's length with the blades whizzing past his nose, he lay on his stomach and positioned it on the ground. Meanwhile I fiddled with the radio-control knobs trying to work out which corresponded with the collective and the yaw pedals on a real helicopter.

I managed to stall it the first couple of times. When we got it going the third time I flipped a switch I'd not tried before.

The thing went ballistic and flew out of the guy's hands towards his face. Within seconds his white T-shirt was bright red. His wife and children were watching as he hit the ground, blood spurting, pumping from his wounds like the special effects in a Schwarzenegger movie.

He looked at me, and in the same tone of voice he'd used when he'd asked 'Can you fly my helicopter?' said, 'Can you drive my car?'

I drove him to the hospital, luckily only five minutes away. The nurses and a doctor took my man away saying, 'We are going to operate immediately . . .'

I had never felt so low. It felt like I'd killed him.

The next day I visited him in hospital and although badly injured he was not in danger. His thumb and half his fingers had been cut off. The fingers had been sewn back on, but nothing could be done for the thumb.

My Swedish friend was cheerful and philosophical about the whole thing. 'Boys play games and boys get hurt,' he said. They are words that have stayed with me.

About six months later I got a postcard in slightly spidery handwriting saying that he had made a pretty good recovery, and that he still bore me no ill will. 'The only thing,' the card said, 'that I need help with, is to put my cuff-links on.'

Boys play games, boys get injured, or in some circumstances very nearly die. On the way back from another trip from up north to Pembroke Dock we were airborne on a brief engine-check test flight following some maintenance. We were also to pop across and have a look at the Soviet spy trawler that was always somewhere off Malin Head in Northern Ireland. You could tell it was a spy ship because of all the discs and domes. There were certainly no fishing nets and the only rod-like objects were self-evidently aerials.

In the aircraft were the observer, my flight commander Neville Gaunt and Jack, our controller. We had briefed the captain, still Tim Barton, at 7.00 a.m. At the end of this he'd made an amusing throw-away remark at which we'd all laughed (because he was the captain). 'Make sure you've got your rescue strop. I saw on breakfast TV that Branson's balloon is coming this way.' Ha, ha. We always carried a rescue strop anyway, but didn't for a moment expect to see the balloon.

As we got on with our tests a message was radioed across: 'We have a large balloon visual five miles north, believed to be Richard Branson's. The skipper wants you to carry out a photo run – return to mother.'

We landed, and the deck crew plugged in communications with the ops room so we could chat. 'Yeah, apparently father wants you to get me some pictures for his kids, his camera is on the way up now.'

The captain wasn't the only one with this idea. Within moments I had three cameras hanging round my neck, and Neville and Jack were festooned with them too.

We took off for the balloon. When we got visual with it we attempted to establish comms, trying every likely frequency. It was odd but we couldn't get through on any. Odd but not extraordinary, so we took lots of pics for the ship's company and thought no more.

Before long the balloon disappeared into cloud. We were a bit bemused but assumed that Branson must have decided to go up to seek better winds or something. Anyway, we'd done our multiple photo run and went back to doing the maintenance checks we'd been on earlier.

Twenty minutes later we heard 'Balloon visual again', so we set off to look. This time it did look as though something was wrong. The balloon was descending rapidly towards the sea and looked out of control.

She was surrounded by half a dozen aircraft: a Sea King, a press helicopter, one with family, one with the support crew and two other light aeroplanes. They were all buzzing around trying to avoid each other. I decided that the best place to be was tucked in as close as possible to the balloon, so I moved in, watching it as it came down.

When it was twenty to thirty feet from the sea, this familiar bearded figure emerged and tumbled through the sky into the water. It was quite strange to think 'That's Richard Branson', just as if you were caught in a traffic jam and his car was next to yours.

Chat from all the aircraft filled two or three frequencies; information was being relayed via the ship. It was chaos and I think we were the only people to have seen what happened. No one knew that Richard and his pilot Per Lindstrom had already landed once in Northern Ireland, hitting a tree, a hedge and some power lines, and that the balloon was now in serious trouble.

We called the Sea King. 'Rescue One, would you like us to pick him up?' There was no reply through the jumble of radio chat. We did not wait long; the water looked cold, so seconds later and despite being without a winchman we were hovering over him.

Later we learned that 'Rescue One' didn't even have a rescue winch fitted, and that a second Sea King was on its way from HMS *Gannet* at Prestwick.

I turned the radio off – it was too distracting – so I could concentrate on Neville's con. He lowered the strop on the winch wire to the bearded figure below. Richard couldn't get the hang of how to put on the strop, first just hanging on to it, then putting his head in it and finally trying to sit on it like a swing. When Neville started to raise him he'd begin to topple.

Branson was clearly well out of it, cold and frightened, and didn't seem to understand Neville's sign language at all. We would get him a bit out of the water, then have to lower him again for fear that he would fall off. Eventually caution was thrown to the winds and we brought him up sitting precariously in the strop.

Afterwards, whenever he gave a press interview he'd complain how, instead of rescuing him, the Navy had tried to drown him. Most ungracious, but for reasons which will become apparent later in this narrative, I'm glad we pulled him out.

When we got him in the back of the aircraft, spluttering and shivering and gibbering, he really was in a bad way. He was trying to tell Neville something but couldn't make himself understood, not least because of the noise. Neville said to me, 'Apparently there were two more of them or something. Dunno what he's on about. Not completely with it.'

I said I hadn't seen anyone else. We'd been very close for some minutes. Only when we got Branson on to the deck of *Argonaut* and away from the noise of the helicopter did it become apparent what had happened. Per Lindstrom had jumped out some time before him and was somewhere in the Irish Sea.

We called the Sea King. 'Rescue One, Branson has been safely recovered to *Argonaut*, he has just told us his pilot jumped from the ballon about half an hour before him, and is still in the water. We are available for search and await your instructions.'

After a while the Sea King observer said, 'Execute search.' He gave us a datum based on where the balloon had come down. We immediately thought this was a stupid place to look because in the time since Lindstrand had jumped – it might have been ten, twenty, thirty minutes before – the balloon would have drifted some distance.

Richard Branson himself was unable to give us many clues; he was in such a state that nothing he said made much sense.

Neville Gaunt reasoned that the place where Per Lindstrom had jumped was more likely to be somewhere near the spot where we'd first seen the balloon climb into the clouds; the abrupt reduction in weight might explain why this happened.

He worked out from the record of his plot where that would have been, came up with his own datum and then radioed the Sea King to tell them they'd be better off doing a search based on his datum. They ignored him and went off to do their own search, while we ignored them as Neville directed me on to his datum.

The plan was to do a standard expanding-square search at fifty knots airspeed, flying a timed run on each leg of a gradually expanding square, with Jack and I looking out of the right window, Neville the left.

There was, frankly, little hope. We were looking for one tiny man in a huge sea. He could be anywhere. A few weeks before we had had an exercise in which we'd practised flying search techniques in the Channel using an orange day-glo dinghy. In one and a half hours we hadn't found it. One small human body, already in the water for up to an hour, fat chance.

We arrived at the start of Neville's search datum and were only seconds into the first leg when I spotted this little pink body swimming towards Ireland in his underpants. It was the most amazing moment, the most incredible bit of luck. The Sea Kings Rescue One and Rescue Two were five or ten miles away and would never have found him, indeed the chances of our finding him were minuscule. Per owes his life, no question, to the skill, intelligence and intuition of my observer and flight commander Neville Gaunt.

Unfortunately we couldn't pick him up because our winch wire had got snarled up on its drum rescuing Branson, so we circled over the pink figure still swimming below in his underpants, hoping he'd be reassured that his troubles were nearly over. We sent for a Sea King but a speedboat had seen us circling and come across to investigate. Per was picked up and taken into Port Rush on the nearby Northern Irish coast.

We returned to HMS *Argonaut*, refuelled and flew to RAF Machrehanish where Branson's ground-support team had been waiting. Richard himself, meanwhile, had had a hot bath in the captain's cabin and departed on another helicopter.

He'd asked Tim Barton to do what he could to salvage the balloon. Naval manuals don't prescribe a procedure for recovering transatlantic balloons, so Tim decided that the first step should be to drive the bow of his ship into the billowing balloon and because of some failed explosive bolts wait for us to pick up Lindstrom's support team before trying to bring the capsule on board. The exercise would be an example of what naval jargon calls a 'seamanship evolution'.

The experts disembarked from our helicopter, which was put away in the hangar. Our job was over. That was when the fun started.

Neville and I had no role to play beyond watching. Andy Underwood, the first lieutenant, was in charge of the operation. There was something about the situation which suggested it was all going to go wrong. 'Just watch this,

Neville,' I said. I was still nursing a grudge against Andy for banning me from shore in Sweden.

The first thing he had to achieve was to cut the capsule free from the balloon. A scramble net had been lowered down the side of the ship for the sailors to work from, and to protect the paintwork. As they worked, the contents of the capsule began to float out – Virgin jackets, a video camera used for the documentary of the trip. Each time something interesting appeared a sailor would stop what he was doing and grab for it.

The capsule was a big object. Full of water, it posed many problems. Andy was the type who would think up a plan and when that didn't work try another, then another and so on. It had to be said there were those around him who knew a lot more about seamanship-type things. On every ship there is a senior rate called the buffer whose specialisation is in fact – seamanship.

Neville and I looked at one another, saying, 'Why doesn't he ask the buffer?'

It was not until Andy had tried and failed with all his ideas that he turned for advice. Still things didn't go right. Every time Andy started to brief his men with a plan something else interesting would float out. The sailors would immediately stop work and concentrate on rescuing it.

He had finally got them all back to work when a whole lot of $100 bills started to float past the ship. Branson had packed some cash, presumably to bribe the natives if he came down somewhere hostile. More sailors instantly swarmed down the scramble netting. Then one of them fell in, so another guy tried to rescue him. Then he fell in too, so all the attention shifted towards rescuing the two sailors.

As a passive onlooker, I found it agonising to watch. Partly from laughter and partly because with all those men and all that sophisticated military equipment, we were dying to suggest something.

It was night before all the excitement had ended and the

balloon and capsule were safely aboard, but by then its contents had been absolutely ransacked. Every removable item had been stashed in some locker somewhere in our ship. They are now doubtless on mantelpieces all around the country. The balloon was not in the best of nick either, patches having been snipped off, and once we got into Pembroke Dock the next day a big trade in souvenirs developed.

Branson and Lindstrom were very lucky indeed to be alive. When they'd first landed in Northern Ireland, Per had fired the explosive bolts to separate balloon from capsule. It had not worked. In this attempted landing they had lost all electrics. The balloon was too large and uncontrollable to land attached to the capsule, so Per had decided to ditch just off the beach and jump into the water, only he missed the beach by several miles and by the time it was Richard's turn the balloon was a hundred feet up again and climbing.

This must have been the moment we lost the balloon in the clouds. He must have been terrified that the semi-disconnected capsule would fall off and he'd plunge to an untimely death. Apparently he first thought of parachuting, then that he was going to die; he had written a farewell note to his wife Joan and their kids.

A fact not mentioned in Richard's accounts of the event is that the balloon fabric was designed to catch the sun's rays and heat up the air inside, thereby saving on gas. If it had broken through the clouds he'd have shot off towards the stratosphere and then only God knows where he'd have come down. Somewhere in Russia where he would have needed his $100 bills.

A couple of weeks later Per and Richard were invited to dinner on board *Argonaut*. Per came but Richard cancelled at the last moment. A shame because I had really looked forward to meeting him properly. That wasn't to happen until much later.

Six

For Christmas 1987 I went home on leave to Mum and Frank's in Wales. Rod, Angus and Stuart were there and a good time was had by all. I hadn't been home all that much over the last few years, never for more than a few days. Once, *en route* to a fighter evasion exercise in South Wales, I put the Lynx down in the garden with a box of chocolates for Mum on her birthday ('. . . all because the lady loves Black Magic . . .') but I couldn't stay for more than a few minutes.

On Boxing Day I was inveigled into a very muddy but enjoyable game of rugby against the local side, Llandeilo. I'd recently started playing for the ship having given it up during flying training after breaking my arm at Dartmouth and concentrated on hockey instead. In the New Year I was to go skiing in Austria. Naval and other commitments had meant that despite my Kandahar training I hadn't been available for the Navy team since I joined six years earlier. This trip included a week's race training, the Navy Championships and, if selected (I reckoned I had a good chance), a chance to represent the Navy in the Combined Services Ski Championships.

I was fully packed and ready for departure towards the Alps when my mother said, 'Trevor you haven't looked at the stable conversion yet.' Mum and Frank had a derelict farmyard half a mile away at a place called The Maerdy where they had converted some of the stables into holiday cottages.

Dutiful son that I am, I got her to show me around. She was

especially proud of the latest conversion. It had been beautifully done and was designed to be fully accessible by wheelchair, with ramps where there had been steps, a large shower room, wide doors and lots of turning space.

The first week's skiing with the Navy squad had to take place on a glacier because of lack of snow further down. A Scottish trainer from Aviemore called Alasdair McGann had been hired to put us through our paces. He was a bit disorganised and I didn't rate him very highly. My brother Rod had been offered the job, but couldn't make it (I think he was retaking some accountancy exams) but he'd have been so much better. One advantage of Rod not being there was that he had lent me his racing skis, albeit well-worn ones from his time on the British junior team.

The day before the championships were due to kick off, things were looking good; probably I wouldn't beat Nick Brewer, but then there was a chance. Nick Brewer and I had last skied together ten years before with the Kandahar. It was he who persuaded the management to call me up.

I'd more or less got the feel of skis on my feet again when we moved to a place called St Johann near Kitzbühel, the championship venue.

Very often at the beginning of the season there is not enough snow but I'd never seen anything like this, the slopes were bare for long patches, worse even than the Cairngorms – known for the worst skiing in the world.

The decision was taken to drive to the nearest resort with snow, a place called Passthurn. What snow there was was icy hard, so getting the slalom poles in was no easy matter, it took a special battery-powered hand drill.

It was the afternoon, about three-thirty, the light was diminishing and there was time for one last run down the giant slalom course before the championship the next day.

I started off well. My skis carved and scraped over the icy snow with some precision as I fought my way down, it felt like my best run of the day. I flashed past the trainer who was watching me from the top of a rise and positioned myself high for the next gate.

What I saw next I simply could not believe; a mixture of rage and frustration instantly filled my veins; there in my path were two skiers just standing, watching me thunder towards them.

'What the effing hell,' I screamed at them as I skied over the fronts of their skis, just managing not to knock them flying. Somehow I managed to stay on my own feet, but my run had been ruined, rhythm, timing, concentration all gone.

What complete idiots. Why hadn't the trainer got them off or warned me? I opted to go back into the course and make the best of what was left but it was hopeless. Again I skied out, confused by some poles stuck in the snow but not part of the course. I was going quite fast, probably about thirty miles an hour, and turned towards the lift. My next thought was 'Shit, the road.'

Skirting the bottom of the piste was this icy road, not that wide, fifteen feet, say. There was no room to stop and I made a split-second decision that my best choice was to try and leap it.

It was very nearly my last thought; I remember my legs coming up in front of my eyes, a dull thud as I hit the ice and then silence. I never felt my legs land and as far as I am concerned they never have. I felt like a disembodied head rolling on and on through the snow. I stopped, face up, and immediately looked around to see if my legs had fallen off; I couldn't feel them at all. It took a moment to realise how ridiculous a thought that was, they could not possibly have been chopped off.

Thank goodness, no blood, I thought as I lay there helpless. I could not feel my body. I could not move, I seemed stuck from head to foot on the snow.

Suddenly I began to feel all alone. I started to get cold and then frightened. Somebody help, I thought to myself. Where's

Nick? Why can't I move? Time seemed to stand still as I lay there waiting for someone to arrive. All I could see was the sky, and the tops of the little fir trees poking out of the snow. A confusing and unfamiliar feeling of anxiety was building up inside me.

Then Nick arrived – he'd skied down in his own time.

'That was some wipe-out,' he said as he bent over me. 'Fantastic crash. You hit the ground like a rocket. Look, you've smashed a ski.'

His voice brought momentary comfort. Only I could not turn to look at him. What had happened to me? I was making a huge effort to calm myself, everything was taking place on a different level, something deep inside me had taken control.

I thought, God I have never been this frightened, why can't I move? It was as if I was glued to the mountain. I could not get up, I could not move a muscle, I could not feel a thing.

Nick,' I said, 'there is something very wrong.' No sooner had I spoken than a searing pain erupted between my shoulders.

'Hang on, Trev, I'll just move your legs.' Nick straightened my legs out and put an anorak under my shoulders to keep me from losing body heat into the frozen road. I could feel only a very sharp pain at the base of my neck, which was probably caused by the freezing snow touching me; I couldn't alter my position to relieve the cold on my neck. Nick's jacket didn't help the pain. All I wanted was to get to hospital where they could find out what was wrong with me and put it right.

I was also probably in the early stages of shock and I was frightened. I could not identify the fear, or what it was I was frightened of, but it came from somewhere very deep.

Nick said that someone had gone off to get help. Team-mates were gathered round, but at a distance; I could hear their voices, but couldn't see them. The pain in my shoulders had become so great and the thought of being strapped to a blood wagon and bumped down an uneven slope by a *pisteur* terrified me.

Then Nick told me that a helicopter was on its way. The word helicopter was a reassuring one for me but though I only waited for twenty minutes it seemed like for ever. I heard it arriving. What type it was I couldn't see, a BO105 maybe.

Paramedics from the helicopter, *pisteurs*, I don't know who, put a collar around my neck and lifted me on to a special stretcher. A German-speaking team-mate interpreted for me as I was loaded carefully into the aircraft. It was a very small helicopter with just room for the pilot, the crewman and my stretcher but none for my interpreter. I felt alone and even more afraid. Neither of the crew spoke any English and I didn't know where I was being taken, or what was wrong with me, and now there was no one to ask.

I remember being taken into the hospital, but not being examined. A doctor explained in broken English that I would have to wait for another helicopter to take me to a bigger hospital in Innsbruck, some fifty miles away from the Kitzbühel one where I now was. There was the cold realisation that if Kitzbühel couldn't treat me there must be something very wrong.

I was dimly aware of the second helicopter flight and then the next thing I remember was waking up inside a smooth white cylinder as I was gradually slid out of it. I guessed correctly that this was a body-scanning machine.

I asked a nurse what was wrong with me, but she either would not answer or spoke no English. People came, glanced at me, said things in German to each other and then went, but no one would stop and talk to me or explain anything.

The Plaintiff was keen to become a Sea Harrier pilot. The last Officer's Report before the Plaintiff's accident (a report dated 24 November 1987) describes the Plaintiff as of above average flying ability, with a buoyant temperament and individualism ideally suited to serving as a Sea Harrier pilot.

I woke up again, this time lying in crisp white hospital sheets. I was free of pain, comfortable and happy. About me were nurses, calm, caring and reassuring. All the anxiety of the mountainside was gone. Even though I didn't know the extent of my injuries, I felt safe.

My first visitors were two physiotherapists who came to my bedside. I noticed that one was quite pretty, looking at her made me feel good. They moved my legs and arms around a bit. They didn't say much as neither appeared to speak English, then they went away. It was strange but comforting. I was unaware of all the tubes coming in and out of me, neither could I feel them, nor could I see any of the equipment which was placed behind my bed. Life-support systems hummed away in the background, but I had no idea that that was what they were or what they were doing.

The next person who came to see me was Dr Inge Braito. She smiled at me in a hugely reassuring way. She had the most beautiful eyes I had ever seen before or, I think, since. She told me she was an anaesthetist and part of the team that had operated on me for six hours. The surgeon and professor would be coming to tell me about it. She also said that my heart had stopped shortly after being admitted; she was not normally in that part of the hospital and had applied a direct shot of adrenalin to my heart. She said that looking at me in the state I was she wasn't sure that she had done the right thing. Her beautiful eyes were misty and filled with sympathy as she said this.

I was getting a first impression that my injuries were serious, but I couldn't imagine what made them so bad that I might be better off dead. I was quite sure I wasn't brain-damaged and it didn't seem to me that I could be as bad as all that. I felt fine as I lay between those crisp white sheets.

'I think it would be better for the professor to explain.' She left, but the image of those exquisitely beautiful, loving eyes stayed with me. I could think of little else for weeks.

The surgeon came to see me next. He introduced himself by saying, 'The professor is coming to speak to you later.'

Everyone who came to my bedside, nurses, physios, whoever, seemed to be building up to the visit of the professor. Meanwhile the surgeon told me about the operation he had performed.

'The operation was successful,' he said, so that was a relief. The fifth and sixth vertebrae had been crushed sending shards of bone in many directions, and these had been painstakingly picked out of the spinal cord. To get at the injury he had opened up the front of my neck, pulling the skin covering a five-inch incision up and over my chin. They had taken a bit of my left hip bone to replace the smashed parts of the vertebrae, also inserting a two-inch titanium plate attached to the vertebrae of my spinal column by four self-tapping stainless steel screws each about half an inch long. These would hold my neck together for ever. It was OK for me to move my head very gently, he explained, but only when strictly necessary.

He left me, repeating that the operation had been a success, but without telling me anything about my expected recovery or the implications of my injury. I had no understanding whatsoever of the implications of a spinal cord damaged at the fifth and sixth vertebrae. Would I ever walk again? I still didn't know. The surgeon's visit was a positive one, leaving me with the question, When is someone going to tell me what, deep down, I strongly suspect? In a way I was happy to wait longer to hear, although part of me wanted to be told. I guess it is a bit like having cancer, but wanting to know definitively if you are going to live.

I waited in vain for the professor. He was supposed to come at two o'clock: a message came to say that it would be more like three, but he didn't come then either. I badly wanted to talk to this man, and every time somebody who looked like a doctor came past I thought it must be him. He was a busy man, the most important man in the hospital, and I understood that I had to wait for him to come and see me when he was free.

Meanwhile confused messages had been circulating about

my condition. My mother was rung up late on the evening of the day of the accident by a naval officer calling from Scotland, who informed her that I had had an accident skiing and that he had no further information. He gave her the number of the hotel in St Johann were we had been staying.

The team captain told her that I had hurt my back in a fall and was in a hospital in Innsbruck, but he did not have any concrete information about my injuries. My mother was very anxious by this stage. If she had been rung up at home by a naval officer in Scotland about a skiing accident in Austria then the accident had to be serious. Being a physiotherapist, she knew the implications of 'hurting my back'.

She rang up Dad's wife, Polly, in America and discovered that Dad was in Europe on business; Polly didn't know where but she'd try to track him down.

At about one in the morning Dad phoned back from Paris. He had discovered all that there was to know at that stage, namely that they had just finished surgery on me. I had broken my neck, and it looked as though I would be paralysed.

He headed straight for Innsbruck and indeed was the next person to appear at my bedside. It was a huge relief to see that familiar face, the one I loved so much. I asked him what he knew of my condition.

He placed a tape recorder on my pillow. He was already thinking about who there might be to sue, almost a reflex reaction to an accident in America. You can hear my faint voice on the tape asking, 'Dad, will I ever walk again?' and then Dad at a slight loss as to what to say but trying to reassure and not frighten me. 'I've spoken to the professor and he says you will be OK. It may take a few weeks, you may have to work quite hard to recover, but you're going to be fine.'

'Dad, am I ever going to walk again?' I repeated.

Again he reassured me, but he didn't answer the question fully. 'You must just wait for the professor, but you are going to be OK, it's going to take quite a long time, we're going to arrange to get you back to England, but you are going to be OK.'

Then the professor finally arrived. He looked like a classic Swiss watchmaker, or perhaps Pinocchio's dad, grey-haired with a reddish, friendly face, a little beard and a large curly moustache, and spectacles which he removed. I had instant respect for him. I could take anything from this man.

He was very composed, very calm, instantly authoritative, trust-inspiring. He asked how I was feeling before starting to tell me about the injury. 'The spinal cord is damaged quite severely,' he said. 'You have lost control and function of the muscles below the middle of your chest. You will not regain the use of your legs. Spinal tissue does not regenerate like other tissue. At the moment you have also lost function in your right arm, but that may return to match that of your left arm.'

'You mean that I will never walk again?'

He looked me straight in the eye. 'I'm afraid not.'

He was so matter-of-fact. The news was delivered beautifully and strangely enough made me feel very secure because it removed uncertainty. Deep down, right from the moment of the accident, I had had an unquantifiable knowledge that the injury was this serious. At least now the uncertainty was gone.

When he went away I thought I should burst into tears, but there were none. My first thoughts were to picture myself playing wheelchair basketball and lifting weights to get really strong. OK, so I can't walk, ski, play hockey, but I can play wheelchair basketball. I couldn't imagine not being active. The professor had said that he was hopeful my right arm might recover to become as strong as my left. I took that to mean that my left arm was completely undamaged. So that was fine.

I'd fallen asleep and woke to a female voice shouting in accented English, 'Trefor, Trefor, breathe, breathe, you must breathe.' Behind me the ventilator alarm beeped continuously.

'You must breathe,' the voice repeated, 'please.' It was the tone of her voice begging, pleading to me, that brought home the realisation that my hold on life was so fragile, that I was teetering on the brink. The pleading in her voice haunted me.

I knew what it was like to struggle for air because up until the age of thirteen I had suffered from bouts of asthma caused by an allergy to dust mites. It felt just the same.

In an instant the meaning of life had never been clearer to me – I so badly wanted to live, I loved life so much and did not want to die. Whatever the extent of my injuries, however paralysed, I saw just how lucky I was to be alive. I resolved then and there to value life, to love it for ever.

It was the passion in the nurse's voice, the fact that she cared so much, which saved me. It is pretty fundamental to tell someone he needs to breathe. As with the proverbial drowning man, life did flash before me, not a series of events as such, but a memory of all the joy and happiness I'd had from so many things in my life and from so many people. The thought of saying goodbye to all that, the option of turning off the lights, was terrifying. I was scared to death of dying. I knew I loved life.

If I was going to live and to breathe, I needed to make a conscious effort to do so, to fight for every breath. For the machine to give me air I had to demand it. The professor had explained that my chest muscles were paralysed; from now on breathing had to be accomplished by a conscious effort of my diaphragm.

The machine could have been set to give me air free of effort, but I would have quickly lost the capacity to draw my own. 'Trefor, breathe, please breathe.'

I heaved on my diaphragm and took in a breath. It was a defining moment; for the next six days I made a conscious and unrelenting effort to breathe. I believe that I didn't sleep at all in that time. I fought to stay awake, fearful that if I drifted off it would be for ever.

It is difficult to get across what this involved; it was like settling into a rhythm for a cross-country run with no discernible finish. I had no concept of time. It was easier going when I had people around my bed, but when they left I set goals for myself to breathe until the next mealtime, say, then until the lights were turned down, then till light seeped in with the dawn, then until the flurry of activity when the day was acknowledged by the staff.

In retrospect I don't think anyone knew the effort I was putting in to stay awake. If they had I'm sure they would have adjusted the ventilator and made it easier for me but as far as I knew at the time I had no alternative. I probably encouraged my subsequent deterioration through sheer exhaustion.

I was helped by visits from Dr Inge Braito, who sat by my bed chatting in a friendly way about this and that. She was a single mother and found it difficult to manage time with her daughter with the long working hours. She told me that my injury would take immense courage to cope with, not just for a few weeks but for years and years to come, for the rest of my life. When she was not there I dreamed of her eyes, just thinking of them filled me with joy.

If I ever strayed into sleep the alarm would come on, and the effort to breathe would start again, powered by this new will to live.

Mum had very reluctantly decided to stay in Wales, having been told by the Navy that I would be flown home soon. In reality I think they were fobbing her off; there was no military machine swinging into action to get me back to the UK, chaos ruled. Meanwhile she sat helplessly at home going through the entire range of emotions from quiet sobbing to complete hysterics.

The hospital had noticed a deterioration in my condition associated with the difficulty I was having breathing. My lungs could be in danger of collapse and the stress of travel might bring on a second, possibly fatal, trauma. If I was to travel, it must be while I had strength enough left from before the accident.

Dad had been given to understand that an RAF Hercules or a VC10 was going to come out and get me, but then it became clear that no such thing was going to happen. Was it considered too expensive, or was the runway at Innsbruck too short? No one seemed to know.

The Crabs have such a bureaucratic chain of command and nine-to-five mentality that nothing was going to happen. The Navy, with only helicopters and Harriers, didn't have the right kind of aircraft to come and get me, otherwise I am certain they would have. Meanwhile my doctors were warning everyone (including me) that unless I was repatriated as soon as possible I might pick up an infection and be stuck in Austria for many months while they fought the likely relapses.

That same week Mum resigned her physiotherapy job in Wales and set about finding me a place in a hospital. She knew of the reputation of Stoke Mandeville near Aylesbury, as one of the best spinal injury units in the world, but was told that there were no places available, especially for me as Stoke was near neither her home nor my naval base in Portland.

My captain from HMS *Argonaut*, Commander Tim Barton, visited Mum, dressed in naval uniform. He stuck to the facts, telling her to get out a notebook and listen carefully to what he had to say. 'You must understand that Trevor has been seriously injured and was on duty. He will need your help and you must pull yourself together. The Navy will only support him for two years. You must understand that that is our system, that is how we work and you must ready yourself to help him.'

He was preparing Mum in as honest a way as he knew for some of the realities of my new situation and the support role she would have to play.

But if the Navy was not geared up to rallying round, Tim's wife, a doctor, was. She made a few phone calls and through some valuable personal contacts managed to find me a place at Stoke.

*

Once I'd been told for sure that I would never walk again all I wanted to do was have Dad at my side and chat about old times aboard his yacht or as children and be made to feel better. His visits made me feel secure and I loved him so much.

He was inhabiting the real world. He wanted to know who was to blame for the accident. If there is an accident in the States, the first thing to discover is whom to sue. Apart from tape recording my version of events he went up to the hotel and interviewed Nick Brewer and whoever else was about, but as an evidence-gathering exercise it was not outstandingly successful. A closing of ranks seemed to be going on, in fact the team members had been instructed not to speak to him about it but to tell him not to worry and that the Navy would be doing a full investigation of its own.

If Dad wasn't notably successful in gathering evidence for a potential lawsuit, I was still very lucky that he had been in Europe at the time of the accident and able to take charge of the situation.

He knew from the doctors that my condition was getting serious and so it was he, rather than my team-mates or the Navy, who took the initiative and arranged a medi-vac Lear jet to take me back to RAF Northolt, paid for by our ski team insurance. At least they had some insurance.

My breathing was becoming more troubled by the hour. The ventilator tube and a feeding tube had been stuck down my throat but it was decided that the arrangement should be transferred to my nose instead for the journey home. This was done with no anaesthetic. A great thick tube with a bend in it was shoved up my nose and round the corner.

There was nothing magical about the methodology, they just shoved it up my narrow nasal passage by the application of brute force, the doctor applying all his strength to get it to go round the corner at the back of my nose and down my throat. It felt like having someone break your nose deliberately at the bottom of a rugby scrum and was far more painful than breaking my neck in the first place. I felt the tube come round the corner and back down my throat. I'd have preferred to get this particular lesson in anatomy from an encyclopaedia; I hadn't realised the nose and throat were joined up quite so intimately.

Next a crew of about six nurses and ambulance men transferred me very smoothly and professionally from my bed to a trolley, taking great care not to jolt the newly applied bits of metal holding my neck together inside.

Dad, by now joined by Polly, was to accompany me back to England in the jet, along with the plane's doctor. I was exhausted, aware of little beyond my efforts to keep breathing, although conscious that something was preventing us from taking off and that Dad was a bit anxious about this. I felt at home in the plane, though. A medi-vac jet may be a far cry from a naval helicopter but all aircraft share certain characteristics; there was the noise of the jet engine and the familiar smell of av-gas that you get at airfields, a smell that I associated with my job and which therefore made me feel secure.

Finally we left. Our departure had been delayed by fog at Heathrow. I remember wishing that I could have been plugged into the pilot's intercom so that I could hear air-traffic control and follow what was going on.

I began to struggle for breath as we climbed. The air pressure in a pressurised cabin settles down at the equivalent to the air you get up a 3,000-foot mountain. Tiredness and exhaustion overwhelmed me as I struggled for air. The medic had an air bag, a simple mechanical device like the rubber inner bag of a football, with which he filled my lungs from time to time, free air like I used to get, gained with no effort, and what a relief that was.

The fog had not lifted sufficiently around Northolt and the patient in the back of the aircraft was struggling. Under radar control our pilot was twice lined up with the runway, descended, then twice had to overshoot because he couldn't see it. Heathrow had all the equipment to bring us in but that too was fog-bound. Aircraft were being diverted to Birmingham and beyond. Polly is a bad flier and despite several G and Ts she was getting a little agitated. I too, as a pilot, however groggy, knew that things were not going to plan. I concentrated on my breathing.

The medic gave up bagging me and put an oxygen mask over my face. After five days of effort I could at last relax. It was the most amazing feeling – I had made it to the finishing line in the cross-country race with no discernible finish. I was so exhausted, the air was such bliss.

Then they began to worry that there might not be enough oxygen to sustain me.

I remembered the long-distance rescue I had done in the Falklands, when I, the pilot, was receiving bulletins from the medics about the casualty in the back. 'I hope this man doesn't do what I think he is going to do.'

'You mean he's only hanging on in there?'

'Well, let's say I'm not that confident.'

We were an unscheduled private jet, but once Heathrow knew of my condition and that fuel was running too low for many further attempts at Northolt we were given clearance to land. I was unloaded down the steep stairs into a waiting ambulance. Somebody said that I had been given special dispensation to miss out customs. The idea of passing through the Nothing to Declare channel with all those tubes hanging off me was sufficiently amusing even to get through to me. Nothing to declare, except my head. Body still out there somewhere on the ski slopes of Austria.

I don't remember much about the ambulance ride to Stoke Mandeville, only that Mum wasn't there when we arrived. I didn't understand why, it was very distressing, I was so looking forward to seeing her. I needed her, I wanted her to hold my hand. I needn't have worried, it was just that the ambulance had taken us to the wrong entrance.

Seven

I woke up in the intensive care unit of Stoke Mandeville hospital on Sunday, 17 January 1988 breathing with no effort at all. Air was no longer going down my mouth or nose, a tracheotomy had been performed on me, and a ventilator propelled the air straight into my lungs through the pipe at the base of my neck.

It was blissful to breathe without trying, but the rest of me was less comfortable. My mouth was sore and dry and my jaw incredibly painful; even moving it slightly was agony.

Breathing through a pipe meant that there was no air to propel over my vocal cords so I could not speak, but then my jaw would have prevented me anyway. I don't know why it hurt so much, I think it was from having the ventilator shoved down my mouth into the back of my throat.

Mum was there and that was a huge relief. If close to tears she never showed it – I saw the strong, determined mother I had always known. It gave me a feeling of strength and security. I couldn't talk but Mum could read my lips, anticipate my needs and speak for me. She would ensure I got the best attention, she knew best. I somehow felt that her agony must be greater than mine. She was hurting for me and for herself. It must have been far worse for her. We were now both living it, but in the state I was in I was unable to think at all of the long-term implications of what had happened. She knew that I was going to need her support for a long time. Five years was what she thought.

'It's pretty bad, isn't it, Mum?'

'Yes it is,' was all she said.

Together we'd get over it. Not just me, but me and my Mum. Nothing more needed to be said.

The first couple of days in the ICU were spent in the quarantine room. It was kept stiflingly hot in there, apparently so that the patient uses no energy keeping himself warm. Most of the time a nurse was in the room with me, sitting behind my bed-head, or in a corner, although the only way I had of knowing if I had company was when I heard the flutter of the pages of a novel being turned.

Unable to question the nurses, I was like a detective trying to work out the features of my habitat. The daylight proved there was a window behind me. I was in a corner because I could see a wall meet the ceiling on my left. I guessed I was high up because there was no traffic noise (I guessed wrong – I was on the ground floor).

For accounts of what happened in intensive care I have to rely on other people. Family and friends visited and various things were done to me and while I can remember some things, of others I have no recollection at all. I guess most people who go through intensive care units don't remember much (assuming they leave alive).

Apparently the room was already stuffed with flowers and well-wishing cards when Mum was shown it before my delayed flight arrived. Anyone visiting me encountered a figure still with suntanned face, still looking like a healthy twenty-six-year-old athlete, laid out in a crucifix with tubes and wires going in and out of everywhere, bleeping lights behind my head, bellows going up and down, heart monitors sending blips across a screen.

The nurses devised a method for me to get their attention, because I could not speak thanks to the tracheotomy and that painful jaw. I had to make a clicking noise out of the left side of my mouth without moving my jaw, and hope that if Mum wasn't there, the nurse would notice. Mum could tell what I needed, and all but one of the nurses became pretty good at lip-reading.

I was incredibly thirsty the whole time, which was partly to do with the heat, but only partly. Massive physiological changes were taking place; already my paralysed muscles were beginning to atrophy for lack of exercise. As they broke down they were effectively being digested into my bloodstream and that was making me thirsty, just as would happen when a healthy person eats an overly large steak. You need water to help the digestion.

The nurses told me that I had to temper my thirst. I was taking in liquid through an intravenous drip, and after a while they supplemented that with water through a straw to my dry, crusty, foul-tasting mouth, but they would not let me have too much in case it caused renewed trauma and made me sick.

Nothing could sate my thirst. After a while some of the nurses began to relent and allow me to take larger sips from the litre jug. Some would let me drink the whole lot. As a treat they would wet my lips with ice.

All that effort in Austria trying to stay awake in order to keep on drawing breath from the ventilator seemed to have robbed me of the ability to sleep. Now I was absolutely exhausted with air being fed to me automatically, but having trained myself not to sleep, I couldn't. I was so, so desperate to sleep, the sockets of my eyes ached with the agony of tiredness.

I asked the doctor who came once a day to give me sleeping pills, but he wouldn't. At night I begged the nurse. She got the night doctor who relented, and at long last I managed a night of unbroken, deep sleep.

The next night I asked again and was refused. I complained in my near soundless voice but the doctor said they didn't want me taking too many, I might become dependent on them, so I lay awake again. After the third night I finally got a prescription for sleeping pills.

At first Mum stayed nearby at the house of friends called Jane and Roger Manley. On the day I arrived back from

Austria, three hours delayed by the fog, she had picked up the *Today* newspaper to find the story of my accident on the front page. It mystified her that I should be at all newsworthy.

FERGIE'S TRAGIC PAL
The Duchess of York was deeply shocked last night after being told that a dashing pilot friend may never walk again after a skiing accident.

The tragic news about Trevor Jones, an usher at Fergie's wedding, cast a shadow over her joy that she is expecting Prince Andrew's baby.

The distraught Duchess interrupted her own skiing holiday to send an urgent message of sympathy to the 26-year-old Navy helicopter pilot.

The Duke is expected at the hospital as soon as Lt Jones is out of intensive care . . .

The article went on to mention that I had been the pilot who fished Branson out of the Irish Sea when his balloon crashed and other details of no possible relevance to my current position strapped to a bed in Stoke Mandeville. The story was in the *Telegraph* and other papers too.

In fact I had only ever met Fergie once briefly and it is doubtful that she would have had much idea of who I was; she certainly didn't interrupt a skiing holiday to send me an urgent message of sympathy.

The staff at Stoke recognise the importance of relatives in the recovery of patients and someone was assigned to look after my mother and get her through the first shock. She was allowed to see me for ten minutes every four hours, and the hospital gave her a room to stay in.

She left me at eleven one evening. I was in a state described in medical parlance as 'critical' but 'comfortable'. Nevertheless back in her room she found she couldn't sleep, she had a sense that something was going wrong with me, so she rang the intensive care unit after an hour or so to be told that I had taken a turn for the worse and that it might be a good thing if she came quickly.

When she arrived she immediately saw a problem that the nurses had not noticed. The ventilator was not balanced properly. I was in considerable discomfort and was mouthing at her, 'Help me, Mum.'

She tried to get the sister to call the consultant.

'But it's two-thirty in the morning. We can't get him before six.'

'Can't you see the bulge this side of his chest? All the air is going into one lung. The other has collapsed.'

She could see that I was in very serious trouble and raised her voice until the nurses saw that she was right and went to get the consultant who finally came an hour later. He told us that my lung had collapsed but didn't seem overly concerned about it. 'We'll get it going again.'

When they couldn't get the ventilator to balance. Mum got them to get another one. After that she didn't return to the room she'd been assigned for five days, not even to sleep, opting to grab what rest she could in the waiting-room rather than risk some mishap while she was away.

It was a great comfort to have her there. It made me a lot less dependent on the nurses, who were constantly changing in shifts and who had other patients to think of. She kept an eye on the breathing tube which could get clogged up with sputum. It was one such blockage which had caused the collapsed lung in the first place.

People began to come to visit. Dad had to go back to the States, but my brothers Rod and Angus came on about the fourth day. They were let in one at a time. Angus describes how weird it was to see me laid out there, naked on the sheet, all my muscles standing out with the definition of an athlete. He took one look at me, felt his head swimming and had to sit down before fainting. Rod was the same.

My brothers' visits were the saddest moments of my whole experience. I had thought about them often over the previous few days and wondered what I would have felt if it had happened to one of them. Tears rolled down my cheeks when I thought of it. In fact they do to this day. Seeing them again I fought hard for control until they left then I sobbed and sobbed.

Old friends from Gordonstoun visited, as did Navy friends, such as my flight commander Neville Gaunt, who flew into the hospital's helipad with three colleagues. I also got a visit from the entire Navy hockey team.

Quite a few made the trip to the hospital to be told that I was not well enough to receive them, but anyone who did battle through only got to see me for a maximum of ten minutes, for fear of exhausting me.

One friend from both Navy and Gordonstoun who visited was Alex Howard. I don't remember this at all but it has changed my life and that of many others. Alex says that he told me that all my friends were rooting for me, that I managed a smile and to mouth my thanks for his visit, and somehow to look optimistic.

He told my mother that of all the people to whom such an accident might have happened I, through whatever inner qualities I possessed, would turn out to be one of the best equipped to deal with it. Even so he thought immediately that I would need a massive amount of support from my friends.

Alex was the son of the Earl of Strathcona and had taken over the running of the family estate on the island of Colonsay three years before, where he had quickly learned how money can dissipate unless it is handled correctly.

As soon as he had left me he went to Mum, Rod and Angus in the ante-room next-door and, taking Rod to one side, he said, 'Look, I know this isn't the best time to think about these things but you're not a wealthy family, and we must raise some money; we mustn't wait, we must start right now while Trevor is still in the public eye. We must cash in on any connection going, because whatever happens this is going to be very expensive and Trevor is going to need money, lots of it, and I

84

can tell you that the Navy is not going to help him in anything like the way he needs.'

Alex had gathered from my father that the insurance policy taken out by the Navy ski team would pay me only £5,000 for my disabilities. If I'd died, on the other hand, my next of kin would have got a million; obviously a mad situation, it should be the other way round.

Rod was still reeling from that first sight of his brother. 'Don't be ridiculous,' he said to Alex about his money-raising ideas, 'Trev will up and about in a couple of weeks.' He couldn't accept what had happened to me and perhaps he had reason to be confused. There had been Dad's early bulletins from the hospital in Austria which implied that I might still walk one day, while at Stoke Mandeville there was another official line, namely that until the trauma surrounding the spinal cord had settled – which could take six weeks or more – nothing could be said with any certainty. Some paralysed people recover movement even several years later.

Medical Report
on
Trevor Jones
by Dr H. L. Frankel OBE

History of Present Condition

On 10 January 1988 while skiing he had a high-speed fall. He was taken by helicopter to the University Clinic in Innsbruck. He was found to have sustained a fracture dislocation of C5 vertebra with associated quadriplegia. On the same day an operation was performed on his cervical spine which was described as 'open reduction and corporectomy, anterior fusion C4 through C6 plus bone graft from iliac crest'. The patient himself has little memory of these days but from the letter that accompanied him it appears that on 10 January 1988 a supra pubic catheter was inserted. He remained on a ventilator until he was transferred to the National Spinal Injuries Centre, Stoke Mandeville on 15 January 1988.

On admission to Stoke Mandeville he was still breathing

> with the aid of a ventilator. He was conscious and it was possible to test his motor power which showed, in the right arm, slight power in the deltoid and biceps, all other muscles were paralysed. In the left arm he had moderate power in the deltoid and biceps and slight power in the long extensor of the wrist. All other muscles were paralysed. There was complete paralysis of his chest, trunk, abdomen and lower limbs. All modalities of sensation were absent below C6 segment although there was a possibility that he could feel on the soles of his feet. His bladder and bowels were paralysed. He had no pressure sores.

There were strings of other visitors, some of whom got to see me, some of whom made a wasted trip, turned away at the door. It's the thought that counts, as they say. Only one person at a time could lean over the bed and attempt to understand what I was trying to say. Some would put their ear practically in my mouth to try to hear, which was useless and slightly annoying. They should have been watching my face.

My old Gordonstoun study mate, Bill Carrington (the one who had got food parcels from his mother which he'd refused to share), turned up one day and I could tell he was nervous as hell. All that slightly arrogant self-confidence disappeared the moment he saw me. He looked white and shocked. Mum stood by him and tried to rescue him from embarrassment, as she did with many guests. 'Trevor's very glad to see you Bill', that sort of thing.

What words of warning she had been giving visitors I don't know, but certainly some friends did look distressed when they came in. Some were speechless, some could not stop talking, some were sad. Most behaved as if I was the same old Trev, and nothing much had happened to me. But then I guess I could not tell if being cheerful was a real effort for them.

The one visitor who pulled that off better than anyone else was Prince Andrew's flight commander, Robin Wain. He just stood there talking, telling me lots of news and Navy gossip as if it were the most natural thing in the world. He didn't come in with a doom-laden face, or look sad or emotional or shocked at my condition, nor did he have a hint of embarrassment about him (neither did he try to stick his ear in my mouth). It was a lovely visit and made me feel as near to normal as I could.

Bill, on the other hand, was far from his usual slightly over self-confident, if quiet, laid-back self. I'd like to have taken the piss out of him, but could barely even smile in greeting.

Uncle David, my mother's brother, brought me an old red and green navigation light off the bow of Grandpa's boat *Kiff*. He set it up at the end of my bed which caused a great deal of amusement although I did not appreciate why. The fact that my sense of humour was in remission made it necessary for the joke to be explained to me: in the ICU there were so many lights flashing here and there, including one on my toe, that Uncle David thought I would benefit from another one.

There were others who, like Bill, found visiting me a difficult experience. Vanda North had shared my cottage in Falmouth and ran it for me when I was away on a ship (or when I was there, for that matter). Her visit was actually the second she'd made, having been turned away the first time after driving all the way from Bristol where she worked as a nurse.

Before I was able to manage solid food, some friends brought up home-made soups. Vanda attempted to feed me some she'd made through a straw. It was too hot and I burnt my tongue. I could tell she was extremely ill at ease and found the sight of me very shocking and upsetting.

She cooled the soup down and held the straw close to my mouth for another go. A misunderstanding occurred and she pulled the cup away from me and spilt it all over the place.

'Call yourself a nurse,' I mouthed. I was only joking, but poor Vanda seemed very upset by the whole experience. She got a cloth to clear up the mess and I think she thought I didn't want her there, which was quite wrong. I did; I was delighted by her visit, but she didn't come again for a couple weeks.

The hospital secretary came to see my mother. He understood that Trevor knew Prince Andrew, would the prince be coming to visit? Mum didn't know. Neither did I. The press were camped outside expecting celebrities a-gogo to pile through the doors of Stoke Mandeville. Could the secretary issue a hospital bulletin? Mum said no.

What did it matter? The press had got quite the wrong idea about how close a friend I was of Prince Andrew. I knew him from school and the Navy, I could ring him up and if he was near the phone I'd get past his secretary and be able to speak to him; indeed he had been an important figure in my progression through the Navy but, regrettably, he never became a close mate like Pete Griffiths or Bill Carrington. Probably it is very difficult for a man in his position to be a close mate of anyone.

While I had been pinioned to my bed, groggy with drugs and shock, attached to all this equipment and not really aware of what was going on, all these friends had begun to rally round.

A week after his visit to me, Alex Howard had rung up Rod again and said, 'What about it?' He wanted Rod to be a trustee of the new charity he thought should be formed, and he repeated his argument that the effort must start immediately, while I was still in the public eye as the tragically injured young man who had rescued Richard Branson and was a mate of Prince Andrew. Branson would be asked to be a patron of the charity.

Rod could see no harm in it and so agreed.

Either Alex or Bill had already contacted Gordonstoun for a mailing list and done a ring round of anyone he thought might know me, and soon they were all ringing each other and anyone else with whom I had even the vaguest acquaintance – a network was developing. Another Gordonstoun friend called Georgia Bailey was brilliant at this. She compiled a database and started to put together a newsletter called 'Trev's Connections'. Great buddies like Angus Buchanan from school became involved.

Bill worked as an estate agent in the Chelsea offices of his stepfather, Lord Francis Russel. His firm offered office space for the new charity once it got going and Bill volunteered to do the day-to-day admin. The charity would be called the Trevor Jones Trust.

In due course the running of it might give me employment, which I would certainly need, not only to occupy me, but because I would need the money to supplement my Navy pension and disability allowances, which even when put together (I was later to find out), would not go nearly far enough.

It appears that a division occurred fairly early on between those who wanted to raise money for me and those who felt the charity should have broader aims. Bill, for example, will say that he is not remotely charitable by nature, but he will help his friends.

It was decided that in the first instance the aim of the trust would be to get me on to my metaphorical feet again before moving on to the subjects of sporting accidents more generally. Car crash victims often have someone to sue for their injuries, sportsmen rarely do.

A further role of the Trevor Jones Trust would therefore be to lobby the insurance industry and get them to market policies with adequate provision for a lifetime of disability.

Alex Howard had contacted a family solicitor, Mike Gascoigne of Brodies in Edinburgh, who suggested that the rules for setting up charities were more straightforward in Scotland. The other advantage was that it would allow me to benefit from up to eighty per cent of any money raised.

Although the charity was incorporated in Scotland, committee meetings took place, so far as I know, in a pub in London, as did most of the fund-raising activities. Apart from the initial impetus, Alex's other major contribution was in paying Mike's fees, some £4,000. Thereafter it was Rod, Bill Carrington, Georgia Bailey and others who took up the running.

The collapsed lung was all part of my generally weakened state. My lungs were constantly filling with fluid which needed to be drawn off and I had started to develop pneumonia as a result of it. A consultant known as Jones the Chest took a look at things and another drug went on my list of prescriptions. By this time I was on about twenty, or so it seemed. There were antibiotics to fight infection, and warfarin to thin my blood (another application is rat poison) thereby preventing the very real danger of a clot forming, becoming dislodged and finding its way up to my brain and causing a stroke. There were saline drips and glucose drips, and a million blipping machines monitoring heartbeat, blood pressure and God knows what else.

I remained on the critical list for three weeks and was aware that details of my condition were being faxed to the Navy every day (just in case). It surprised me that I should be described as critical. I was on a ventilator maybe, but I felt fine. I certainly had no way of measuring the description of me against what was expected.

Then one day the nursing sister told me the word had changed to 'stable'.

Dr Frankel decided that it was time to begin weaning me off the ventilator. Dr Frankel is a pioneer in spinal injury management. Many spinal units around the world base their practices on those he inherited and developed from Dr Ludwig Gutman at Stoke Mandeville. It isn't so long ago that there would not have been much that could be done to save the life of a tetraplegic (or quadraplegic; the words are interchangeable. 'Tetra' is Greek and 'quad' is Latin for four, as in four paralysed limbs. A paraplegic is paralysed in two limbs). Before the Second World War the life expectancy of a tetraplegic would have been eighteen months at best.

On the 31 January the nurses informed me that it was time

to start learning how to breathe again. 'When we disconnect the ventilator try to draw breath. Imagine where it's coming from, deep down below the chest, focus on your diaphragm. We don't expect much, maybe two breaths, then we will reconnect you and try again say six breaths, just a few seconds to begin with. Take it really slowly.'

The ventilator was unhooked and I tried to draw breath. In the ten days that I had been on the ventilator at Stoke my diaphragm had weakened and the breathing reflex had disappeared. I had literally forgotten how to breath. How can anyone forget how to breathe? It was a strange concept to grasp. 'As easy as breathing' is not an expression I shall ever use lightly again.

I was nervous about them turning off the ventilator. The struggle in Austria was fresh in my mind, and Dr Frankel and the nurses had made clear the enormity of the task ahead; breathing was nothing like riding a bike, it would take several days, weeks even. The moment came and, staying as calm as I knew how, I heaved and gasped and under a minute later was plugged back into the ventilator, totally and utterly exhausted. They left me to sleep.

I got my first visit from Jimmy Savile early on, which was good for morale. He has a flat at Stoke Mandeville and makes sure that he talks to every single patient (he raised the money to build the spinal unit; the trust he set up owns it, but it is run by the NHS).

The only other stranger to visit me was a retired naval officer who claimed to have met me on HMS *Brazen* at Naples. I'd never been to Naples on any ship, so I wondered if he was visiting the right man. I had, however, been on her for a few weeks during my leave when I had hitched a lift from the Falklands to Maryland to go and see Dad. Prince Andrew was the ship's helicopter pilot and had fixed up the trip, and I remembered word of her visit to Naples earlier in the year.

'If you don't remember me, perhaps you remember my

daughter,' the man said. Of course I did not, but could not tell him so, and just lay there watching him and listening and wondering why he was here. He introduced himself as Charles Wylie.

Later it emerged that his interest had been raised because the son of a work colleague of his from Allied Dunbar (who was a close friend of Georgia Bailey's mum) had also broken his neck.

It did cross my mind that he might have come to sell me a pension scheme or something, which in fact he did about two years later, but in due course Charles Wylie became a good friend and closely involved with the Trevor Jones Trust.

'Do you play chess?' he asked. I hadn't virtually since Gayhurst. I wouldn't have had the energy to play a match there and then, but he proposed a postal game which we duly embarked upon, at the speed of a second-class stamp over the next two months.

Apart from visitors there was no entertainment beyond sleep, my imagination and the white ceiling. They tried to rig up a TV for me but I could not see it as I had to lie on my back. First they tried to fix up a system of mirrors, but they couldn't get them aligned properly. Then someone came in with some prism glasses which enabled me to see the television beyond the end of the bed. When I stared at the ceiling my gaze was redirected towards the screen.

After weeks staring at a white ceiling it was a welcome diversion to have a television. There was the build-up to the Five Nations rugby and believe it or not, one of the week's highlights was *Ski Sunday*. The glasses were not very comfortable – their weight hurt the bridge of my nose and slightly distorted the picture – but they were a godsend.

Best of all, during the afternoons there was a season of Second World War movies on a naval or airforce theme, usually starring Richard Attenborough, Jack Hawkins or John Mills, real old classics with proper story-lines, budding romances and happy endings. It was the perfect escape.

*

On the second day of learning how to breathe again unassisted I managed a few minutes. It helped a great deal knowing how long I'd done, which gave me a target to beat. They told me of a guy called Darren Lillywhite who was managing ten minutes, and I set myself the task of beating that.

Later, when I moved out of intensive care, I was introduced to Darren. He was far more paralysed than me and was likely to be on a ventilator for the rest of his life. What breathing he manages for himself is achieved by heaving his shoulders and at the time it was only for a few hours a day.

One day, alone in the intensive care unit, my right leg shot up into the air, as if it had been given a massive electric shock. I was very alarmed by this. The movement had been completely spontaneous, I'd certainly made no effort myself. I clicked my tongue at the nurse to get her attention.

She explained that it was an involuntary muscle action that was quite normal. I was told it was a good sign, it showed that things were working much better, although not necessarily a sign that I was going to regain the use of my legs. Whether or not any improvement was likely in that department could only be said for certain when the traumatic swelling around my spinal cord had subsided after two months or so. Meanwhile, spasm of this kind was something to which I would have to become accustomed, it was to do with my nervous reflexes which don't involve the brain.

Much of this was explained by Dr Frankel who told me that occasionally someone came in completely paralysed and walked out without lasting ill effect. He was telling me this as he tapped a pin on to the back of my hand.

'Feel that?' he asked, but he already knew from my lack of response that I felt nothing.

In charge of the intensive care unit was a nurse of West Indian descent, Sister Beatrix. She ran the place with a rod of iron, or so I imagined. I could see nothing beyond the ceiling, so all my impressions were formed by what I could hear and I got this image of a slightly authoritarian matriarchal kind of figure. When she was actually dealing with me she was different, a brilliant and instinctive nurse, with an extraordinary gentleness about her quite different from the way she handled her staff.

By the end of a six-hour shift I felt that I had got to know that day's duty nurse well, far better than I would meeting someone at a drinks party, say. There was just one I didn't like; she was an abrasive young woman with a Midlands accent, in charge of me for several shifts.

'You'll be in a wheelchair for the rest of your life.'

I was angry but could say nothing.

'You think you are going to walk again?'

I lifted an eyebrow and mouthed my agreement.

'You won't and I'm afraid you must get used to the fact.'

I wanted to shout at her, 'You little bitch, you're wrong, just watch me,' but I couldn't.

The intensive care nurses have to look after a wide range of accidents and illnesses, and they aren't necessarily the most knowledgeable about spinal injuries. From time to time Sister Rose and her team would come down from St Francis, the acute ward in the spinal unit, where it was planned that I should go next. They called in because of their expertise in lifting, moving and washing people with neck injuries, which was noticeably superior.

Sister Rose inspired immediate confidence as she and her team worked. She said I'd be far better off in the spinal unit where there were lots of people in a similar predicament. She told me what a good team of nurses she had on St Francis, that they were looking forward to having me and that my bed was ready and waiting. I too began to look forward to the day when I would be transferred.

On the fourth day of learning to breathe I was determined to extend my record further. I was bringing to it the same attitude that had got me to the end of a cross-country course or a batch of press-ups. I was doing well when suddenly it all started to go wrong. Fortunately Mum was in attendance and spotted that I was in difficulty: Dr Frankel also happened to be passing.

He took one look and said, 'You've overdone it, Trevor. Now both lungs have collapsed.' He gave me a little lecture about the dangers of pushing the body beyond its limits.

He didn't show any alarm but after he had had a chat with Mum her expression seemed to show that she was very worried.

In fact she had been told there was a chance that I might not last the night. I was in serious trouble again and Mum was told to get in touch with Dad and warn him to be on stand-by.

They put me on a new type of ventilator, the first of its kind at Stoke, just out of its wrapper. Only the technician who set it up knew how to operate it. The machine could regulate the level of moisture introduced into the lungs, whereas the one before had pushed in dry air which was part of the reason I had been getting so thirsty. It seemed to do the trick, and there was far less trouble. As Dr Frankel promised, they got my lungs going again, and after a few more days I returned from the critical list to the stable one.

Eight

On 4 February, twenty-five days after the trachy, I was fully able to breathe on my own, the natural reflex had taken over again and I was taken off the life-support machine for the last time. On the 9th, almost a month after my accident and a week after my last little relapse, it was decided that I was well enough to be moved into the care of Sister Rose at the acute ward, St Francis. I felt a bit like a small boy who has heard things about big school and is looking forward to it, but is a bit apprehensive. I wondered how I would cope.

She came to get me with a team of nurses and a trolley, and within half an hour I was in my new bed. It was strikingly peaceful compared with the intensive care unit. How people hanging on to life get better with all that harsh white light, bleeping noise and stifling heat is beyond me.

After their accidents most people go straight into the main rehabilitation wards for a lengthy period of bed rest, but those of us in the worst shape would go via the acute ward, or traumatic care unit, for closer nursing attention before any attempt at rehabilitation. I was getting better, was off the critical list maybe, but I was still very weak and had a long way to go before being out of danger.

St Francis ward had just five beds, one on its own, the others in bays of two. My head still had to be kept immobilised as it had been in the ICU. A break at the fifth and sixth vertebrae meant that I would be able to move my head in due course like anybody else, but despite having a metal plate in my neck, I was being treated conservatively. For the moment it was propped in the right position by sandbags (dressed as pillows so that I would not look too reminiscent of a London shop front during the Blitz). These bags had to be adjusted every few hours to stop pressure sores where they touched my neck or shoulders.

With an immobile head I was still obliged to pass my time staring at a spotless white ceiling, but there was one major improvement on the ICU, namely that my view was broken by a telly on an arm over the bed, so I could dispense with the prism glasses. There was also a radio equipped with earphones, and piped music if you wanted it.

Unfortunately I couldn't operate any of this without asking a nurse (or Mum). They provided a remote control clicker to change channels or the volume but there was no way I could use the bloody thing, even if it was placed directly in my faintly operable left hand, as opposed to my completely inoperable right one.

There were faint signs of movement in the right arm, but nothing I knew how to control; messages from my brain didn't seem to get there. I could move my left arm a little bit, but all ten fingers remained utterly paralysed. Stoke might be at the cutting edge of care for the spinally injured, but an adapted telly control was something to which the (presumably) able-bodied designer had given no thought at all.

In St Francis I became far more aware of my surroundings, my visitors and what was being done for me (or to me). Alex Howard's sister Emma, another old Gordonstoun girl and a first-rate cook (also a trained counsellor for the terminally ill, although I didn't know that), came regularly, bearing soup. She was so keen that she even borrowed her brother's new BMW without asking him, crashing it one day on the elevated section of the M40. That's devotion for you. (To me, not Alex.) She was uninjured but the car was a write-off, and as she wasn't properly insured and hadn't asked his permission Alex made her pay him back which took her several years.

Georgia Bailey bounced in regularly, also bearing soup. The

message had certainly gone out about soup, I was being overwhelmed with the most amazing and varied recipes of the stuff. Georgia had become a successful options dealer in the City since school, but had done time as a cook on charter boats so she too made good soup. She is a girl who is rather small but with features which are rather large (personality, voice, bosom). When she came the ward would echo with her presence. For somebody without a girlfriend, I did have a lot of very supportive friends who were girls. There is a lesson there probably.

One slightly sad thing of which I was not aware was that Alex hadn't asked Georgia to be a trustee of the Trevor Jones Trust. There was a bit of a personality clash going on, brought on by his feeling that she was monopolising me. Bill Carrington thought such differences silly; she might be almost over-enthusiastic, or even a little bossy, but she was a fantastic support to me in hospital and afterwards. In terms of visits and acts of kindness, big or small, she did more than anyone.

On Valentine's Day I was sent a vast number of red roses, more than could readily be counted, although after various attempts by the nurses and my mother a consensus emerged that there were a hundred and thirty-five. I had absolutely no idea who they were from, but as it was such a large gesture perhaps I should have guessed.

I couldn't begin to tackle the well-wishing mail I'd been getting, but I did dictate a letter for my mother to send to Dr Inge Braito in Austria, telling her what an inspiration she (or rather her eyes) had been. I wanted her to know that she had done the right thing in saving my life.

The regime began to change. While I was in intensive care they had concentrated on keeping me alive but in St Francis ward the emphasis shifted. They still had to keep me alive, but they also began to educate me about my condition, and to look for signs that they could start to build on whatever functions I had left, or might yet return.

Mum and I clung to the hope that the two months during

which the trauma subsided around my spinal cord would see a return of movement even in my legs. I think Mum had greater hopes than I did. The professor in Austria had been very definite that I would never walk again. The bone had so completely crushed the cord that I knew there was no hope, but if I ever said so to Mum she'd say, 'We've still got time. The power of the mind is infinite; you must believe you will move your limbs again, force the channels open.' She made me pretend I was on a bicycle. 'Think really hard you are going to pedal. Begin with your right foot, now let's see you move it, just a little, that's it, push.'

Once I thought I had managed a fraction of a movement in my feet. 'Did you see it, Mum?'

'Yes, I think so. Keep trying. Never give up. Believe you will get better and you will. We've still got four weeks.'

Sister Rose told me that my days of being washed on the bed were over, I was to take my first shower. I was very apprehensive about this, reluctant to leave the safety of my bed (something I hadn't done yet) and confront my paralysed body. Sister did her best to build up the occasion but the reality didn't match.

The sheets were peeled back, four nurses lifted me on to a shower trolley and I was then wheeled off through the ward to the shower room with a sheet over me. In the shower room this was removed, then I was gently hosed down. Even though the performance was as professional and as sympathetic as it could possibly have been I felt acutely uncomfortable and self-conscious, like a piece of meat on a butcher's table, or a body on the way to an autopsy. I had never felt so naked and helpless, and lacking in dignity.

If I could have avoided it I would never have gone for another shower again, but I had to come to terms with such occasions, and school myself to look forward to them and to treat an ability to look forward to them as a goal to be achieved, a personal landmark just like the struggle to breathe unassisted.

Physios visited daily to manipulate my joints. It was a process that had started in Austria but I only really became conscious of what was being done to me and the reasons for it in St Francis ward. Calcination of the joints, for example, occurs very quickly after an accident, and it is important to keep them moving so that when eventually you do get up they will still bend.

They also adjusted my position every few hours. Pressure sores resulting from your body weight being in the same position are one of the greatest dangers to a paralysed person, you can even die of them. A small pink patch quickly becomes red. Before long the squashed flesh begins to die, then it can go gangrenous. I was later shown pictures of rotten bottoms, shoulder-blades, penises, heels, and told that it would always be one of the most serious threats to my future health. Once the skin and flesh are dead, that's it, they will not heal or regenerate.

To counter this danger I was on an electric turning bed. Every four hours the inclination of the bed was altered so that the pressure points changed, and the nurses also took great care to ensure that the sheets were flat and there were no creases in my skin.

When they came in to do this they first moved the urine bag over to the other side of the bed so the tubes were all draining downhill. Bladder and bowel were as paralysed as everything else below C5/6 level, so a urethra catheter tube had been fed up my penis. In Austria they had given me a supra pubic catheter which drained my bladder through a tube leading out of a hole cut in the middle of the pubic hair.

A new item of vocabulary entered my daily usage. I remember as a boy reading a very compelling book called *118 Days Adrift* about a family who got stuck in a life raft after their yacht had been sunk by killer whales in the middle of the Pacific. The author had rather coyly referred to 'bowel movements' and it took me a while to realise what he was on about, viz. the difficulties encountered by the family and crewman in having a really good unencumbered crap. This is one joy which paralysis takes away from you.

The word 'paralysis' needs some explaining. A lot of functions below the broken fifth vertebra worked autonomously, including nervous reflexes which don't involve the brain. So if you clonk me on the correct spot on the knee the leg will jerk just like a normal person's, because reflexes of that kind go to the spinal cord but not to the brain (and never did). I am paralysed in the sense that I can't tell my limbs what to do. So being paralysed you no longer crap, you have 'bowel movements', which have to be programmed and managed.

In ICU, once removed from the ventilator, the hole in my throat was plugged by a device resembling a large golf tee. On St Francis they inserted a talking tube, still shaped like a golf tee, which helped produce some sound when I spoke. Gradually it was replaced by a smaller one as the skin closed in until it was literally golf-tee sized, then finally, about a month later, they took that out and stuck a bit of elastoplast over the hole.

It was wonderful to be able to speak again and be heard, at first with help from the special tube. Then with the elastoplast in place, air from my lungs could cross my vocal cords for the first time for one and a half months. For a while my voice was very soft and raspy, my larynx having received a thorough battering one way or another over the last few weeks what with trach tubes and feeding tubes, not to mention major surgery on my neck.

Friends said it made me sound like a South African, which is unkind to South Africans. It was more than two years before my voice returned completely to normal.

There were various little events which indicated progress. The doctor said that I could have my first solid meal, which was something to look forward to after all those soups brought by Mum, Emma, Georgia, Vanda. You name them, they all seemed to know that it wasn't flowers or champagne, but good, wholesome, home-made soup that I needed.

These soups were great compared with getting your sustenance unnoticed down a tube inserted in whichever orifice was handiest at the time (all the same to me, I couldn't feel a thing apart from the one that had gone up my nose).

The solid meal arrived. The orderly put down the tray, removed the metal lid and left.

'What have they got for me, Mum?' I was really looking forward to it, and so, on my behalf, was she.

'You asked for a solid meal . . .' She sounded really quite cross.

She held up the plate for my inspection. It was steak and kidney pie, with a thick and dry crust of pastry, in fact not much steak or kidney at all. It looked disgusting, the worst kind of school food imaginable. I had a go at it, but it was impossible, especially as my jaw was still sore. Solid was the word for it.

Mum was very annoyed and went off to have a firm word with the kitchen. As she said, food is as important for morale as for nutrition; diet was crucial to recovery, hence all the home-made soups.

About ten minutes later another plateful of food came up, this time macaroni cheese, which might have been a better solution, had it not clearly been sitting around in some forgotten corner of the kitchen for a while. It was every bit as hard and dry as the pie crust. We gave up. There was still a bit of soup left in the fridge so Mum went off and warmed that up. Also the pudding accompanying the solid meal was soft, some raspberry splurge of some kind, so she spooned that into my mouth.

In mid-February Dad visited again. Richard Branson had very kindly written offering him free travel from New York on Virgin Atlantic but I think Dad preferred to pay his own way. My brother Stu, however, who at the time lived in New York and was broke, accepted.

Dad was able to report on progress on the legal front. The

hospital had recommended a solicitor called Douglas Stewart who specialised in personal injury cases. Stewart had advised that there might well be a case for the Ministry of Defence to answer.

It's perhaps not immediately obvious why someone who injures himself having fun skiing should be able to sue for damages.

There are two requirements needed for successful litigation: firstly you need to prove negligence; secondly the people you sue must be able to afford to pay. It was fortunate in many ways that I was at work at the time of my accident – the kind of work I joined up for: sport. The Navy or Ministry of Defence or the Treasury (ultimately the same purse) could certainly afford to pay.

There were so many factors leading to my accident; we were skiing in poor snow conditions so should the slope have been closed by the ski lift company, or should the trainer have selected a more suitable site?

There was poor supervision of the course; there were the two people standing on the piste right in my way. Shouldn't the trainer have made sure they were moved, or should our course have been marked off?

Then I'd apparently been distracted by rogue slalom poles incorrectly positioned, causing me to follow the wrong course when I tried to get my rhythm back. Again was this the fault of the trainer, who should have ensured that the course was properly marked out, and that displaced poles were put back in their proper place?

An altogether separate question was whether the Navy were negligent in not taking out adequate insurance cover for permanent total disability. There were many questions to answer before a case could be prepared and fought under the terms of British law.

The Navy were conducting their own internal inquiry and obviously their findings about the adequacy of the trainer's supervision would be important. It turned out that the

Ministry of Defence pleaded the need for confidentiality on grounds of national security and would not agree to let us see it.

So there would be loads to keep the lawyers going: first of all a fight to get the Navy's report, second to argue about who was responsible for the accident, and only then (if successful), an argument about the quantum of the damages. Fourth, and the biggest worry of all, was the matter of paying the solicitor's bills in the first place. Getting legal aid was going to be the first battle.

This was all too much for me to take on board in one go, in fact I was completely ambivalent about it all. I just felt so lucky to be alive that I had no bad feelings towards anyone. The idea of a lawsuit to get money was quite distasteful. Money was not important; I had life.

Fortunately for me, my dad knew that my only real chance of getting the funds needed for my future was to sue.

Dad had also met the new trustees of the Trevor Jones Trust, which seemed to be taking shape. The trustees were Alex Howard and Angus Buchanan for their Scottish connection, Mike Gascoigne the solicitor, brother Rod and Bill Carrington.

On St Francis ward there was an attractive Irish nurse called Annie O'Leary. From the outset the appearance of a good-looking nurse, physio (or in the case of Inge, doctor) had improved my morale. Annie had a lovely face but because I was still supine in bed gazing at the ceiling, I had no idea whether she had a good figure or nice legs, though I supposed she had. More than that she had a wonderful character, with a wicked sense of humour. I thrived on her company.

She would spend a lot of time chatting to me. It emerged that she came from a small village on an island called Valencia near the Kerry coast. On my last trip in *Yoldia* I had anchored just by her family home, a tiny cottage near the bridge to the mainland.

She seemed to take a shine to me and to use every excuse to be with me. If someone else was feeding me she'd always offer to take over. I began to look forward to her shifts more and more, she was the first person since my accident to make me laugh.

'Are you going to marry me and give me your children?' She'd say the most ridiculous things. If female friends such as Georgia or Emma came to see me, afterwards she'd play very jealous. I say she'd *play* jealous but I think she might actually have *been* jealous. There was something a little unfulfilled about her, but I couldn't put a finger on what (metaphorically speaking; physically I couldn't put a finger on anything). Perhaps it was that she was from Ireland and didn't have many friends around her, maybe she needed a man.

I think my mother was concerned at the developing relationship. Dr Frankel told her not to interfere. 'Don't worry,' he said. 'It's perfectly normal. Lots of our patients end up marrying their nurses.'

Thoughts of Annie began to displace the image of Dr Inge Braito and her extraordinary eyes.

I once said to a nurse that since I was never going to walk again I might as well have my legs chopped off to save having to cart them around the place; being lighter I would be more manoeuvrable. For some reason none of the nurses or physios found this suggestion at all amusing, they thought it was a sick idea, except for Annie, who took it a stage further, volunteering to undertake the amputation herself if no doctor would agree. She talked of the saving in shoes and wear on trousers and how much more convenient a package I'd be.

She'd come up to me and say, 'And how is my favourite legless patient today?' before embarking on feeding me my latest solid meal.

'You know, I think you and I could be made for each other,' she'd say. There would be a pause before she added, 'No, I couldn't possibly go with a man who doesn't finish his pudding.'

There was a sadness about her that indicated that she was only half-joking. Every time Georgia swept through, voice booming, making everyone laugh, Annie would say, 'My God, Trevor, every time I come to see you, you make sure you are with a beautiful woman. You're not interested in me at all, are you?'

The ever-professional Sister Rose seemed to disapprove a little of the amount of attention Annie would give to me to the detriment of her other duties, so one day as she was spooning food down my throat I was disappointed but not surprised to hear her shout, 'Nurse O'Leary, leave Mr Jones, will you please, I've got something else for you to do. Nurse Solleveld will take over.'

A slightly less feminine hand than usual reached for the teaspoon and started to shovel food in my direction. I couldn't really turn my head to examine this new creature to decide if she'd be worth chatting up or not. It is obvious that if you are immobilised in bed then the prettiness of the nurse is a key source of entertainment, but in this case I was put in an immediate sulk that one of my pleasures had been taken away from me by Sister Rose's bossy removal of Annie. I took a mouthful before the new nurse gave me the chance to examine her. Frankly I was pretty pissed off at Sister Rose and wasn't bothered either way.

Then I got a glimpse of her face. Or rather his face. It was Guy Solleveld in drag, the helicopter pilot from HMS *Endurance*, the prankster who had faked that emergency landing on an iceberg. There he was dressed in a very badly fitting nurse's uniform, black tights, suspenders, hat and bright red inexpertly applied lipstick, looking for all the world like, well, I would like to say a cheap tart, but that would be wrong. He looked like a bloke in a nurse's uniform.

I hadn't had a great deal to laugh at by that stage of my recovery, but now I nearly choked on my food as the tears rolled down my cheeks. It was a long time before he could feed me the rest. God knows how I ever mistook him for a nurse.

He stayed just long enough not to exhaust me with good humour and as he went asked if I needed anything. I was drinking a lot of Perrier at the time, so I said I'd like some Perrier.

Guy had left the Navy at about the time of my accident and was retraining nearby as a pilot for British Airways. So the next time you are flying British Airways across the Atlantic, and a man dressed in an air hostess's uniform comes out of the pilot's cabin, take no notice. It is probably just my old mate Guy Solleveld acting out some deeply personal fantasy.

A few days later a large case of Perrier water arrived in jumbo-sized bottles, more than I would normally drink in a year, and with it a copy of an article from *Flight* magazine which he said he thought might interest me.

The article described another tetraplegic called Philip Scott. His paralysis was at about the same level as mine, C5 or so. Philip was attempting to adapt an aircraft so that he could learn to fly. I found the story interesting but fanciful as I lay stretched on my bed, getting accustomed to the little movement I had left, hoping more would return; flying again was the last thing I had on my mind.

The physiotherapist's role is central to everyone's rehabilitation. Mine was a girl called Fiona and for as long as I remained in bed it was her job to visit daily in order to move my limbs, a process known as passive movements. I had some control of my left arm, but as yet none over my right. None the less there was still a hope that as the pressure caused by the swelling around my spinal cord subsided, my right arm and wrist might one day be as good as my left, as the professor had forecast in Austria.

It would be a couple of months before a regime of exercise was introduced; in the meantime these daily visits would also give us the opportunity to get to know each other. The patient–physio relationship is very important, I was told.

One day Fiona came accompanied by her junior. 'This is

Caryl Houston,' said Fiona, 'spelt C-a-r-y-l,' as if this was a matter of great importance.

'Hello C-a-r-y-l,' I said. She was slim, with thick brown hair, young. She looked about eighteen and had a distracted day-dreaming look about her. As far as I was concerned she was the prettiest girl I'd yet seen in the hospital. Brown eyes full of life, slim, sporty looking. It was enchantment at first sight.

Fiona disappeared, leaving Caryl to exercise my various bits.

I did my best to slow her down. There is not much to do lying in bed, nothing in fact, and so if entertainment became available at the bedside then it was a personal challenge, which became a game, to try and keep it there. 'My right shoulder is rather painful, so please be gentle with me.' Pause while C-a-r-y-l carried out the exercise, having to lean right over me, concentrating hard at what she was doing and taking great care. I could smell her scent and my senses were alerted by her closeness, electric, in fact. 'This is fantastic,' I thought.

Caryl had a slightly Australian accent and so I asked her about that. She was English, but her family had moved out there when she was a teenager.

'So what were your parents doing in Australia?'

'Dad's a gynaecologist, he got a professor's job in Sydney.'

'Why Sydney?'

Etc.

I wasn't all that interested in her gynaecologist father, who had done a stint at a hospital in Sydney, as I attempted to engage this obviously very shy girl in conversation. I thought she'd be relatively easy to chat up and I wasn't entirely wrong.

If I timed it right she'd forget to continue doing the exercises, better still she would be holding my hand in hers while she answered. Meanwhile I was in the privileged position of watching this lovely creature work. I just lay there thinking, 'This Caryl is absolutely gorgeous', while throwing in the odd 'And so is Bondi Beach really all it's cracked up to be?'

in the hope it would throw her off her work. I couldn't keep my eyes off her, but then since she was doing her job I didn't have to, she was there working on me, officially for ten minutes, but I managed to spin it out for fifteen, sometimes twenty. Fiona was actually a far better physio, but that wasn't the point.

I must have been making some sort of improvement because on the third weekend of February Mum felt she could go home for the first time in the nine weeks since my accident, not exactly for a well-deserved rest – she was entertaining Rod and five friends down for the England–Wales match at Cardiff Arms Park – but for a break at least.

She was away just a couple of days and back on the Monday. It was decided that I was getting well enough to move onwards and upwards to St George's ward. It worried her that I was to move on from St Francis less than three weeks since both my lungs had collapsed and she said so forcefully but unsuccessfully to the ward sister. Sister Rose had gone on holiday and Mum thought that I should stay put at least until she got back.

The lovely Annie often used to say, 'What'll it be like for me when you've gone up to St George's? How will I cope?'

The day came, 29 February, a leap year day. For me it was like a bereavement. As she leant over me to help transfer me on to the trolley I whispered in my damaged voice, 'Annie, I'll miss you . . .'

'You'll what?'

'I'll miss you.'

'Dear God,' she said, 'you'll forget me in five minutes with all those women around you.'

'What women?' I said.

No sooner had I spoken than somebody arrived who I had hoped more than anyone would visit: my old girlfriend, Sarah Slight.

Since I'd disappeared across the Atlantic leaving her on

Bermuda I'd barely seen Sarah. Quite deservedly I had got the boot for my behaviour, but it had taken me a long time to get over her. I had had various girlfriends over the years, none serious, and whenever I was between them, it was Sarah's photo that went back up again on my cabin wall. Too late, I now apologised for what I'd done and told her I'd thought about her a lot since we'd broken up and hadn't really been able to go out with anyone else.

She said she wished I'd got in touch. She was so natural and it was lovely to see her, but sadly, for us the moment had passed.

Nine

St George's ward is one of the three main rehabilitation wards. It is on the first floor of the hospital; each ward has two bays of six beds for men, two bays of two beds for women and five or six single rooms. This is not a sexist policy, it just reflects the fact that most spinal injuries happen to young men.

The causes of spinal injury are many and various. Most are from car and motor-bike crashes, the other major category is sporting: rugby, horse riding, judo, cycling, winter sports, diving into murky water or swimming pools without checking the depth.

After that the causes are completely random. Slipping on newly washed floors or banana skins, falling off scaffolding, bullets, falling downstairs – there are a million ways to break your neck.

There was a lot of chat one day when news came of the arrival of an eighteen-stone Black man who had broken his neck in a freak weight-lifting accident, dropping the bar on himself. He was so heavy that the hospital needed to buy in a special bed for him. His name was Sean Jackman. I had started to get to know him shortly before I left. He'd served in the Army for a while but was out by the time of the accident. He had a great sense of humour and a character I could relate to, and later we were to become friends.

The funniest – wrong word – accident I heard of was of a bloke who was staying with his mistress, and had slipped on a wet floor while going for a pee in the middle of the night. He broke his neck on the loo bowl, and never came back to bed.

The mistress went to investigate and found herself with the dilemma of how to get the man to hospital without his wife finding out, which, given the seriousness of the injury – at that point unappreciated – was impossible, because like me the guy is now tetraplegic.

Disgust at adultery overruled sympathy for injury and the man's wife left him and petitioned for divorce. At the last count there had been a happy ending to the story; she forgave him and they currently live together as man and wife. Adultery, however, is now more of a challenge.

Few accidents are so unfunny that they don't offer some variant on the banana skin theme but the saddest one I heard of was of two young brothers scrapping playfully on the sofa where their mum had left her knitting needles. One boy skewered himself in the neck and is now paralysed. I broke my neck in a risky sport, but to suffer such a freak accident with a knitting needle, that is bad luck.

A day after my move to St George's in March I had a visit from a couple of Gordonstoun friends, at least one of whom, call him Rick, was visibly unsettled by the sight of a much reduced Trevor.

That particular day I wasn't feeling great but then I had grown fully accustomed to not feeling great; the lack of a feeling of greatness did not necessarily signify much about my physical state that I didn't know already (namely paralysed for life, incontinent, won't walk again, etc.).

What was great was to have attentive visitors, and Rick was at his most attentive when trying to catch something I was attempting to say with my still feeble voice and the funny 'South African' intonation.

'Chunder' is a maritime term deriving from 'Watch under', something the man who has not yet got his sea legs shouts as he discharges his last meal through the open porthole, so that the passenger with his head out of the porthole beneath doesn't get it in the neck. Perhaps it was something of that order that Rick was having difficulty hearing me say, I really can't remember, but I have an unforgettable memory of the fountain of rust-coloured vomit that shot out of my mouth and all over him, his head and shirt in particular.

'That's a nice way to treat your visitors, eh? We come all the way out to see you and you throw up all over me.' He went off to clean himself up. It was then that Jerry explained about Rick's own recent experience in hospital having a testicle removed and suggested that after this he would probably never visit a hospital again.

The same day I got a visit from Melissa Woodard, her mum and her dad, now promoted to Commodore. I was chuffed to see Commodore Woodard; he was a very busy, senior man and he had taken the trouble and time to visit me.

As a family they know how to have a laugh. Past events are painted up to become huge, hilarious sagas. They were giving this treatment to the dummy deck party when I'd abused the loan of the captain's car, or perhaps they were reminiscing about my arrest in Gibraltar (I'd been found not guilty) or the time at the Dartmouth Ball when I was dancing with Melissa and she'd asked me to do up the zip at the back of her dress which had begun to slip down. I had undone it instead at which point the DJ had turned the spotlight on to us, catching me undressing her in the middle of the dance floor.

Whatever it was we were talking about, Commodore Woodard, who is a very funny man, got me laughing. In fact they got me choking with laughter as I lay in bed, still weak and quite ill, without the strength in my shoulders or lungs to laugh properly.

It is no exaggeration to say that I nearly laughed to death. I could have died from the weakened state in which laughing so much left me. I was repeatedly sick for a couple of days before Dr Frankel and a doctor specialising in intestines agreed that my symptoms probably indicated a duodenal ulcer (without cutting you open they can't be sure).

I'd survived barely a couple of days in St George's ward

before being shipped back down to St Francis where once again I was plugged back into various drips and taken off solid food, this time for three more weeks.

When the lovely Annie O'Leary saw me there she said, 'So my prayers were answered.'

'You wanted me to come back?'

'Did I say I was praying for that? You grew it just to see me, didn't you, Trevor? When you get better you'll grow another one for the same reason, isn't that so?'

I had an unexpected visit from another Gordonstoun contemporary while my health was being restabilised, a visit which touched me greatly, from Tim Knatchbull.

He and his identical twin brother Nick had been thirteen or so when I was head of the new boys' house at school, their first year, my last, just before I became Guardian. When I left I'd gone off on the Dragon's hockey tour of Canada, where the papers carried news of the death of Nick in the IRA bomb which killed his great-uncle, Lord Mountbatten, on a fishing holiday in Ireland.

I hadn't seen Tim for eight years. I didn't know him especially well because he was so much younger – I was more the contemporary of his older brother Philip – but there was that enduring image of the young identical twins doing everything together down to one applying the polish to the shoes, the other buffing it off; inseparable.

When I'd read about Nick in the papers I was a fairly typical immature eighteen-year-old without a serious care in the world. I had no A-levels nor any clear idea as to what I wanted to be when I grew up. Neither fact bothered me.

I didn't know how to react to Nick's death. Should I write a letter? If so, what should I say? The whole world would be writing to them, what possible difference could a letter from me make and besides, what could I put in it which wasn't clumsy or liable to make things worse for Tim?

In the end I did nothing.

I was very conscious of this when Tim came to see me. I felt a terrible sense of guilt, but I also felt terrifically humbled by the trouble he'd taken. He was twenty-two and had just got a first-class degree from Oxford; we had nothing obvious in common beyond having been at the same school nine years before. We barely knew each other any more. I'd ignored his suffering and given that I had been his head of house and school, and therefore bore some responsibility towards him, it had been at best a lazy failure of mine, at worst a cowardly one.

Tim talked about his murdered brother. He told me that he himself had suffered a lot. The first few years after the death had been so, so difficult, he'd had an enormous sense of loss. He was getting better but the hurt didn't go away and probably never would. He told me that most people would avoid the subject of Nick, steer round it, almost as if he hadn't ever existed. He explained that he would rather they didn't ignore what had happened, and would like to feel that he himself could talk about Nick without making people feel uneasy.

It was too soon after my accident for me to understand fully why he had taken the trouble to come and see me. I think that he wanted to share the grief he'd experienced and the way that he'd had to deal with it; he also knew the value of the support he'd had from people at the time of his loss and wanted to give me that.

The visit meant a lot to me. One of the interesting things about my accident was the way in which unexpected people popped out of the woodwork to support me; and you never knew who those people would be. If my accident had happened to a friend instead of me, I wonder if I would have done anything to help? I hope so, but I was so selfish then, it's quite possible that I would have done nothing.

Once my ulcer was under control it was back to St George's. I missed Annie, but she did drop by to see me on the odd evening, dressed in civvies.

It wasn't the same as it had been in the ward in which she worked. There was still the disapproval of the senior sister, in this case sister Anderton, but often when she came I was being attended by a nurse, or visited by a friend such as Georgia. We were no longer as free to chat as we had been when our little relationship could be entered into under the guise of her supervision.

I got Mum to go out and buy a bracelet for her. That was quite a difficult thing for me to do. In the past if I'd wanted to buy a girl a bracelet I'd just have popped out and got one but now I had to do it through my mother. I was very self-conscious and not a little embarrassed asking my mum to do this.

Unfortunately, soon after I went to St George's for the second time, Annie came to tell me that she would be leaving Stoke Mandeville and heading back to Ireland. 'I'll come and say goodbye nearer the time,' she told me. It was a sad moment for me, I'd grown very fond of her.

The staple source of entertainment remained the telly. I didn't have my own individual one over the bed as in St Francis but there were two communal ones in our six-bed room which we were able to view, at least I could when they had my body tipped in the right direction.

By this time I had seen enough television. It seemed to be on the whole time, there was no choice about what to watch. The season of naval epics had ended, rugby internationals were only once a fortnight and the normal fare had begun to get on my nerves. Sometimes the two tellies would even be on different channels, both with volume turned up high. I could not understand the almost religious devotion of everyone to the twice-daily episodes of *Neighbours*. I would have buried my head under the pillow if I could. To this day the theme music makes the hairs on the back of my neck stand on end.

On board ship I'd usually have had a book on the go and

would have liked to read now. The problem was not only that I couldn't turn the pages, but to read I need a peaceful environment. On the ward there was too much coming and going. My occupational therapist (OT) set up a device called a page turner which could hold a newspaper or magazine and turn the pages at the press of a button, a button which presented problems of its own. But I discovered that I still did not have the strength or composure to read. Instead I listened to talking books and thoroughly enjoyed becoming involved in titles such as the *Kontiki, Kane and Abel, Great Expectations* and best of all the Asterix stories.

My bed space in St George's was getting very colourful. Each patient has a section of wall behind the bed to which you can pin cards and pictures. It can end up looking like one of those mass tributes after a soccer stadium disaster and mine probably did, but I couldn't be sure because I couldn't turn round and survey it.

On the ceiling above every bed was a curved track, supposedly at the suggestion of Margaret Tebbit (Norman's wife who had been in Stoke's spinal unit after the Brighton bomb). The idea of this was to carry a mobile. It was a good idea, but most remained empty.

Some patients have posters put on the ceiling, which is more logical than having them behind your head. I didn't have posters but fish. Tropical fish, big ones, an entire shoal of brightly coloured soft toys, each about two feet long. These were fixed to the ceiling with drawing pins giving me a completely mad but restful mobile to look at. They were the gift of the ever-supportive Georgia Bailey who had spotted them on a Caribbean holiday and, inspired by the empty track, felt that what my bed space needed was fish.

In the bed next to me was a nineteen-year-old paraplegic called Pete Byrne, who'd come to St George's a couple of days after me. For nearly two months since the accident, apart from a couple of visits, I had been isolated from other patients. Despite being in a similar predicament to me it seemed I had little in common with Pete and I was nervous about making the effort to speak to him.

He had quite a few visitors who were very noisy and I had him and his friends categorised in my mind as being the rowdier kind of soccer fan. When you first arrive in hospital you get a lot of visitors and his bedside was very busy. In fact at times the whole ward bustled. In addition to visitors there were half a dozen nurses on the move at any one time, various orderlies, a houseman or two, the ward clerk, porters, professionals of one specialisation or another coming and going, and of course those patients able to wheel themselves about.

I too had a lot of visitors but they were generally a more restrained bunch, differing noticeably in dress and speech.

I felt uncomfortable when his rowdy friends visited, more than anything because I felt left out. It's awful when the guy next to you has visitors while you don't and worse when his visitors ignore you, which to start with they did. I also hated myself because my voice was weak and because I lacked the confidence to join in. These feelings I kept inside my head while lying there, blaming them on Pete to whom I still had barely spoken.

The feeling was mutual. I'd spend half my time facing his way, before the auxiliaries came to turn me to face the other way. If my face was in his direction he'd pull his curtains slightly so that he didn't have to communicate with me, or place the water jug on the trolley between the beds so that our mutual line of vision was blocked.

So there we lay, in an uneasy stand-off which lasted almost a week, only occasionally looking in each other's direction. At least Pete, if he caught my eye by mistake, could turn away – me, I was stuck facing him.

It was Louise who broke the ice. She was a jovial West Indian cleaner, and when she breezed in the ward immediately seemed a jollier place. She had a beautiful and happy face. She was probably a well-preserved forty-five, but if she hadn't had a seventeen-year-old daughter, I'd have thought she was in her late twenties. She had a huge, hooting laugh which lifted your spirits. She went through the ward taking no prisoners on the dust front and left the place sparkling.

When she dealt with us she was gentleness itself. She had an instinctive understanding of our needs. She would always ask if she could get us a drink or do anything and it was a blessing when she was working the patch of floor in our bay, for she was always more eager to do things for us than the nurses, so she was easier to ask.

It is such a strain asking for little things, like to have the tape in your walkman turned over, or for a piece of fruit. You have to shout 'Nurse' quite loudly and then wait. Sometimes the nurse makes you feel that you are interrupting more important work, or makes you wait and wait, which rams home your dependence. It was particularly hard for me as I had always been self-reliant; even in the Navy I hated asking ratings to do things that I could have done myself.

After a while of 'Please nurse, would you turn my cassette over?' you think, Why bother asking? It's an attitude which breeds idleness and resignation, two demons who seemed determined to camp in my head. After a while you become reluctant to ask for things, particularly if it means shouting and making a spectacle of yourself. They were just two of many little demons that needed to be sat on if I was to take control of my situation inside the hospital, let alone outside.

'Trevor, you good-looking feller, you get better, y'hear, an' help me sweep this place.'

Louise got Pete to tell her how he had received his injury and I overheard. He had been working as a barman in Switzerland. He and a group of mates one night decided that it would be a good idea to remove one of those large bits of padding like a high-jumper's crash pad which swathe the bottom of chair-lift pylons. These are placed to protect skiers who might run into them. It was obvious to Pete and his friends that the thing would make an excellent toboggan.

Four of them got on it. There was a steel fence at the bottom of the nursery slope which they knew they had to be careful about. Pete described the last thing he remembered as they hurtled down the slope in the dark: 'That's fine, we're going to miss it.'

The pad obviously did hit the fence, though he couldn't recall the blow. Two of them walked away unharmed, Pete had broken his back, paralysing him from the waist downwards, and the fourth guy was killed, so I suppose Pete was lucky. The attitude 'I was lucky, it could have been worse' was one that sustained many of us. It did not help to think, I was unlucky, it needn't have been so bad. The truth depended on your state of mind at any one time.

I was surprised to hear how Pete had been injured, it gave us something in common and I started to see him in a different light. Louise knew my story already and aluded to the fact. 'It's funny how you two side by side now, had accidents out there in the snow,' she said. So I then told Pete all about it.

Our accidents had happened on the same day. A busy day in the Alpine hospitals. Pete had stayed in Switzerland for a couple of months under a Dr Weissler, himself an Aston-Martin-driving paraplegic and apparently the man to be under in Switzerland.

Pretty soon Pete and I discovered that we shared a similar and slightly macabre sense of humour. We had an acute understanding of each other's predicament which no one else had, so that sometimes when friends visited we'd carry on our banter as if they were not there, sharing all our private jokes – appalling behaviour thinking back on it, but a defence of sorts against the horror of what faced us.

Pete's analysis of this is quite good. There are two ways of dealing with a catastrophic accident of the kind we had both experienced. The first is to accept what has happened, that you will never walk again, that you have been fabulously unlucky and that life will never be the same, in short, that from now on it's going to be a bit of a pisser. This leaves you depressed and listless.

The second is to enter a phase of denial, over-compensate by being falsely cheerful, pretend that life will be as full as it always was, indeed that new opportunities may present themselves. Denial is far more fun. As far as Pete and I were concerned denial was where it was at.

Before long, no one could shut us up.

The game of postal chess against Charles Wylie came to an end. Mum had bought me a magnetic chess set, but it wasn't very good as the pieces would fall off as she tipped it up for me to examine my position. Also my powers of concentration were just not there. That's my excuse anyway; after a closely fought end game, Charles had checkmated me.

To mark the occasion he came to visit me again. He was keen to be of help, telling me that I had to replan my life in every department, financially, emotionally and physically. He ran up a loose financial plan for me, although at that stage it begged too many questions to be really useful. The Navy were still employing me, but that would probably not last. I would have to retrain and start a new career. It looked as if I would receive a service-attributable disability pension in addition to the statutory welfare benefit but it was unclear how much this would be and equally unclear what my needs were actually going to be. Whatever they were, I felt confident that the Navy would do the best for me. After all they always had.

Bill Carrington et al at the new Trevor Jones Trust had started to raise funds for a van and the Navy were raising funds for a lightweight manual wheelchair, which would cost about £1,300. The insurance company had said they would pay out the maximum amount for personal injury: £5,000 (in addition to refunding the medi-vac jet and other fees). I had also got a cheque for £240 for my missing ski pants (I never did find out what happened to them) and for Rod's broken skis.

There was the question of where I would live when released from hospital. Mum and Frank had their holiday cottages at The Maerdy, one of which was, as I had seen, already adapted for wheelchair users. There was also talk of an extension to her house in Llandeilo which Frank wasn't particulary in favour of. I wasn't his son, after all.

Then there was the question of who would look after me. Certainly £5,000 insurance money would solve my care and accommodation problems for about three minutes. Mum couldn't be expected to devote all her time to me.

There were so many things to think about, so many ifs, buts, maybes. And I was ill and lacking in energy. Where to start the process, what to start it with. If I tried to think about it I went dizzy and so I shut it completely out of my mind, it was something for later.

Friends had realised that I was incapable of confronting my situation which is one reason they set up the Trevor Jones Trust. Charles Wylie had also quietly involved himself with that, but the incredibly useful thing that he did was to make me confront some of these issues. He drew up a Navy-style 'Appreciation of the Situation'. It was a very short piece of paper, so simple, which he typed out and sent to me.

Suddenly my goal, in bold black-and-white print, became obvious: 'To Achieve Maximum Independence As Soon As Possible.' It was posted above my bed.

Then there were sub-objectives to achieve, just six of them:

1. Mobility.
2. Housing.
3. Care.
4. Employment.
5. Exercise and health.
6. Recreation.

Much of this remained abstract while I was in hospital, but once I was out it became a focus. For such a bland-looking list it was very inspirational, something which I always had in mind, as I gradually started to pick off the objectives one by one.

There was a seventh sub-objective developing which didn't feature on Charles Wylie's list, but probably should have been under (7.) – relationship with Caryl, Fiona the physio's junior.

Whenever Fiona visited me Caryl would be there learning, always shy and a little aloof, or more accurately, distracted, off in her own dream world somewhere. It made me want to get to know her better.

I confided in Pete that I thought Caryl was the loveliest creature I had ever seen. Not that I needed to tell him anything; it was obvious I was besotted. 'Trevor, have you noticed that dove she wears?'

I had, obviously. I'd noticed everything about her including the small brooch of a dove but it had no particular significance for me.

'She's a born-again Christian, Trevor.'

I didn't mind. Born-again Christians had never been quite my cup of tea, but Caryl could have been a tree-hugging druid for all I cared.

I began to look forward to physio sessions not for the prospect of physical improvement that they offered but for the hope that Caryl would be detailed to work with me.

Thoughts of the delightful Annie O'Leary in St Francis began to recede, as did the recollection of the beautiful eyes of Dr Inge Braito in Innsbruck.

Ten

On 20 March 1988 I reached the age at which traditionally you are considered to be in your prime: twenty-seven. I had lots of cards and quite a few visitors, in addition to my mother who continued virtually to live at the hospital, Rod and Angus, Georgia, Vanda, Emma and a few others. Dad, who had recently returned, had bought me a set of antique tools for woodworking, a somewhat eccentric present in the circumstances. But what on earth do you get your recently paralysed-for-life son for his twenty-seventh birthday?

Mum smartened me up for the guests. She allowed me to check my appearance in the mirror for the first time and what I saw shocked me. My eyes were hollow, my hair long, I had lost over two stone, my limbs were wasted. I looked old.

My brothers sang 'Happy Birthday' and in the middle of it Annie O'Leary's face came into my line of vision. She sort of hovered, not wanting to intrude on a private party. She waited for one group of visitors to go and then just as they did another lot bowled in, so she was robbed of a one-to-one chat. She managed to sneak in a word, 'Just to wish you . . . you know . . .'

She did not kiss me, but unpredictable to the end, left in the middle of a conversation and disappeared with a little wave without turning round so that I wondered for quite a while afterwards if she would come back and finish her goodbye. I'd like to have thanked her for everything she'd done for me.

A few days after my birthday another paralysed patient called

Caroline Beauthier came to see me. She was on St Patrick's ward, one you go to shortly before discharge, where levels of nursing are far reduced. She had heard of me and sought me out for various reasons. She was a very pretty South African girl of about twenty-five who had worked briefly as a ski instructor before her accident. The accident didn't happen on skis, though; she had been following a motor rally in South Africa in a helicopter when the aircraft's engine failed. They were low and it had come down heavily. 'You and I should have swopped accidents,' she said.

Her mother was divorced and had married one of the wealthiest men in South Africa, which I believe was how she had been able to afford to come to Stoke as a private patient.

She soon became a semi-permanent fixture at my bedside, arriving almost the moment breakfast was finished. She had a light-weight wheelchair which she could push confidently and quickly herself. I was still on a turning bed so she would come to whichever side I was facing.

She was a very physical person, would touch me and hold my hand, checking it for movement, encouraging me, hoping to find some twitch of muscular activity.

She had come to the hospital at the same time as me but was paraplegic and making faster progress because her break had been much further down the spine. Almost the first question any two people with spinal injuries ask each other is, 'What level are you?'

I am C5/6, which means the break is around the fifth and sixth cerviacal vertebrae. Former Superman Christopher Reeve is C1/2, otherwise known as the hangman's break because that is the point at which the noose snaps the neck of the criminal. It is almost the highest break from which survival is possible but Christopher Reeve has no use of his arms at all, cannot move his head even. One of the quirks of his break is that the phrenic nerve which should control his breathing leaves the spinal cord between the first and second vertebrae, so he is likely to be on a ventilator for life. When he speaks he has to catch the out breath, then stop as his lungs are filled again by the machine. If the break had been slightly lower that nerve would have remained intact, allowing them to implant a device like a heart pacemaker which would trip it off and control the diaphram for breathing.

After the seven cerviacal vertebrae there are twelve thoracic, then five lumbar and finally five sacral. Caroline was an L1/2 so she had full use of her arms and indeed was learning to walk with callipers although like anyone who breaks his or her spinal cord she would never make a complete recovery.

She was certainly very attractive, blonde, perhaps one of the best-looking girls who had ever shown an interest in me, but I didn't especially fancy her. She didn't make my heart miss a beat as Sarah Slight had, or now Caryl.

She seemed almost to want to adopt me. She was fascinated by my condition and the differences with hers. She'd touch me everywhere wanting to know what I could feel and what I couldn't and watched for signs of improvement in my condition. On 12 March, for example, Mum's diary records, 'Tiny flexion index finger. Tiny adduction left thumb discovered by Caroline. Tears to my eyes.' Wonderfully clinical language, meaning 'Trev twitched his big finger today.'

'Caroline was very excited to discover that I could move my thumb and thought it was a sign of more recovery to come.

Mum was very good about not hovering around my bed when I had a visitor and as soon as Caroline arrived she would quietly make herself scarce.

Caroline would rest her head on the bed beside mine and we would share our predicament in its entirety. She was much better at expressing her thoughts and feelings than me, I was very reserved in comparison, but she would egg it out of me and it helped greatly expressing what it meant knowing I would never walk again.

We talked of our relationships with our mothers, fathers, family and lovers, past, present and future. Tears would often flow down my cheeks, but without an accompanying strong feeling of emotion; they were just tears.

Caroline did not shed a tear when with me. She had an incredibly practical way of dealing with her situation. I was inspired but also a little perplexed by the optimistic way in which she was coming to terms with her injuries. She never complained, and talked about the future as if she had never had an accident. In Pete Byrne's words, she had denial down to a T.

Quite a lot of the time we didn't speak at all, but were just together, holding hands, saying nothing but if I was ever upset her presence was fantastically comforting.

She was amazingly frank about her own state. She told me she could feel part of her legs and backside, but had no feeling at all in her vagina. With sex as she knew it out of the window she was exploring new ways to have a physical relationship.

I enjoyed the thing for the companionship more than anything. It was thus a huge surprise when she leant across me one day and said, 'Do you mind if I kiss you?' It was very strange, I didn't feel any passion to speak of, it was like two good friends kissing. I say 'one day' as if there was a bit of a build-up, but if memory serves me correctly, it was within a couple of days of her coming to my bedside.

Meanwhile Caryl's visits to the ward would stir up more excitement in me than my smooching sessions with Caroline. I wondered if she had picked up on the fact I was attracted to her and if there was any possibility of her feeling anything for me. If she did, she never gave the slightest indication.

She would sometimes visit the ward to work on other patients, I would watch, mesmerised by her pretty face, her small sporty body, her innocent and sweet, sincere manner and the way she always put everything into what she was doing. I felt positively jealous as she climbed on to the bed opposite to get a better position to work from. Was he flirting with her? It was unbearable. She then left the ward. She'd have been there twenty minutes and not so much as glanced in my direction. I don't know why, but I felt I might one day have a chance.

Sister Anderton, in charge of our ward, was a good nurse, but not my favourite. She disapproved of the way Caroline and I carried on together, but there was nothing she could do. We were consenting adults in private (once Caroline had pulled the curtain round the bed).

There is one other major personality worthy of mention in St George's ward. One of Georgia's fish fell off the ceiling and Pete Byrne and I, who talked gibberish to each other most of the time, decided that the fall must have broken his neck and that he couldn't move a fin.

We christened him Freddie the Fish. Pete had also been given a soft toy by somebody, a walrus who was called Freddie the Walrus and Caroline gave me a tortoise which Pete threw on the floor one day for no good reason other than that it amused him to bully the soft toys. Thus in our little fantasy world Freddie the Tortoise had a broken back for which Pete even made a splint one day down in the OT department.

But of all the Freddies it was Freddie the Fish who was the star – he was very popular in the ward.

Freddie played a crucial role when Fiona announced that after nearly three months of bed rest I was ready to get up into a wheelchair. My first sit-out might have happened earlier but for a deep vein thrombosis in my leg. It was not something I noticed because I couldn't see my legs when I was in bed but a blockage in a blood vessel made the left leg swell up to the diameter of a football. Thromboses are apparently quite common in the bed-rest phase of recovery from a spinal injury. The lack of exercise means that clots can form because the blood stagnates instead of being moved about the circulatory system and broken up as it would be by an able-bodied person. Mine happened despite being on blood thinners.

Getting me up involved more than just taking me out of bed

and plonking me in a wheelchair, patting me on the head and saying, 'Well done Trevor.'

The first part of the process involved about ten days of gradually sitting me further and further up in bed. Having been on my back for all that time my body had to reaccustom itself to being vertical. There were a couple of dangers in rotating me through ninety degrees. The first was that my body weight would immediately make it more difficult to lift my ribcage and breathe and the second that the rush of blood would likely as not make me pass out. The muscles were no longer helping to pump blood round the body, the heart had to be given the chance to take up the load.

It should perhaps have been a day of triumph. I was dressed in real clothes for the first time, a shirt and a pair of trousers being wrestled on to my frame. I had to wear a tight elastic stocking over the leg with the deep vein thrombosis. A urine bag was then strapped to the other leg and with that came the realisation that it would be with me for the rest of my life. I thought of my old grandfather when I had last seen him six months before, and my feelings of sympathy seeing him immobile with his catheter bag beside him. It was quite a hard moment.

I was lifted by Fiona, the lovely Caryl and another physio with Mum in attendance. My legs shot out in front of me in spasm, something that happens as a reflex unless they are in the sitting position bent at the knees. Then pain in my right shoulder took over, a sharp, searing pain. I winced and frowned, trying not to cry out, but it was unbearable. Caryl took the weight of my arm, which helped a little. There was a brief moment of triumph when I realised I was not dizzy, then I felt myself passing out as the blood left my head. Caryl and Fiona tipped the chair back and my feet up and I stayed conscious. I was working hard for breath because of the extra weight on my diaphragm.

Pete and Caroline joked I wouldn't make it. 'Fat chance Trev,' said Pete.

'Go for it,' said Caroline.

Then I passed out. I had been in my wheelchair for no more than a few minutes before I was put back to bed.

The next day I managed something like ten minutes but the shoulder pain made it impossible to last longer. What had caused the inflammation in the shoulder socket nobody knew but the pain was overwhelming. Caryl tried to find out whether the cause was more serious than a weak atrophied group of muscles supporting more weight than they were used to.

She found an angle for the arm which hurt less supported by pillows, then tried out various systems of bandaging, binding and propping the arm up. It was discovered that one pillow was not enough and two pillows were too many. Then someone thought of Freddie the Fish sitting lonely on the window-sill and he was found to be exactly the right size.

From then on I was got up every day. The shoulder was strapped up and as the pain gradually eased I could stay sitting up for longer. Sitting for the first time in months was a weird sensation. The perspective was changed because my eyeline was horizontal for the first time. Everything and everyone looked different. I could see the nurses' legs and my own bed space. I was very much struck by this (the bed space, not the legs, although those too). It was amazing how you could be in a room for so long and be unfamiliar with it, simple things like the disposition of cupboards, shelves, or the distance between beds.

When friends visited they always asked if there was anything I needed. At first I would say, No, it was just great to see them, but later realised I was missing a trick and asked for champagne. Because of the medication I was on there was a general ban on alcohol. 'What, even champagne?' I'd said querulously to Dr Frankel, hoping for permission to crack open the bottle someone had brought me. Somewhat surprisingly he said, 'Champagne never did anyone any harm.' Thereafter the word went out that the only thing Trevor was allowed to drink was champagne. Louise used to complain about it. 'How can I clean out your cupboard with all that fizz, tell me. It beats me, Mr Trevor, how come you drink that nasty stuff.'

Then there was Guy Solleveld's case of Perrier which I told him had caused the duodenal ulcer. Overall I had had fantastic support from my friends. Looking around the ward for the first time I could see that my bed area was easily the busiest. I had literally hundreds of cards behind my head. A dozen would be more usual. I had teddy bears, other gifts, not to mention the fish mobile over my bed space giving it life and character.

I felt for fellow patients who barely anybody bothered with beyond close family (if they had one) and realised for the first time how lucky, or privileged, I was. For some the only visitors were nice old ladies from the League of Friends or hospital volunteers. Some had no cards at all.

On my third day in the wheelchair I managed to stay sitting for half an hour, an hour for the fourth and within a week I could be left in a chair for several hours at a time.

These first few days in a chair were very confusing. In part I was occupied dealing with the shoulder pain and the effort of breathing. To speak I had to take a big breath and talk while expiring, pause, breathe again, then repeat. Consequently I did not say much, which in turn made me feel left out. I kept looking down at my legs, bent and still, I could not believe it was me. Then there was the vulnerability. Having left the safe haven of the bed, where I was at least in charge of my own space, I was now having to share space with other people, to interact and start relationships with everyone, based on different terms. My identity of myself – young guy, fit, naval pilot – was not entirely there any more. Who was I?

Every half-hour or so a couple of nurses, usually one man, one woman, would come and lift me above the seat and hold me there for ten seconds. This was to allow blood to circulate and prevent sores developing. The experience was not pleasant and served to heighten my feelings of incapacity. At first the ward staff took responsibility for the timing of this but it was soon handed over to me.

By the first weekend the new and confused feeling at the change of perspective had subsided a little. I was sitting in my chair for five hours. I had some strength in my left arm, none at all in my right, but insufficient in either to move the chair even a little bit. Eating was hard. A leather strap was wrapped around my hand which would hold a fork or spoon. I could chase my food around the plate but had barely enough strength to lift it to my mouth. I'd catch a few mouthfuls, then need five minutes' rest.

Cleaning my teeth, too, was hard. I had a brush fixed to my hand by the same strap. Two or three brushes, then the arm would sag, spent, and the nurse would finish the job off.

Weekends on the wards were very quiet, many went home, and for the first time I had no visitors to occupy or entertain me and it started to really get to me. The nurses had got me up and had left me sitting at the end of my bed, with my back to the window and facing the wall ahead. I could see the nurses at their desk at the end of the ward, but I was alone.

Very quickly I became bored, I wanted to do something, but I was just sitting there alone staring at the wall, full of feelings I could not work out. Frustration welled up inside me and when a nurse came down the ward towards me I sarcastically asked her to turn my chair around so I could stare at a different wall for a while. When she did just that I somehow could not tell her I was just joking. Perhaps I wasn't. It seemed I could do nothing for myself and no one could do anything for me. Not even share my joke.

On the Monday, I told Caryl that I was going mad in the chair, and asked if I could have an electric one. She said she would look into it. Each day I made my point but for one reason or another nothing happened. It was Dr Frankel's general philosophy not to provide electric chairs. Apart from the expense, they encourage dependency. You could see his point for a paraplegic like Pete maybe, but my arms were so weak I could see nothing to gain from this experience other than the humiliation of dependency.

By the time I saw Dr Frankel on his weekly ward round at the end of the second week, I was feeling pretty desperate and hugely frustrated. I let him know it, pulling together all the words I could to explain just how I was feeling.

He turned to the head of OT who was with him and said, 'Isn't there that chair donated about a year ago? He could use that, couldn't he?'

Amazingly, electric chairs were a rarity in the hospital; this one was a manufacturer's sample which had been forgotten and stashed away in a storage cupboard.

It was a decent Levo chair from Europe, not the embarrassing NHS one with the sewing-machine motor. I wasn't able to use it straight away, various modifications had to be made so that I could control it. There was enough movement in my left arm to move a joystick, but my hand kept falling off it so they made a wooden V for me to lean it on. In addition, Freddie the Fish was not working so well as an armrest, so the workshop also fashioned a full-length rest out of sheet metal which they padded out for my right arm.

The chair was instantly liberating, suddenly I had the run of the ward and beyond. Pete and I would go on expeditions to other parts of the hospital. He had his arms but he did not yet have the powerful shoulders that many paraplegics develop so I towed him around the place, each with our respective Freddies, the Walrus and the Fish.

St George's ward was on the first floor but there was a lift, one I appreciated because I could actually press the buttons myself. It gave me a unique feeling of empowerment, controling that lift. Most of the general hospital is spread out at ground-floor level in what, from the outside, looks like old army huts joined together by covered corridors. You can go quite large distances without ever going out of doors.

I was up and ready to start my rehabilitation, preparation

for a return to society. The OT department was down the lift and several kinks in the corridor away. There, I was in the capable hands of Michele who had an array of objects at her disposal for training. There were boxes of little aids, specially shaped bits of plastic for fitting over a hand with a cunning spiral bit coming out of the top into which you could slot a pencil, crafty devices for holding a coffee cup, that sort of thing.

On a larger scale there was a computer room, lathe room, dummy kitchen, dummy bedroom, real lavatory. One object that takes you by surprise the first time you see it is a sawn-off car, no boot or bonnet, there for practising getting in and out of. Outside, OT even have a small bungalow where you could go and stay with relatives and practise living at home.

The first task was to develop a grip. I had no use of my fingers but I still had the extensor muscles in my left wrist, which meant I could lift it against gravity. This formed the basis for what is known as a tenodesus grip, whereby if you place your wrist on a surface, palm down, then lift the hand, the thumb and forefinger fall together.

Michele had a refined instrument of torture to help me develop this, a solitaire board with large wooden pegs on it. I had to manoeuvre my hand over the board, then drop the hand on to a peg and pick it up, transferring it across and placing it in the appropriate hole. It was at first incredibly difficult. To see me would have been a bit like watching a three-year-old child play with a toy grab-digger crane. In all my months in OT I never did have the mental energy to win a game of solitaire. I had to concentrate too hard on lifting the pegs which were made smaller and heavier as I progressed. The goal was to use marbles, but that took many weeks.

The other thing I was made to do in OT was sand my own sliding board. This was a plank of mahogany about three feet long which could be placed as a bridge between bed and chair, or car and chair, to aid the transfer. It had to be thin at each end so that there would be no edge to stop me being slid across, and very smooth. My right arm was rigged up in a sling hanging from a gantry above so that together with the left I was able to move the sandpaper back and forth.

About the same time as starting all this I was taken off to the gym for physio for the first time. Hitherto I had had it done to me passively on the bed or in the chair on the ward. Joy of joys, Fiona told me that Caryl was no longer under her direct supervision and I was to be her very first patient. I could gaze at her longingly, one to one, for up to three hours a day every day. On my first day I managed sixty revolutions of the arm cycle, a device attached to the wall for exercising the arms. Because I couldn't hold on to it she had to bind my hands on with bandages. 'Ouch, you've got that bandage too tight,' I'd say. That would keep her working on me for a bit longer while she readjusted everything.

While I did my revolutions she'd go off and look after another patient and then I'd work myself to the point of exhaustion, all the time anticipating her return to release me. Across the gym there might be twenty or thirty people doing various exercises. To the uninitiated it might look as though they are doing nothing; if you popped into a fitness club you would see the members frantically pumping iron, whereas at Stoke a lot of people look as though they are doing nothing but in fact I doubt there is a gym in the country where people work harder. There are some patients standing in frames, for example, or being tilted upright on tilt tables; they are apparently doing nothing, they don't have splodgy sweat marks under their armpits, but they might be working very hard at breathing against unaccustomed gravity.

Standing is an important part of rehab. Initially it is for the circulation. I was put on a tilting bed in the gym on which they gradually tipped me up over the space of about two weeks. Once I could manage it without passing out they would lift me into a standing frame.

This is a wooden box-like structure with straps for your knees, backside and chest. The idea was that it would stop my bones weakening, and would help the kidneys and other organs to drain properly. At first, breathing once standing was very difficult because of the extra weight on my diaphragm.

There were four in the gym, usually all occupied. A lot of paras would listen to their walkmen while they stood. For a tetra it would take determined organisation to manage a walkman and was not worth the hassle.

Other patients could be practising transferring themselves from a wheelchair to a bench which physios call a plinth.

Another part of my rehabilitation took place at the hydrotherapy pool. This started the moment the hole in my neck healed up (otherwise I would have sunk).

The sessions were only once a week, and I really looked forward to them so I had to hassle the nurses to get me ready in time because they operated a tight schedule, one patient at a time, and if you missed your slot that was it.

It was an old pool and sometimes cash problems meant that it had to shut, which was a shame as hydro was exceedingly good value. It was run by two marvellously salty middle-aged ladies.

Transfers were all smooth and professional, their attitude helped you forget the usual feeling of being just a lump of meat, helpless and half naked. They lifted you from wheelchair to hoist and lowered you into the warm water and the arms of the waiting physio. Just once it was Caryl, which was excitement itself. All the time they kept up the chat:

'You take the bottom, I'll take the top.'

'Fair enough, I'm much happier with the bottom.'

They'd remove my leg bag and put a spigot in the catheter and at the end of the sessions they'd have you changed very quickly.

'You had those off pretty smartish.'

'Not much we don't know about getting a bloke's pants off,' would be the reply, echoed with laughter.

Once in the warm water the physios would give my limbs a good stretch. I had a float to keep me buoyant, and would try to swim. My left arm had some strength, and with the support of the water I could slowly move the right, so I could propel myself a bit but mostly round in circles.

I had a confrontation with Sister Anderton one day. You're in hospital and all these wonderful nurses effectively save your life. None the less a sort of resentment can build up. While at Stoke Mandeville, Margaret Tebbit had been a 'difficult patient', so the rumour had it. There is an underlying message being delivered to you when you are told that another patient is 'difficult'; it is hoped that you will think to yourself, 'Gosh, I wouldn't want to be considered difficult by everyone, I'd better conform.'

Since leaving hospital Lady Tebbit has become quite a good friend and I doubt she was difficult as such, only demanding of quite basic things. She was probably less accepting than average, and would make more of an effort than most to get things the way she wanted, especially when they were denied.

I had agitated and got an electric wheelchair; I suppose that made me difficult. After more agitation I got them to put a hand cycle up in St George's ward so that I could train myself at weekends and when a nurse complained that it squeaked too much I told her to go and get the effing thing oiled. Why should I stop? I was trying to improve myself.

Sister Anderton had been getting on my nerves for ages. She disapproved of the attention Caroline had been giving me, and as a result had been making snide remarks to me and, I thought, to her staff on the ward. She was also at times less than civil towards Caroline.

One day I had more or less finished feeding myself lunch and Caroline was putting grapes into my mouth. Sister Anderton walked in and said, 'Stop feeding him, he can do that himself.'

'I'll bloody well choose who feeds me and when, you can clear off and mind your own effing business.' Quite strong language by my standards. It was the first time I really blew my top with anyone.

There is quite a high turnover of nurses in spinal units, probably because it is hard work which can be dull and repetitive. It is nothing like as exciting as an intensive care unit where the patient could haemorrhage massively or die at any given moment.

For an auxiliary, on the other hand, the work might be more rewarding than the average because you'd get to know the patients. Many of them had been on the spinal wards for years and knew more about our injuries than the nurses. There was one, however, whom I didn't like at all, a guy called Ron. I think he may have been chippy because he had been in the ranks in the Army, so there was some inter-service rivalry as well as the fact that I'd been an officer. The tables were turned. He was needlessly rough, I think a bit of a bully. 'I wouldn't wish your injuries on my worst enemy,' he'd say.

There was a party on the ward one evening, I think to celebrate its fifth birthday. I was acutely self-conscious in my wheelchair as I sat with Caroline adjacent, her head on my shoulder while the music from the disco played.

I was well overdue for a pressure lift and asked someone to get a nurse. Ron came through but instead of taking me out into the corridor to do it in private so I wouldn't be made a spectacle of, he said, 'You've got to get used to it, sooner or later,' and to another orderly, 'Here, give us a hand, grab his legs.' I could do nothing to stop him.

It was the culmination of various things so Pete and I decided to put in a joint complaint about him. Pete began typing our letter on the OT electic typewriter. It was difficult to complain about staff on the ward because Sister Anderton was a loud, proud person who clearly enjoyed her power and was likely to take it personally, possibly to our detriment. So half-way through we changed our minds and instead I had a quiet word with the nursing officer. The guy was a bully, we had to do something. I doubt that it was our complaint that did it, but he left not long afterwards.

Most of the auxiliaries were not like that, they were, in a word, wonderful. One was a guy called Angelo who had been on the ward for years. Sadly he died recently, far too young, fifty-something. He was an enormous Black guy, six foot six, a man for whom the expression 'gentle giant' was coined. He never had an unkind word for anyone, and when he was dealing with you it was with kindness and respect and you always knew you had his full attention. His hands were like shovels but they were magic hands. If you had any kind of urinary or bladder problem you didn't call a nurse, you called Angelo who seemed to have a touch which could get everything going, or rather flowing, again. Once I felt as if he had saved my life after my catheter blocked, causing sweating and the most intense pain in my head – as though it were being run through by a knitting needle – an experience known as Autonomic dysreflexia.

Eleven

Four months were up and it had become apparent that I had regained almost as much movement as I was ever going to from any diminution in the swelling around my spinal cord. There were, however, a couple of further tricks beyond spasm to be played on me as a result of my injury, however.

The involuntary spasm in my legs, although reduced by taking a drug called Baclofen, remained. Every non-doctor knows the knee reflex where the nervous impulse goes from knee to spinal cord and back without going near the brain, but there are many others. One with major implications for tetraplegics results from the way the ball of your foot reacts when it touches the ground, a sort of 'cat on a hot tin roof' reflex. Sudden pressure on this part results in the leg recoiling as it would if an able-bodied person trod on a cactus.

A bit of spasm of this kind, I was told, is a good thing. It keeps the muscle bulk in your legs and the blood circulating. Many paras don't get so much spasm and as a result their legs will waste away and become very thin. It is the paralysed legs' way of doing their own exercise. On the other hand when the ball of the foot treads on its imaginary hot tin roof the leg shoots straight out in a spasm, often arriving high up between the legs of the attending nurse and shaking violently, causing great excitement and occasionally fits of giggles. Then there is the problem of straightening the leg again which I have to ask someone else to do, and which takes considerable strength. For some tetraplegics the spasm is very debilitating. It can be sufficiently violent to throw you out of your wheelchair.

Spasm was one thing, but what no one had warned me might happen as the swelling around the cord subsided was phantom pain, a constant all-over burning in my legs and all the bits I couldn't feel. Dr Frankel said that he could not prescribe painkillers as they would not work. The pain was literally in my mind, something to do with the way my spinal cord had been broken; the pain originated at the break, not in the limbs I could apparently feel.

At Stoke it was easy to feel sorry for yourself but also easy to realise how lucky you were. There is always someone around the corner worse off. Darren Lillywhite, still only seventeen years old, would probably be on a ventilator for the rest of his life. He had phantom pain too. This pain has no apparent cure. It is constant and all over, and it was hard to accept that I would have to spend the rest of my life in unremitting discomfort and that nothing could be done about it.

None the less I was making some progress. I could sit up in the electric wheelchair for about eight hours at a stretch provided I periodically leant right forward or was lifted to relieve pressure. The routine of physio and OT was dominating the day and to begin with was all-consuming.

During long sessions Caryl and I talked and joked a lot, we were getting on really well. I even felt I was getting closer to her at an emotional level. She certainly would give me no positive sign but I was sure she was interested in me. She even referred to my seeing Caroline which surprised me. Caroline was due to leave shortly, and I could not stop myself from looking forward to saying goodbye. Caryl had totally taken over my thoughts, I now really thought I had a chance.

As soon as Dr Frankel cleared me to go out of the hospital on visits, Georgia came up with a proposal to take me out to a Fleetwood Mac concert at Wembley Arena. I managed to persuade both her and Caryl that as it was my first outing I would need my physio along for the concert just in case. In the end it became quite a party with Pete, his sister Fi and Caroline, 'my girlfriend', coming along too.

In preparation for the trip Caryl had to teach me how to transfer into a car from a chair using the sawn-off Vauxhall Astra in the OT department.

The standing transfer is the technique used to enable one person to get a paralysed person into the front seat of a car. It is not difficult but takes a bit of practice. The head nurse of the spinal unit, Mrs Rogers, had married a former patient called Michael. Michael preferred to be driven as a passenger in a normal car rather than seated in his wheelchair in a van. He was more paralysed than me and used a chin-controlled wheelchair. He'd spend a day a week at Stoke talking to patients and was a great inspiration.

I had once watched Mrs Rogers get him into their big white Mercedes. She would take his feet off the foot plates and place them on the ground, then swing his chin control out of the way and pull him forward to the edge of his seat. With her hands behind his backside, and her knees round his knees to lock them in place, she'd stand him up with her, then turn and lower him gently into the car seat, then lift his feet into the foot well and adjust his clothes to make him comfortable, before putting on his seat-belt.

It was incredible to watch this controlled and fluid movement. Michael would just hang there, this intelligent, caring man. I felt sad, really sad, then I realised that I was looking at Michael, a man, paralysed like me. Is that how people would feel when they looked at me?

Caryl had only just learnt the manoeuvre herself, being still quite an inexperienced physio and I her first patient. The standing transfer is very intimate. She positioned my chair beside the open door and I watched her as she took my feet off the foot rests and continued just as Mrs Rogers did.

I could have practised this all day with Caryl and I did definitely get the impression that she was in no hurry either.

Next she had to put her head under my armpit, arms

around my body and stand me up, our bodies clamped together. That was the theory. Half-way across the whole thing began to go wrong. I slipped slowly out of her grasp but she just managed to catch me in time, somehow ending up stuck clutching me by my neck, unable to move for fear of dropping me and damaging me further.

She had to shout for one of the OTs to grab me and help me back into the chair, while she extricated herself. It didn't hurt and I didn't mind. My neck was held together by titanium and perfectly strong enough. I was in Caryl's arms, that was the main thing, and even if dangling by the broken neck it was everything I had dreamed of.

On 24 May Georgia came to take me in her BMW to the Fleetwood Mac concert at Wembley. The standing transfer by Caryl was accomplished to perfection and accessories were loaded into the car to ease the journey: a moulded foam neck brace, pillows for my right arm, Freddie the Fish, urine bottle, pads for elbows to stop sores, a sheepskin rug to protect my increasingly bony back and a selection of pills to control spasm, blood levels and this and that. If there was a disappointment it was that Caryl had to drive her own car loaded with Caroline, Pete and respective wheelchairs.

The BMW seats were wonderfully comfortable compared to the two bits of canvas of a wheelchair. It was a fantastic and beautiful early summer's evening. Round the M25 Georgia seemed to be driving so fast, at least a hundred – I was unaccustomed to the speed – but the speedo read only 70 mph. I was elated by seeing the countryside alive with early summer colour and the yellow rape fields, my senses freed after five months indoors.

The concert was good, as you'd expect. I felt very humble, insignificant even, being pushed through the crowd of thousands of people. I could see few faces, only midriffs and backsides.

Just three days later I stayed away from the hospital for the first time for a weekend. This was at the house of my Uncle Dave, Mum's brother, and Aunt Terry (these days, now they've moved to Wales near Mum, Dai and Tel). Cousin Danny was there and so of course was Mum herself. George, Terry's dad, lent me the annexe to their house next door which had a room at ground-floor level for me to sleep in.

I'd been in hospital four and a half months but was a long way from being prepared for going home, so this weekend was like a practice for the real world, but not too urgent. Dr Frankel was talking about my being there for another six months.

It was a great weekend for me, surrounded by family and friends. It was also a harsh lesson in some of the difficulties which would face me when I got out. Mum and Terry had arranged a district nurse to come in and help in the mornings, particularly with my bowel programme.

When the nurse arrived she first emphasised that she was doing us all a big favour by coming out to help at all. Then she said she already had a spinally injured patient and knew what to do. I tried to explain that the needs of each spinally injured person differed widely but like many nurses she was of the 'I've been doing this job a long time and I know best' persuasion.

It is not quite accurate to say that I can feel nothing below my break. I do have some all-over sensation on my body, so that I can't feel a pinprick but can sense it if somebody places a hand on me. In other words I can feel a finger up my backside and I don't like it.

She wouldn't follow my instructions – she knew best – and tried a manual excavation using her finger when I told her not to. The upshot (or rather downshot) of it all was that the sheets and bed ended up needing a good wash. Then once I was up in my chair I had a bowel accident and had to be cleaned up again.

From this experience I began to learn how I need always to assert myself. Nowadays whenever someone says 'I know what to do', or they automatically start to take charge, warning bells start ringing. It is amazing how other people want to take control of you, decide things for you. That was something for which life in hospital was to blame, already I had become partly institutionalised.

Twelve

In June Caryl had just bought her first house, jointly with her brother Graham, an instructor officer in the Navy. We were discussing it one day in the gym when she said in the light Aussie accent I loved so much, 'When we've settled in a bit you must come round for some supper.'

I could have died with excitement, but the gym wasn't the place so I went through my exercycle routine with a new vigour.

Meanwhile Caroline was at the end of her stay at Stoke. She was going on vacation to the US, then for more treatment to Israel where, apparently because of the troubles, they had some pretty progressive ideas on rehab for spinal injuries.

She had even talked about us setting up home together when I left. Her mother was buying a big house near Regent's Park and having it adapted. I doubted she could really feel that strongly for me, and tried to imagine what it would be like – two disabled people living together. It would be too much.

When she left the hospital it was a sad day for me; she had been an excellent friend. Life might have been a whole lot more simple if I'd been in love with her rather than Caryl. 'I'll write to you and phone you,' she said, '. . . if I can get through.' The phones had always been a problem, not properly adapted for tetras, and there was only one between the twenty-five or so of us on the ward.

Caroline was all dressed up and ready to go with her mother, a woman in excellent nick for her age. She looked more like an older sister.

Caroline was an inspiration in the way she tackled her disability; she seemed fearless, there was no way it was going to stop her from doing anything, or so she said, and I could see it was true. Although I was sad to see her go, part of me was glad. She had dominated and monopolised me to some extent and her departure left me free to concentrate my attentions on Caryl.

The day at Caryl's, the day I had been looking forward to more than anything, arrived. Her house was a short walk away through the hospital grounds, on an adjoining housing estate. Her brother was there to help lift my chair over the doorstep, we chatted briefly about mutual naval acquaintances, then he left.

There I was alone with Caryl, it was so quiet after the hospital, peaceful and private. The room was tiny and simply furnished, it felt odd after the busy ward. Almost a culture shock.

She was wearing jeans and a cotton shirt, she looked gorgeous, her mood, as usual, radiating forth. She could not hide her concern about her cooking, whether it would be OK. She was so sweet, I would share her worry though not caring what she served.

The meal itself was a culinary disaster, she couldn't cook to save her life. The spuds were hard, the chicken tough, the sauce bland, the Black Forest gâteau acceptable but only because it came from the supermarket and she couldn't do anything wrong with it.

'How is it?' she asked self-consciously.

'Wonderful, never tasted anything like it.' There was absolutely no irony intended, I was in a state of euphoria just at being there. She could have served me ram's testicles in brine and I'd have thought it delicious.

After dinner we ended up talking about my accident. As I told her my initial thought about playing wheelchair basketball it came home to me how very much worse my injuries were than I had envisaged and how I had been living in hope ever since. Even basketball was out of the question, I did not and would never have the upper body strength. I wiped my moist eyes.

Then we started to talk about our families. At mention of the word 'brothers' the tears just poured down my cheeks. It's difficult to explain why the thought of my brothers upset me so, and why it still does. I'd been the eldest and always wanted to be setting an example, showing them the way. It was one thought that always creased me up; what if it had happened to one of them? I imagined how upset I'd be and what I must be putting them through now.

I could see she felt for me. She said, 'Would you mind if I gave you a hug? Can I sit on your lap?'

Would I mind! 'You're the physio. If you think it would be OK . . .'

Then she started kissing me. I was very surprised; I had had my head so filled with her for so long, then all of a sudden it happened in a way I could never have expected.

It was quite different from what I had imagined it might be. There was no surging feeling of passion or of lust. All that sort of thing was disconnected at C5/6. I'd anticipated a great sense of relief but there wasn't that either and yet the desire I felt for her was definitely physical, or chemical, or something. I was uncomfortable at what was happening and euphoric at the same time, but it was a measured euphoria. I couldn't begin to analyse why. It might have been that the physical element and accompanying hormonal surge (and surge in the trouser department) had gone, it might have been confusion at my state or because of being overwhelmed with my situation.

All that I know is that since my accident everything has been different; after twenty-six years of learning what made my body tick I was having to start from scratch. Being kissed by a girl I was mad about was one more of those experiences which was different and I didn't know why.

Next morning Pete asked, 'How was dinner with Caryl?' or

'the lovely Caryl' as he called her. He looked at me knowingly, as did Louise. They could not possibly know, I thought. I was happy and nervous, a different man even, but was I so transparent? I had to wait for a whole weekend to see Caryl again. Obviously I looked forward to Monday but equally obviously I was apprehensive. Would she take any notice of me? Would she think she had made a big mistake? Would she backtrack frantically?

When the moment came I entered the gym, looking cautiously around for Caryl. She had asked someone else to treat me for some reason, in fact it was another two days before I saw her. The apprehension was killing me.

On the third day she came into the gym late. I had already been strapped to the weights by someone else. After about five minutes, without glancing at me first, she made her way over. I could sense her embarrassment. All she said was, 'Good afternoon, Trevor.' She barely looked at me and seemed deliberately to decide to treat me in a group of patients, making private conversation impossible.

After the physio session I haunted the parts of the hospital where I thought Caryl might be. I saw her several times that day but she was steadfastly professional, refused to make eye contact and got on with her work as if nothing had happened between us.

This uneasy stand-off continued for a couple of days. She was my physio so she couldn't avoid me but she seemed to go to great lengths to keep me in a group with other patients, or give me tasks working out alone. If possible she would even get another physio to help transfer me back to the chair, after which she'd beat as hasty a retreat as possible, or so it seemed to me.

A few days later I was alone in a corridor when she walked past.

'Caryl, we must talk,' I said urgently. There was no one else around and she couldn't avoid me. She just said, 'It can never be between us, Trevor.'

'Why?'

'I can't ever go out with you.'

'Tell me why.' But she wouldn't, just repeating that it could not be.

I could not see why. Maybe it was because I was in a wheelchair – Caryl had only ever known me as a disabled person. My self-image was still of this young, fit sportsman.

In some ways my mind-set about being in hospital was similar to that when I'd had my cartilage op after twisting my knee three minutes into the hockey match against the Army. I'd be in a wheelchair for a while, it would improve, then I'd leave and get back to normal, wouldn't I?

On reflection, obviously I could see that being with a disabled person was probably not every little girl's dream, and I would not much have fancied my chances at the local disco but there were many stories of patients marrying their nurses or physios. What could be more normal or sensible? During a protracted period of therapy there is not much that patient and therapist aren't going to end up knowing about each other and any triumphs of progress are going to be experienced together.

But the following days were misery to me. I was sure she'd kissed me out of more than mere sympathy, for goodness' sake, and now she ignored me. If she passed me in the corridor she was too busy to stop.

Finally I got her on her own in the gym one day and pleaded with her to agree to talk things over. She said she'd meet me that afternoon in the Outpatients department at the far end of the hospital. People from the spinal unit hardly ever went there.

'Trevor, I can't go out with you, it wouldn't be professional,' she said. I did wonder if Alison, her new superior, might not be making disapproving noises. I had told no one about my infatuation with Caryl, but it was getting so obvious that some of the other patients had even started to take the piss out of me.

I told her I accepted that part of her difficulty was that she had a professional relationship with me and that a personal one might cause ethical problems. 'But I'm not going to be in hospital for ever. I'll be out soon and leading a life which, with a bit of help, will be nearly normal. What's really bothering you, Caryl?'

'I don't want to hurt you, Trevor.'

This puzzled me. 'But how, Caryl, can your affection hurt me? It does me a lot of good.'

The discussion ended there, unresolved. She said she had to get to an appointment. She wasn't fobbing me off, she had an endearing conscientiousness about her work and left me in the corridor pondering how I could persuade her she wouldn't hurt me.

Pete said that he was going to give it five years out of hospital to see if life would be bearable, and if not it was off to Beachy Head.

I agreed – five years was a fair crack, I might see him there. On the other side of the ward was Carl. He was about Pete's age and a born-again Christian. The summer before he had dived into a gravel pit without checking the depth and broken his neck. He went on and on about Jesus, often reading aloud from his bible. So far as he was concerned he had no complaints about his situation, it was simply the will of God.

'Why,' Pete demanded of Carl, 'was your God so keen for you to break your neck?'

'How should I know, I just trust Him.'

I said I didn't know what Carl saw in a God who enjoyed people breaking their necks and Carl said God didn't enjoy it.

'Why did he do it then?' asked Pete.

'To make me a better person.'

'If your God is all-powerful, couldn't He have improved you without breaking your bloody neck? I mean, Carl, my mum tells me that I'm a nicer person since I broke my neck, but I don't suppose she would have done it on purpose just for that.'

'With God there aren't any accidents.' Pete had wound him up thoroughly.

None the less, when it came to the Beachy Head plan Carl was up for it with the rest of us, he had a good sense of humour too.

As the days went by the plan became more and more sophisticated. We'd argue over what car to use. Pete favoured a 2CV, Carl something bigger, a Renault Espace with leather seats and tinted windows.

'Then we could sell tickets for the spare places. Gary would come, wouldn't you, Gary?'

'What?' said Gary.

Then the conversation would start all over again. It was somewhat disjointed, as we could not see each other from our respective beds, each staring at the ceiling. Only Pete was up in a wheelchair.

The two-hour physiotherapy sessions with Caryl had now become agonising, emotionally as well as physically. If she was dealing with someone else I could gaze at her adoringly from a distance; if she was working on me, it was even worse.

There was another guy who seemed to have a crush on her. I remember thinking, What chance has he got, he can't even sit up straight in his chair.

I imagined Caryl's parents, or her brother, saying, 'Pull yourself together, Caryl, you can't possibly go out with him, it would be a disaster for you.'

Then I heard on the hospital rumour mill that a male physio called Tony had taken Caryl out to dinner. I couldn't imagine what she could possibly see in him, except that he was able-bodied. OK, so he could trot down to the corner shop and get the newspaper, help her move house, whatever, but he was so boring, no sense of humour. Caryl and I had such fun together, surely it was more fun than being with him. Jealousy burned away within me.

It then struck me that Caryl might not want to go out with

The four boys. Me, Stuart, Angus and Rod

Aged 19, with Sarah Slight, in the Caribbean

No. 14 Pilots Course during training on 705 Squadron

With Dad at the presentation of 'Wings' at R.N.A.S. Culdrose

Penguin spotting by Sea King in South Georgia

Ignore him and he'll go away

Delivering chocolates by helicopter to Mum on her birthday

The Virgin Challenger capsule on board H.M.S. *Argonaut*

Yoldia. Home during my time at Portland

With Neville Gaunt after rescuing Richard Branson
and Per Linstrand from the ditched Virgin Challenger

With the Royal Navy ski squad.
The last photo taken of me before my accident

The journey home

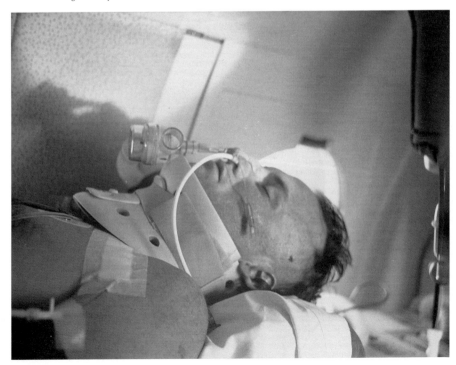

Home with Mum for the first time after hospital

With Sir Jimmy Saville at a fundraising event in London

Cartoon by Claire Minter-Kemp sold for £3000
at the launch of the Trevor Jones Trust

TREVAMOBILE N° II   MINTER-KEMP.

The Trev-mobile – Freedom

With Anneka Rice during the scuba diving trip to the Red Sea

Back on the slopes in Sweden.
Don't be fooled, the contraption was potentially lethal!

Sailing off Miami in the winter of 1992

Last photocall before flying across the Channel

Take off

Arriving at the Rolli fly-in. Exhausted, but happy

The Next Challenge

me because she loved me. What if in her mind going out with me might raise my hopes of marrying her to unrealistic levels, when despite what she felt for me it was impossible?

I clung to this hope, and as the days passed it did seem to me that she had begun again to spend more time with me, to talk more normally and to enjoy my company. She did enjoy my company, no question, but she was trying not to.

I started to do extra physio, although Caryl was only partly the inspiration for this; I also was feeling more determined to get stronger.

Caryl and I still had not successfully thrashed out the details of what was happening between us. It looked to me as if she wanted to go out with me but could not bear to be judged unprofessional by her peers. She was, I think, confused by her own feelings. It was a sort of 'Stop it, I like it' kind of situation. She had told me she could not go out with me, I did not believe her but decided to cool off her for a bit.

She'd said she was going to Henley with her father who was a rowing blue and a member of the Leander Club. My own father was over from the States, so knowing that she would be there I suggested to him that Henley might be a nice idea for a day out, and I asked Janet, one of the occupational therapists, to come along too.

I suppose these days I'd be done for stalking.

It was a lovely hot day as we milled around the steward's enclosure where everyone was getting very well oiled and having a thoroughly good time. The OT was from New Zealand and someone with whom I'd have had far more in common if I could have got Caryl out of my head. Then, as we were watching a race, Caryl suddenly hove into view.

She was on her own and came over to say 'Hi'. I introduced her to my father – I'd perked up considerably. Dad of course hadn't a clue what was going on. She was wearing a very pretty summer dress and one of the shoulder straps had fallen revealing her bra strap. It was very endearing, so like Caryl to be wandering around the enclosure completely unaware. She stayed a short time, then said she had to get back to her father. Sigh.

On 4 July 1988 Frank drove Mum and me to London for the official launch of the Trevor Jones Trust. Richard Branson had agreed to be its patron and the other celebrity guest was his balloon pilot Per Lindstrom. The event was combined with the opening of the Broadgate Wine Bar in the City. There were loads of City suits there, and Branson, dressed casually as ever, sprayed the crowd with champagne, partly, no doubt, an act of revenge for his unhappiness at the way the Virgin group's shares had performed after flotation. He'd just bought them back.

It was the first time I'd seen him since the rescue. There was an auction to raise funds for the Trust. Claire Minter-Kemp, a cousin of Melissa Woodard and family friend of Alex Howard, is a very talented artist. She had painted a cartoon of the Trevmobile especially for the occasion – a wheelchair turned into a wine bar with champagne bottles for exhausts, a big umbrella and mechanical corkscrews coming off the side. It was number two in a series of five, each with a different theme. A chap bid £3,000 for it, and at the end of the evening he gave it to me.

Georgia said, 'That bloke lost his job this morning.' It may have been the end of the eighties, and a time when reckless generosity of that sort was still possible, but what a guy. If I was going to break my neck and have my friends and their friends rally round, then 1988 wasn't a bad year in which to do it.

A few days later Mum took me up to London again to see school contemporary Jason Connery's first-night appearance in a West End production of *Journey's End*. He had always got a lot of stick at Gordonstoun for being Sean's son. There were quite a few friends in the theatre foyer, some of whom I had not seen for years.

I was amazed that Jason was starring at such a prominent

venue; I think it must be difficult having such a famous actor as a dad and having to prove yourself on your own merits. Of course to old mates it was just Jason up there warts and all, exactly like a school play, but he acted well and was in complete control of his part. If the performance was compelling, however, it failed to keep me awake. I was so exhausted with one thing and another that half-way through I drifted off, only waking when the applause started at the end. There had been a collective unspoken decision among my companions to let poor Trevor sleep and not nudge him awake.

I was very irritated at this and it was Mum who got the brunt of my frustration the whole way back to Stoke – my poor mum who did so much for me. 'Why the bloody hell didn't you wake me up? I came all this way and everyone thinks it better I should be allowed to sleep.'

This period was quite a difficult one for Mum. For the first few months she had virtually moved into Stoke Mandeville hospital to support me. As her diary says, 'Trevor starting on rehab. Somehow I have to let go and keep caring.'

I still needed her, but I needed her less, or rather in a different way, which included giving me a bit of space. She understood this very well, indeed so much so that she had got herself a job nearby as a physio at a private spinal injuries clinic called the Paddocks, so that she could both learn more about the whole field and occupy herself while still being near at hand for me.

Also I was taking my distress about Caryl out on her. As another diary entry says, 'Trev v. miserable and I am so distressed by his crying it weakens me for days.'

For the next week or so an uneasy stand-off continued at our physio sessions. Neither Caryl nor I knew what was going on between us, I think we were both equally distressed, only she had a job which fully occupied her. I was possessed by my thoughts morning to night. Then one day Caryl whispered something I had been longing to hear: 'Meet me in casualty at 5.00.'

Despite the longing I spent the whole morning dreading meeting Caryl in the romantic surroundings of the casualty department. I felt sure she was going to put an end to our faltering relationship.

To my dismay she had the same lengthy explanation as to why the thing was a no go: it would not be professional. 'Even being here with you now is wrong. I'm sorry, Trevor, but I can't be going out with you again.' These were the words that came out of her mouth, but they sounded unconvincing and I did not believe what she was saying.

I attempted to persuade her that a relationship with me need not interfere with her work, if she could believe she was doing nothing wrong. I'd have said anything, in fact I did, arguing the toss with her, back and forth.

Suddenly she came out with the blinder: 'Then there is the fact you are not a Christian.'

'Yes I am,' I said.

'But you are not born again, in the sense that you lead your life for Christ. Jesus is the most important thing in my life and I need someone to share everything with.'

I was not exactly sure what she was talking about and said, 'You're not going to let religion get between us at this early stage. I'm not talking marriage, Caryl, all I know is I spend every moment thinking about you, we get on great and have a lot of fun together. At least we could give the whole thing a try, see how it works out, it may not last, but at least we could try. Anyway, if it came to something, why couldn't I become born again?'

After an hour's heated, passionate discussion – no, negotiation – we fell silent.

'OK,' she said suddenly, 'let's give it a try.'

My heart started buzzing. 'What?' I said, hardly believing my ears.

'I must go,' she said, so we started back to the spinal unit.

'Are you sure,' I said. 'You're not going to change your mind.'

'Quite sure.'

'Right, brilliant.'

We stopped to go our separate ways.

I was elated. 'Then give me a kiss.'

This horrified her, it was back to square one, an outrageous suggestion. Like, What? Here?

'No,' she said.

'But why not?' I felt crushed again. 'If I could grab hold of you and kiss you I would.'

'I can't kiss you in public.'

I realised I had to explain my frustration, that I couldn't articulate my affection in a natural way. If I'd been able-bodied I'd have put an arm around her and just given her a quick kiss to seal our agreement but I couldn't do that from my wheelchair. I felt so frustrated that possibly for the first time I could not do something I wanted to do really badly.

Then she suddenly leant over me as if to straighten my collar and kissed me on the cheek.

After that we went out in the evenings and at weekends quite a lot, although not as often as I'd have liked because Caryl played netball and had bible-study evenings among other commitments.

Pete, I and a few others formed a bit of a group: with our respective physios, we would sometimes all go down to the pub together in the evenings. Stoke Mandeville has a strange effect on its long-term patients.

As Pete's analysis had it, denial is where it's at. It's far more fun than acceptance, and all round the ward would be people deep in denial having the time of their lives. The thing about being in hospital struggling over a grave disability is that you can forget all the things that used to weigh you down when you were on the outside – your family, your mortgage, the difficult relationship with your boss, what to wear, the electricty bill, what to eat, everything. While you are in hospital everything is beyond your control or your power to influence it. It is like being a child again.

All your responsibilities are suddenly put on hold while you fight this major disaster that has befallen you. The only person you have to think of is yourself, the only time-scale is today. Provided, that is, you are in denial. So, many patients, once partly mobile, have a ball.

I reminded Pete recently of another patient at Stoke Mandeville, a little Egyptian girl called Mae of whom I was very fond. I think she was too young to include in our Beachy Head plan, being only eleven years old. Mum had adopted her to some extent because all her family and friends were in Egypt. She was a bright, sparky character, a bit loopy in a self-defensive sort of way, with this big guffaw of a laugh typical of those tetraplegics whose chest muscles are paralysed (I laugh like that too). The laugh comes from the bottom of the throat. She'd arrived at Stoke a couple of months after me speaking no English but she had learnt incredibly quickly. Later, when friends like Georgia came to take me for a stroll around the grounds we'd take Mae too.

'Trevor,' she'd say, 'I'm only eleven years old, so young and I'm going to spend my whole life like this. I just can't believe it.' She had dived into a swimming pool and broken her neck and was tetraplegic like me. And yet she was, as I say, bright, perky, funny and optimistic.

'Bloody hell,' said Pete. 'Did she say that? That's incredibly advanced, it goes beyond denial. She said that aged eleven, just five months after her accident? My God.'

Thirteen

I wanted to take Caryl out to dinner for her birthday so I invited her to a very highly rated local restaurant called The Bell in Aston Clinton. 'What time shall I pick you up?' she asked.

'No, you don't pick me up, you always pick me up, I'll pick you up.'

'But how? Don't be silly.'

I was determined to show I would not always be dependent on someone. I hired a white Mercedes taxi from a local firm. Being big, it was easier to get me into it and there was room in the boot for my wheelchair.

It was the first time I went out without someone taking me. As far as I knew, it was the first time any tetraplegic at Stoke had taken himself out. It felt like a big and risky adventure – you could call it my first 'first'.

We went by a cash machine, then a florist's, then to Caryl's house. She was impressed, I think, more by the fact that I had got myself there than by the flowers or where we were going. I had never taken anyone to such a fine restaurant, able-bodied or not. The pleasure was heightened by the contrast with the hospital. We had fabulous food and champagne which I paid for myself with my own credit card and scratchy signature and more important than anything, Caryl's company was divine.

Shortly afterwards she told me that she was going to Australia for a wedding and to catch up with her friends. That put the frighteners up me. Although she was English, much of her upbringing had been out there and it would be natural for her to want to return. The job of physio at Stoke Mandeville would be typical for your average itinerant Aussie stacking up cash for the next part of a world tour.

She said she was going for three weeks. To me, whose hospital time horizon was limited pretty much to today and the day after, three weeks was a lifetime.

She had often talked about going back to live in Oz. Her close friends were there and, I feared, an old boyfriend. 'There are a lot of things I need to straighten out whilst I'm away,' she said cryptically.

'Are you sure you're coming back?'

She laughed. 'Of course I'm sure.'

She visited the ward to say goodbye and gave me a tape of favourite songs. It was the first thing she had ever given me and, as she must have spent a while compiling it, I was thrilled. She said, 'Don't worry, I will be coming back.'

Once she was gone I convinced myself that at worst she'd go down under and fall in love with somebody else, and at best she would return and finish with me. My anxiety was too much.

I withdrew into myself, stopped chatting with Pete and Carl, began to feel down, fell ill even and was ordered to bed, where I stayed for two weeks. While in bed I played Caryl's tape of favourite songs over and over. I kept on having to ask the nurses to turn the tape over.

Then one day the post arrived and I could see a jumbo-sized postcard of an Australian beach.

I didn't dare read it, convinced that it would say she was settling in Australia again having found some hunky surfer for Christ and that it was all over between us. When it was finally held up for me to read, it said only that she was having a good time, meeting old friends and that she had become a lot clearer in her thoughts about us. This was as enigmatic as it could be and I didn't feel at all reassured.

In early August, when I'd recovered enough from the absence

of Caryl to be out of bed again, I went off home to Wales for the first time since my accident, staying at The Maerdy stables, Mum and Frank's wheelchair-accessible holiday cottage.

A houseful of friends came to stay too, people like Vanda North and my old Navy friend Pete Griffiths, wife Emma and her sister Lucy and old school friend Marc Koska from Gayhurst days.

I left Stoke driven by Frank, with Angus in the car too. I'd just bought myself a computer, my first. It was small and battery-operated. I played with it the whole way down to avoid talking to anyone. Mum had got an old nurse in to help and she had put me to bed. I was lying there at the converted stable cottage and what tipped me over was the image in a full-length dressing mirror of my empty wheelchair. Suddenly all the tears I'd bottled up for months in hospital started to pour out and I cried and cried.

Then Frank came by, probably to say good-night but, seeing me crying, he said, 'Now come on, Trevor, pull yourself together.' At that particular moment it was exactly the wrong thing to say.

I screamed at him to eff off and get out of here. I don't think I'd been as angry since those two holiday-makers had skied across in front of me moments before my accident. I did stop crying, though.

The next day I was fine, surrounded as I was by friends. We made a trip to the theatre in Swansea and, during the week, not really knowing what else to do, I began a routine of physio down at the local hospital.

At the end Marc drove me back to Stoke. It was a very busy time because only a few days after that Mum drove me down to the first big Trevor Jones Trust event I ever attended: a cricket match at the Duke of York's barracks in Chelsea. It was arranged by Bill Carrington between a Gordonstoun Old Boys XI and a bunch of local Chelsea estate agents.

It was a very hot day and difficult for me to keep cool because another of the things that goes wrong when you break your neck is that you lose the ability to sweat and regulate your body temperature. I was very pleased to see that Sean Parry-Jones and his family had set up camp on the boundary.

Sean had already visited me once in hospital. He was the first tetraplegic I got to know who had been injured for some time. He was the same age as me but had broken his neck in a rugby accident while captain and head boy at Llandovery College. His injury was a bit lower than mine, C7, which meant he had more strength in his arms and could get himself in and out of a wheelchair unaided. Like mine, his body thermostat was substantially broken and he busied himself with keeping us both cool by the application of spray from a mister for house plants and a bag of ice.

Sean was an inspiration to me. He drove his own car and for a while lived alone, determined to show that he could do it. For some time he did, at fantastic cost to his body. For example, when it came to his bowel movements he'd position himself over the loo, then attempt to insert suppositories with a special applicator. As he had no feeling, he quite often ending up stabbing himself in the wrong bit, causing serious damage. Then he'd sit waiting for them to work, sometimes for several hours.

Nowadays he has someone round to give him a hand every couple of days but still manages to live substantially alone. For a person who can't hold a knife, he is dead impressive around a kitchen, knocking together a good lunch without any help at all. He has always been an inspiration to me because of his determination to get on with his life and because of his great sense of humour.

After the cricket match there was a dinner in a restaurant called La Finezza off Sloane Square. I left half-way through, absolutely knackered by the heat and the excitement, by having to talk to people I knew, or to friends of friends who had heard about what had happened to me and come to wish me well. The cricket match raised £4,500 for the Trust and ran as an annual event for another five years.

Caryl was back but still had a week of holiday left which she took with her family on the Isle of Wight. I rang her up and invited her to the ballet at Sadler's Wells. She'd said she liked the ballet so I thought she wouldn't say no to that. I fixed up the whole thing: tickets, the lot, including tracking her down at her holiday location. This was no negligible feat because I had not wanted to share my plans with everyone by using the ward phone and had stuggled for hours with the one in the foyer, trying to get the coin into the slot.

From my point of view the occasion was a great success. She watched the ballet and I watched her watching the ballet. Then we went back to my brothers' house in Clapham where I had taken to staying for the odd weekend.

There was no one there and Caryl transferred me to the sofa so we could be closer; half-sitting, half-lying we talked a bit and cuddled a bit. Self-concious as ever, Caryl would sit up and straighten her clothes every time someone walked past, even though the curtains were closed. Apart from that she gave me her undivided attention. It was bliss.

The next week Bill Carrington visited again. He wanted to talk about the vehicle he thought the Trevor Jones Trust should in due course be buying me. Being still in hospital, struggling with my rehabilitation, I had little direct involvement in the various schemes being dreamt up on my behalf, but certainly the success of the cricket match and Broadgate Colony wine bar opening meant that a first capital purchase could be considered.

Bill was basically in charge of all the admin, but he had his enthusiasms (admin not necessarily the top of them) and what he is most enthusiastic about is cars. (Bill still hasn't learnt the lesson that speeding earns you points on your licence, and that too many points lose you your licence. In my time I have written several letters to magistrates on his behalf to argue that the loss of his licence would be a grievous loss to the voluntary sector.)

His first project was to research the best and latest wheelchair-accessible car. I think he probably wanted it to be a bit of a surprise, so he didn't consult with me at all. He had already decided that what would be just the ticket was a converted Renault Espace. He could have got the standard conversion relatively quickly, but thought that what I should really have was the LE GTi version.

A £3,000 deposit was paid and the thing was ordered, all this before I myself had even met the specialist driving instructor or taken advice at Stoke Mandeville. In fact at the time I was not yet aware of the specialist advice available, but faced with all that enthusiasm and grateful for – or humbled by – everyone's efforts on my behalf, I agreed.

All these jaunts add up to a picture of someone not in hospital much at all, which is not the truth. It was just weekends and the odd evening that I went out and quite often, even usually, the experiences left me so whacked that I needed several days to recover.

Meanwhile the tedious business of rehabilitation continued. I was doing my best with building up the strength in my arms. Every little thing helped, from feeding myself to using the exercycle, from lifting weights (little ones), to fencing or work in the hydro pool. My dexterity improved in playing Michele's wretched solitaire game. There were many other exercises as well, like hours of stretching, or balancing on the edge of a plinth. There was the standing frame in which you are strapped.

Then there was the educational side, the meetings with naval resettlement, the psychologist, training on computers, driving, information about wheelchairs. It all added up to a lot of activity, but any improvement I made was incremental, tiny little advances that I barely noticed.

One of the senior nurses, a lovely Irish lady, Mrs Ward,

who had been at the hospital thirty years, had spotted the competitive streak in me (don't know how!) and encouraged me to organise a pool tournament involving patients, nurses and auxiliaries. Obviously I couldn't hold a cue on my own, so I paired myself up with Pete. The cue had been slightly adapted by building up the thickness a little and adding a velcro strap and Pete would hold the rest, or the end of the cue. I would motor my chair into position and with someone holding my shoulders direct Pete: 'Left a bit, right a bit, gently now, hold it, now.' It was a knock-out tournament and to everyone's amazement we won – there is even a photo in the *Aylesbury Gazette* of us clutching our trophy to prove it.

Of all my sporting achievements, playing hockey for the Navy, being captain of this and that at Gordonstoun, this was the most satisfying.

I had been invited back to Gordonstoun to take part in a fun run, or walk in which the Trevor Jones Trust would be the beneficiary. The whole school did a sponsored walk on a 10-kilometre route around and about Elgin. It had been organised by the boys and girls, the idea originating with one of my teachers, Ben Goss, who in my day had been the master in charge of the Surf Life-savers.

I was amazed, because although I loved the place and had fantastic respect for Ben, in the ten years that I had been out of there I had done barely more than send the odd postcard to a teacher. I had made little effort to remain in touch.

The run was organised for a Sunday so Rod, Bill and a few others flew up with me the day before.

Ben Goss, who is a runaholic, pushed me in my wheelchair over the entire route. I don't think he quite realised how delicate I was. The whole experience terrified me, with the chair crashing over bumps, or getting its wheels caught in drains.

Ben is one of those people for whom the expression 'larger than life' was invented, but incredibly kind and generous with it. His enthusiasm for anything is such that he doesn't immediately hoist in all the implications of a particular course of action. In this case running off with a wheelchair containing Trevor, who is unable to sit up properly and will tend to fall out. On the other hand he is a master of improvisation and as there was nothing available at the start of the course, anything at hand was used, such as plastic carrier bags in strips to pin back my legs and waist.

I found the whole experience unnerving as Ben, incurably jolly and singing at the top of his voice, hurtled me around the course. Being September and Scotland, the weather had become pretty cold and this, combined with my inability to shiver or do anything to keep myself warm, meant that by the end I was chilled to the bone.

I went to bed exhausted but the next morning Rod had me up and into chapel for 8.15. There was a telling moment when Ben and some boys lifted me on to the central platform to address the school.

It was something I had done many times as Guardian, but now I was very nervous indeed, with all my frailties to the fore as I went on public display in a big way for the first time. Within Stoke Mandeville I could cope, but outside, my self-image was confused and as a result I was very unsure of myself.

I was expected to speak; they'd raised all this money, so Ben was certainly not going to let me off the hook, knackered or not. I had to thank them all for it, however vulnerable and self-conscious I felt.

I said a few words, something like how much the school was still a part of me, what it meant to come back nine years on and have the support of all you boys and girls. I related to them something about the school motto 'Plus est en vous' – there is more in you than you think – and how my friends from Gordonstoun had set up the Trust and how your friends sitting around you now will always be your friends however many years pass without you seeing one another, such is the strength of your shared experience at Gordonstoun.

The school record at the end of the year published several poems that moved me. Amber Roome described that morning in chapel thus:

> Helpless,
> Undignified,
> A thousand pairs of eyes,
> staring.
> Terrified,
> the words begin to flow,
> silently,
> without hope.
> Sad faces,
> compassion,
> relief,
> then joy.

That visit was the start of several individual initiatives for fund-raising by the boys and girls. A lot of money was raised for the Trust by selling T-shirts or from cheques solicited from Gordonstoun old boys and girls.

The weekend over, I returned to Stoke Mandeville with Rod and took straight to my bed. It was a week before I recovered.

My relationship with Caryl was lurching all around the place. She took me to meet her parents one weekend for lunch. I wasn't quite sure what my status with them was: Caryl's new boyfriend or just her patient from the hospital. I felt very ill at ease and self-conscious, but that probably had to do with the fact that that was the way I felt in any context outside the hospital. Generally I would be so tired that I'd find it hard to make any kind of conversation. I didn't have much small talk and it must have been difficult for them too.

But Caryl was a delight. Whatever my status, she was so excited about having me meet her parents and carefully made sure that the conversation always included me, however quiet and withdrawn I was. I adored her even more, but I couldn't help wondering what her parents must think. Somehow I got the impression they were a bit concerned about their daughter's relationship.

So that was Caryl on a good day. On a bad day, especially in the hospital, she would almost ignore me. She was so sensitive about the rumour mill and imagined, as she worked with me in the gym, that everyone was staring at her.

We went to the Albert Hall for a Prom one night – famous love duets from opera. When she delivered me back to Stoke after midnight, she took me up to the ward, kissed me good-night, opened the door, gave the chair a shove and scarpered, leaving me rolling gently to a halt stranded some forty feet short of the nurses' desk.

This emotional roller-coaster began to get intolerable and I started to think I should leave the hospital. Early in October the weather got colder so I was going out less. The summer season of Henley or the Proms was at an end, so I was quite often stuck there at weekends twiddling my thumbs (well, you know what I mean).

There were little highlights like Guy Solleveld, this time not dressed in a nurse's uniform, but coming to give a talk to the patients about our trip to the Antarctic aboard HMS *Endurance*, sad in a way because it reminded me of what I'd lost, but fantastically appreciated. There isn't enough of that sort of thing at Stoke Mandeville.

Dr Frankel thought that it was too soon for me to leave. My early trauma had held me back a lot, and he felt I still had much to learn, a lot to achieve in terms of physiotherapy. Possibly I should stay until the New Year, twelve months on from my accident.

My body was now constantly on fire with the phantom pain, a sensation a bit like pins and needles all over my body, or as if I was sitting on a block of ice. In so far as I can feel anything it is pressure. I can't feel a pin sticking into me, but the pain I feel is worsened by pressure.

One night, in considerable discomfort, I called for the

nurse and asked her to turn me, but she refused, telling me that I would have to wait another two hours until the next four-hourly turn.

Raising my voice I demanded to see the senior night nurse. Eventually she arrived to tell me I would have to wait. I was furious and started shouting at her to get the duty doctor. They turned me.

I went to see the spinal unit's psychologist, Dr Paul Kennedy. On my second visit I reluctantly opened up and told him what was really on my mind and making me depressed, namely the problems of unrequited love I was having with Caryl, then finally I told Dr Frankel that I needed to leave, explaining that I had fallen in love with my physio.

'But that seems to me like a good reason for staying. It is not unusual for patients and staff to fall in love with each other.'

Dr Frankel too advised that I stay. I had been so ill when I arrived that I was still well behind what I should one day achieve. But I was insistent and there wasn't anything much he could do to keep me there

I didn't fully explain to Caryl that the biggest factor in making me leave was the emotional agony I was going through over her. Probably she understood. There was so much energy and tension between us, whether sexual or just embarrassment, or unresolved conflict, it was unbearable. I had to go.

Mum had offered to let me live in The Maerdy stables, which was vacant until Easter. I didn't really want to live in Wales where I was likely to get bored by the lack of friends of my own age, but there was nothing else available, especially at short notice. I couldn't live in the house in Clapham bought with Rod and Angus. It wasn't properly accessible, besides which there would have been no room for a care assistant, and I'd need one of those full time. Neither would I qualify for a council house in London, having never actually lived there. So Wales it was.

A farewell party was held in the hospital canteen. Jimmy Savile came down from his flat for it. He's someone who attracts strong views. I think he's taken too much for granted by his detractors. Yes, you can make fun of him for wandering around in his tracksuit with all that jangly jewellery, and no, he never draws breath when talking, but he's a showman, that's his job. And over the years he's achieved fantastic things for charity. More important, he has changed the lives of countless individuals for the better. I think he's brilliant.

I asked him about the Trevor Jones Trust and what its aims should be. I was ill at ease at being the recipient of charity, because of the way I was brought up. Just as my Dad never made use of the free pass from Virgin Atlantic – as many flights as he wanted – he preferred to pay.

I asked Jimmy what he thought about us building up the Trevor Jones Trust as a national charity for the benefit of others. His advice shocked me a little as it was not really what I wanted to hear.

'Get your own life back together and look out for yourself. That's where you should concentrate, leave the thinking about other people to us guys.'

Behind the superficial-looking showman is a deep, intelligent, plain-speaking and straightforward person. One way or another he's seen and experienced a lot more than most and he's wise because of it.

Caryl was at the party but I had little chance to talk to her.

'You will come down to Wales to see me, won't you?'

'Maybe,' she said, enigmatic to the last. The person who actually drove me away from the hospital was the ever-faithful Georgia Bailey along with Vanda. The date was 11 November 1988, eleven months and a day since my accident.

We'd been invited to supper by Richard Branson at his house near Oxford. I wanted to thank him for all his kindness to my family and for being a patron of the Trevor Jones Trust. Georgia and I had had a conversation in which she'd asked,

'What do you want to do, what above all else do you want to do?'

I thought about it and gave a very literal reply. 'Above all else what I want to do is sail around the world.' The Whitbread Round the World race was in the news a lot at the time.

No plan is too mad for Georgia so she said, 'Why don't you ask Branson if he can help?'

There was a good family atmosphere round the table, relaxed, informal. His wife Joan stayed at the table while Richard put the children to bed. Joan said, 'I can't remember the last time he did that.' The children, aged five and sevenish, were playing up something rotten: as soon as he got one to bed the other would slip out and come and hide under the dining table. Richard would come looking and we'd pretend we didn't know where they were.

I thought about my sailing idea all the way through dinner, then finally plucked up the courage to say, 'There is something I want to ask. I'm interested in getting sponsorship together for a Whitbread campaign.'

'Trevor, how much would that cost me?'

I'd read somewhere £4 million, so that's what I said.

Richard kept a straight face. 'Right now, it's rather more than I could afford. But if you want me to write any letters to anyone, Tracy Edwards say, then I will.'

It was a such a natural reply to a completely outrageous request and the wonderful thing was that he took me seriously.

After three months the patient was mobilised into a wheelchair and completed his rehabilitation and he was discharged on 11 November 1988. At that time he was still paralysed in his hands, chest, truck, abdomen and lower limbs and confined to a wheelchair.

On examination I found his condition to be as follows:–

GENERAL CONDITION:
Good.

Cardiovascular System:

No abnormality detected.

Respiratory System:

Diaphragmatic breathing otherwise no abnormality detected.

CENTRAL NERVOUS SYSTEM:

Fully conscious and alert, memory good.

Cranial nerves:

No abnormality detected.

Motor function:

Upper limbs: In his right arm he has good but not normal power in the deltoid and biceps. He has very slight power in the extensor carpi radialis longus. (He can move his arm forwards and outwards, he can bend the elbow but can only straighten it feebly. He can just cock-up his wrist).

In his left arm he has good power in the deltoid and biceps and slight power in the triceps. He has good but not normal power in the extensor carpi radialis longus. (He can make the same movements as on the right but somewhat stronger.)

All muscles of his fingers and thumbs remain paralysed.

Intercostals: Paralysed.

Abdominals: Paralysed.

Lower limbs: Paralysed.

Sensory Function:

Light touch severely impaired below C6 segment but present throughout.

Pinprick absent below C5 on the right, C6 on the left.

Spasticity:

He complains of severe spasticity of the chest, trunk, abdomen and lower limbs and he takes Baclofen 20 mgs four times a day to try and reduce this.

Pain:

He complains of pains in his hands, wrists, chest, abdomen, legs, buttocks and groin. He says this burning pain is present all day, every day and is worse when he is feeling low in the evening and is often bad at night. None of the treatments we have tried have been successful in reducing this pain.

Sexual function:

He has reflex erections but no psychic erections and no emissions.

Bowel Function:

Etc.

Fourteen

I was very busy immediately after leaving hospital. There was a fund-raising hockey match between Gordonstoun Old Boys and Old St Andrews university students, and then there was to be a big dinner at the Lord's conference centre organised by school friends Alistair Scott and Malcolm Stewart.

But just before that I'd flown up to Glasgow with Suzie Huntingdon – my girlfriend from my first year at school – to go to Angus Buchanan's wedding. The plane arrived late leaving us no time to change. Changing in a taxi is difficult enough for an able-bodied person as Suzie demonstrated, wrestling into her wedding outfit. Then she had to attend to me, stripping me then reassembling me as my legs shot all over the place in spasm. Passers-by looking in must have wondered who was raping whom, while the taxi-driver sat patiently and politely, looking around, pretending not to look in the mirror.

We just made the door before the bride. We stayed overnight at the RAC Club where the reception continued well into the night, and after no sleep caught the midday shuttle, arriving at the hockey just after the start.

We watched for a bit, but I was getting too cold, so Suzie pushed me off to a nearby pub, telling the others to join us after the game. After an hour, there was still no sign of anyone. She left me sheltering while she went off to look for them. It soon emerged that they had gone. The dinner was supposed to be a black tie do, but neither of us knew where. Frantically we tried to contact somebody by phone, but of course they were out. By the time we got through to someone who knew what was going on, it was nearly start time and we were going to have no time to change back into our posh clothes.

Finally Suzie and I arrived at a party already in full swing. I was overwhelmed by the people I met there, friends from Gordonstoun, friends from the Navy and friends of friends. I had no idea so many people I knew would be there.

It should perhaps have been a celebration of some kind because I was out of hospital, but I felt as I had felt with Caryl's parents, multiplied a million times. I felt I had nothing to hold my head high about and was self-conscious that all these people had come to raise money for me. I didn't like it; I'd never liked being made a fuss of or being the centre of attention (unless I had had a bit to drink and was playing the fool on my own terms). I hated being the subject of charity.

Once we'd finally arrived, I no longer wanted to be there. I was so tired I could not find the considerable effort needed to be positive about the whole thing. I felt different; I was not only in a wheelchair but also the only one not in evening dress.

People would come over and say 'Hi Trevor, how's things?' or 'You're looking well', or 'You look great', or 'How are you?'

I could say nothing, my head was empty of thoughts. One by one everyone came up to me. I tried to smile, listen and nod but my voice was still weak, the room noisy and I just could not think what to say, so we had these stilted conversations one by one or in little groups, with me in my wheelchair, in a corner, my back to the wall, while all about us raged a pretty damned good party. Above all I was absolutely knackered.

I put on as brave a face as I could and don't think that I was rude to anyone, but the conversations were superficial, especially as, like it or not, I was the centre of attention, and they were pleased to come by and briefly wish me well. I needn't have worried. Virtually everyone was pissed and happy.

At the end of the dinner there was an auction of items

donated to raise money. There were plenty of items you might want to own, but everything went for far more than it was worth. Bill Carrington did a great job conducting it, whipping the crowd up into a frenzy, a surprising performance because despite his apparent brash self-confidence he is naturally quite shy.

At school my brother Rod had rejoiced in the nickname 'Scrote' on account of his sporran-like appendages. He was wearing a kilt (we Joneses have a remote claim through one grandfather to wearing one), and an auction started in which the boys were bidding for him to show whether or not (the usual joke) he was a real Scotsman and whether, in terms of the magnificence of these appendages, he lived up to his reputation.

Then Georgia Bailey started a bid on behalf of the girls for him not to show his all. The bidding leapt ahead in £20 slices, then as it flagged in £5 slices until eventually the boys won with a knock-out bid of £402.50, or some such price. Amidst wails and screams of horror – I think it was horror – Rod duly showed his all, and yes, for that night at least he was a real Scotsman.

After that all hell broke loose in the Lord's conference centre, normally the venue for staid cricket dinners, where the wit extends to jokes about slipped catches at silly mid-off. Not that I am suggesting for a moment that wit was in the ascendancy on that particular evening, it was just that everyone was pissed, and anything and everything was treated as uproariously funny. At one stage a bog roll was sold for £200 all for the benefit of the Trevor Jones Trust.

After the auction Georgia Bailey kept coming across to try to get me on to the dance floor and I kept refusing. I couldn't dance so what was the point? She wanted to push me around in time to the music. Others kept asking me the same. After a while she asked if there was anyone I would dance with, already, I suspect, knowing the answer.

Part of me still had a candle burning for Sarah Slight, the

girl I had abandoned in the Caribbean after Dad's wedding, so when she came and asked I relented. She sat on my lap while Georgia pushed the chair, soon a conga formed that went around the room, all these people in their twenties having a ball, a fantastic party, and despite trying not to, I ended up enjoying myself.

After the dinner Sean Parry-Jones drove me back to Wales. He had a Ford Escort adapted with hand controls to operate the brake and accelerator. To me Sean was what we'd have called at Dartmouth a Sea Daddy, someone who knew the ropes and had been through it before.

The back of the car was loaded with our two wheelchairs, our luggage and half a dozen pictures which Sean hoped to trade at Carmarthen auction the next day.

Half-way down the M4 we stopped at Membury service station for some petrol which was fine because someone would fill up the car for us.

'Do you fancy something to eat?' asked Sean.

I looked at him knowing there was no way either of us could get anywhere near our wheelchairs, let alone the Happy Eater or whatever it was.

'Don't worry,' he said. 'You've got a thing or two to learn, Trevor. Just you watch closely. There's a technique which I've refined over the years. You've just got to know who to ask.'

He wound down his window and let half a dozen people go by. 'Ah, here he comes, here's our man. Excuse me, sir,' he began, but before he could get any more words out the guy had walked straight past, completely ignoring him.

'OK,' he said, undefeated. 'Here we go,' as another man approached. 'Excuse me, sir, we're both in wheelchairs and can't get out, would you mind asking the waiter to come out and help us?'

The guy said, 'Sure, fine,' and disappeared. Ten minutes later, no sign of anyone.

I said, 'Let me have a go, Sean.'

'No, no' – because Sean likes to be in charge – 'Excuse me sir, we're both in wheelchairs, could you get us a waiter . . .'

The guy said, 'So sorry, I'm in a bit of a hurry.'

Finally he got the attention of a fourth guy. 'No,' the guy said, 'I won't get you a waiter. I'll get it myself.' Sean offered to give him the money but he'd already gone. We sat there uncertain whether we'd been abandoned again while I took the piss out of him for his technique which he'd refined over the years.

And then the chap came back laden with coffee, doughnuts, sandwiches, everything we'd asked for. He put the sugar in for us, opened the wrappers and wouldn't leave until he was sure there was nothing more he could do for us.

Before I left Stoke Mandeville Mum placed an advert in *Nursing Times* for a personal care assistant. I invited half a dozen applicants to the hospital for interview and offered the job to Jenny Ray. Jenny was young, strong and had experience working in a spinal unit. She seemed ideal.

She couldn't start immediately so my mother got someone else locally as a stopgap. She was Irish, in her fifties and fussed around me like an old woman. It's certain she meant well, but living in my mother's adapted cottage with this woman going 'There, there, Trevor, now I've cooked a lovely supper for you' wound me up thoroughly. It was not a good start to my life of dependency on care in the community. Mum saw the problem pretty quickly and we let her go. This still left us with the problem of who was going to help me. It would have been too much to expect Mum to be my full-time carer; in fact it was out of the question. Her own life had been turned upside down by my accident as it was.

I was aware that Mum and Frank's relationship had been a bit distant even before my accident but things were worse now. He was resentful that his partner (they'd never married) was spending so much time looking after her son. Also her son was occupying The Maerdy stables, the adapted cottage which was supposed to be part of their joint holiday cottage business, and apparently he went on and on at her because of what it was costing.

To find a new stopgap carer Mum placed an ad at the local job centre in Llandeilo. There were several replies and after a bit of vetting we selected a guy called Isaac Romanov.

He was an odd-ball selection in some ways. He was distantly related to the Russian royal family and entitled to call himself Count. He was very intelligent, with PhDs in two different subjects, so I suppose I should refer to him as Dr the Count Isaac Romanov. His most recent job had been as a supermarket shelf stacker.

I think he was drawn to the job because he was going through a patch of his own soul-searching and was interested in my predicament. He himself was a classic stage-camp gay with a brash, working-class boyfriend down in the valley, his bit of rough.

He took all his duties very seriously. He'd put a pinny on to cook and charged around the kitchen in a way that made me laugh. Expectation would build as you heard all the effort and flurry and clanging in the kitchen, only for him to emerge proudly bearing sausage and beans on toast. For a gay man with artistic sensibilities and into the better things in life, he was a hopeless cook.

He had a vast general knowledge and understanding of things. He'd question me especially closely about my recent experiences, but the process of talking these things through made me quite upset, tears would come to my eyes and then he'd be filled with contrition and embarrassment.

He was funny when doing my bowel movement, which involves surgical gloves and the application of suppositories. The night before I take laxatives, and the next morning my carer dons surgical gloves, rolls me on my side and gets things rolling with the suppositories. Nice work if you can get it, it isn't.

Isaac, for all his other personal qualities, found this whole aspect of his employment a bit difficult. I could tell this even though I could neither see what was going on, because I faced the wall, nor feel it because, well, I can't feel. He had on his pinny and his latex gloves and I talked him through the procedure, which had to be performed every other day.

After a while I became conscious that I was talking to myself, a silence in the room indicating that Dr the Count Isaac Romanov was no longer with me. Then as suddenly as he'd disappeared he'd be back, making out that everything was just fine but sounding slightly distressed.

The mystery as to where he was going was solved by the arrival of my mother, who found him outside quietly throwing up into the flower bed. 'It's awful, Margaret, thank God you've arrived . . .' and so from then on Mum quietly took over and did my bowel movements for me, leaving Isaac to make cups of tea. Afterwards he would get me dressed and into my wheelchair.

Isaac was just a stopgap carer, filling in for a couple of weeks. He'd reduced me to tears talking too directly about my problems, was a hopeless cook and not up to dealing with my business end. He sounds like the carer from hell, but when he left I missed him because he was amusing, intelligent, good company, and of all my former personal assistants he is one of very few with whom I have remained in touch.

His company was stimulating, and goodness knows, my brain had had little to occupy it at Stoke. The Woody Allen joke is 'My brain is my second favourite organ'. If he were paralysed it might become his first favourite, and having Isaac around was good for mine. My powers of mental attentiveness had slipped massively at Stoke where all your responsibilities were taken care of for you.

Caryl did visit me. I spent two whole days in bed building up my strength. Isaac was at his most attentive as he nursed me. Ever sensitive, he'd soon picked up on how important this visit was for my morale.

I went into a decline when her arrival was delayed for a day by a blanket of dense fog over Southern England and Wales. Isaac drove me to Cardiff on Saturday, we met Caryl off the train, had lunch and then he made himself scarce whilst Caryl and I went to watch Australia play Wales at the Arms Park. It was a cold day and Caryl stood behind me in the wheelchair enclosure. We were alone together for the first time since my leaving hospital. I still had no idea how she would react so when she put her arms around me and squeezed, I relaxed for possibly the first time in months.

Afterwards we went back to The Maerdy and Isaac took the rest of the weekend off.

Jenny Ray, my new carer, was a qualified nurse, had experience in a spinal unit and was very confident about her work, whereas Isaac had been learning on the job. By comparison she was immensely competent. I was glad to be dressed and up quickly, and to be able to go out with relative ease.

My vehicle had not yet arrived so we mainly travelled around in her Peugeot 205, and she was expert at transferring me in and out of that.

Every day after breakfast she set up my computer for me and I occupied myself tapping in an address book. When I wasn't doing that I flicked through books on Christianity given to me by Caryl.

Jenny was, as I say, a very competent carer. The only big problem I had with her was the moment when *Neighbours* came on the telly each day. If she was helping me do something it would come to an instant halt and on would go the telly. The problem was not only that the sound of the *Neighbours* theme music sends the hairs creeping up the back of my neck but that I was helpless to do what I wanted for that period of time.

The year ended with various activities. Mark Dowie, a colleague from my time in the Falklands, was now teaching at Dartmouth. He invited me to the Dartmouth Christmas Ball. I was keen to go, but needed Jenny to get me there, help get me changed, to bed, toileted etc. I invited Georgia as my partner and Mark, thinking it was best to involve Jenny, organised a young midshipman to accompany her. We stayed at Mark's flat and it was a wonderful event, bringing back lots of happy memories. Only a year before I had been at the same ball with Melissa Woodard, fumbling with the zip of her dress in the middle of the dance floor.

Jenny and I had to share the same bed. I don't snore but she did and she was very pissed. Since my accident I have been a very light sleeper. I'd wake her and tell her to stop snoring, she'd stop for half a minute, then roll over and start again.

I was still feeling my way with what can loosely be called my staff. Most friends then felt that the carer should be integrated. If Trevor was to come to a ball then the carer would be invited too and made to feel part of the occasion.

I'd begun to feel that this was the wrong approach. It would have made me feel heartless to say anything so I didn't, but I really didn't want my care assistant around if at all possible. If I went out I needed her to enable me but not to become an extension of my social circle or a burden. On return from the ball I was forced to sit patiently in my chair waiting for her to sort herself out, handle her stumbling over me with too much drink inside her and then lie awake all night as if in the rhino pen at the zoo.

Bill was disappointed to discover that the Renault Espace was not ready for me as planned and so for Christmas he had arranged the loan of the adapter's demonstrator model. My brother Angus was despatched to bring it down to Dan y Cefn.

At this stage I had never seen it before, not even pictures of it. My reaction when I saw the demonstrator was that I didn't like it. The roof was raised in a way which made the car stand out massively.

The first outing was on Christmas Eve, when I was loaded into it to go to a drinks party at friends of my mother. Immediately I felt awkward and exposed. I had to enter by a big lift into the boot of the car; the roof had been raised but seated in my wheelchair I could not see out of the windows. There was no way into the driving seat from the back and it was too high at the front to be able to do a standing transfer or use a sliding board. It looked like a Popemobile, everything about it drew attention, a classic crip-van.

We arrived outside the friends' house in Llangadog, where I was pushed out on to the lift at the back. I noticed a couple of passers-by stopping to watch. Like at the Lord's dinner but on a smaller scale I felt self-conscious, part of a circus freak show, and I didn't like it.

I got Bill to see things from my point of view, I think. We had a slightly brutal conversation about it.

'I don't want to go around looking like a cripple,' I said to him.

'But you are a fucking cripple, Trevor.' It was perhaps reasonable to point this out, but the look of the thing was important to me. OK, so I'm a cripple, but I don't want to look like one.

I'd already seen a better vehicle, a Volkswagen Caravelle. The order for the Espace was cancelled – the car didn't work for me at all. Paul Cassidy the adapter for the Volkswagen, drove one down the very next day – amazing, given the time of year. With him operating the pedals I had a little drive. It was a vast improvement so one of those was ordered instead. Bill insisted he could get the vehicle itself for a better price – probably true – and obtained one which was sent up to Paul in January.

The Trevor Jones Trust also lost the £3,000 deposit they'd paid to the Espace converters. I suppose the latter were a business, not a charity, but everyone at the time was furious.

Several lessons were learnt from this experience, not least that before doing anything on behalf of Trevor the one person you ought to consult was Trevor himself. Everyone wanted to do stuff for me rather than enable me to do things for myself.

Christmas itself was fun, if a rather emotional affair,

surrounded as I was by a very supportive family. Mum tried to make it as normal as possible and it nearly was except that there was an inescapable pall of sadness or shock in the air. Only Frank was oddly silent; I think the whole thing was too much for him, and he spent the entire time splitting, carrying and stacking logs. I never did see what Mum had seen in him.

For New Year's Eve Caryl came down, as well as Vanda North, and Marc Koska appeared out of the blue with a girl he had met a couple of weeks before, announcing they were to marry. Given that we were seeing out a pretty ghastly year a good time was had by all, with champagne and 'Auld Lang Syne', so much so that Mum's diary entry comes out with the opinion: 'Trev can be happy in a wheelchair . . .'

Fifteen

New Year, new beginning, or so it should have been. Stuck in the adapted stable cottage at The Maerdy I began to get very down. I couldn't see any kind of life ahead of me. The obvious conclusion is that I was depressed about my disability – of course I was – but also there was my love, passion, obsession, infatuation, call it what you will, probably a bit of each, for Caryl. I was consumed with thoughts of her and yet she'd left me with no idea where I stood. I thought about her the whole time. The only thing left in my life, it seemed, was love, and yet that too was out of reach. I was so completely overwhelmed by my disability with no confidence about Caryl, or calling friends, or about a job or even something to fill that particular day. My thoughts turned to suicide.

I needed Jenny to open the door for me, dress me, and whatever the weather I seemed to be frozen solid. I was stuck in a corner of Wales near my beloved mother, but had no friends nearby, few visitors, and felt isolated from all the things I loved about life. I thought of the other tetraplegics at the residential unit at Stoke Mandeville, many of whom sat around passively and acceptingly. They offered little inspiration or hope to me, only a vision of despair.

I got myself into this self-perpetuating obsession with killing myself, and thinking about how I could do it. The irony was that I couldn't think of any way. I couldn't reach the sharp knives in the drawers. Even if I had been able to get hold of one I couldn't grip it. I'd have scratched my wrists, not slashed them. I thought of falling on an upturned knife, but there was no way I could have propped it up with enough force for it not to be knocked over by my falling body.

At that time I was unable to get my upper body upright again if I fell forward at the waist, so another idea was to fill a wash basin and get my head into it. I'd be stuck and I'd drown. But I couldn't get into the bathroom on my own. On one occasion I was left in the bathroom alone with a full basin of water and I tried out my drowning theory, but the rim of the basin was at a height that blocked my chest and I couldn't get my head into it. In any case the water wasn't deep enough and I would just about have been able to get my nose in, and that was it.

Another idea was that if Jenny left me in the garden I might have a chance. A pretty stream runs through The Maerdy garden and I thought I might be able to tip the wheelchair down the bank, then with luck I'd fall face down in the water, *finito*. But then the water wasn't very deep either and I'd have insufficient strength to aim the chair down the right bit of the ditch. In any case there was nearly always someone nearby. Jenny would have rescued me.

I got even more depressed. I was so pathetic I couldn't even kill myself.

During the empty days there was one connection left with Caryl; these were books and tapes on the New Testament which she'd left me and they were perhaps the only thing that lifted me above my suicidal thoughts. I was such a thoroughly confused young man. As I read the books and listened to the tapes I found that a sort of spiritual awakening was occurring.

Mum had bought me a boxful of old tapes from the attic and there was one song by Roger Whitaker I listened to over and over again. Partly it was because I couldn't turn the tape over but mainly because I found that the very simple but revealing chorus line was all that anyone needed to know: 'God is love, love is God.'

That picked me up. I also had a Tracy Chapman tape which would always bring a rise of emotion and tears to my eyes. Fantastic voice, great songs, but listening to it seemed to represent the hopelessnes of my relationship with Caryl.

There was a break after Christmas but then Caryl began to visit most weekends. She would always come with a friend as a sort of self-imposed chaperone. She would lie on my bed for hours into the night and we would talk more openly about our relationship, but she always returned to the spare room where her friend was. It drove me nuts.

I was beginning to learn how being a Christian was central to her life and what being born again meant to her. When she came to see me we could chat about what it signified. Better still, while I was trying to be a Christian I discovered I had her full attention, she loved explaining the whole thing to me. She told me how she was praying to God that I too would one day become a Christian. She was at last showing genuine signs of returning my feelings. One weekend when she eventually felt comfortable enough to visit alone, the knot of torture and angst within me began to unwind. We even started to share the beautiful pine double bed – for so long empty beside my single hospital framed one. Waking up beside her was one of the greatest pleasures of my life.

My only previous experience of Christianity had been in the school chapel (I never bothered with it in the Navy) where parts of the Bible, the New Testament especially, were read out to us every morning. Sometimes I'd listen, sometimes I'd day-dream, but looking at these stories again I was surprised at how familiar they were. They must have been sinking in quietly. My biggest preoccupation had been whether we were going to win the rugby match on Saturday, chapel had no particular relevance for me.

Now that I had suffered I had a first real understanding of what the New Testament especially was saying. It spoke to me and made sense. It talks a lot about the 'poor', for example, and I identified with this. I'd never been poor, in the Navy I'd even had a yacht. I still wasn't poor in some senses – I had warmth, food and shelter and a lot more money than most other tetraplegics – but I felt I had lost a lot, at times that I had nothing. My new needs, basic human needs, which I had always been able to take for granted, overwhelmed me.

It's difficult to explain, but I drew great strength from my belief in God. Worldly riches and material goods meant far less to me now and my faith, which I had always held but which had been dormant for so long, kept me going at a time when I felt empty inside and truly desperate. Through Caryl and the books of the New Testament I discovered a spirituality of which I had never previously had need.

There remained, however, a conflict between Caryl's public kind of born-again Christianity with which I was uncomfortable and the much more private religion I was finding for myself.

She said she was going to a Christian festival during Easter at a Butlin's at Minehead on the north coast of Devon with some of her girlfriends. There would be three and a half thousand born-again Christians.

I wanted to be with her and plucked up the courage to ask if I could come too. She was delighted at my interest and I was delighted at her delight.

I took as my care assistant a man called Gill, my mum's gardener. It was one of the very first trips in my new Volkswagen Caravelle which I'd been waiting for impatiently. It had taken a lot of work to convert so that I could drive it; for example, there needed to be an air-assisted throttle and brake on the same lever, push to brake, pull to accelerate. My wrist was put in a padded crutch, with my elbow resting along the door.

I was appalled at the cost of it: £12,000 for the VW, then adaptions to the vehicle costing £6,000 or £7,000 (lift system, recarpeting etc.), plus further adaptations particular to me (£3,000 more). I couldn't believe where the money had gone but it totted up on things like £60 for a hand grip on the steering wheel, just a piece of metal, shaped yes, but not high tech.

The cost was horrendous when you think you are committed to that sort of outlay for the rest of your life. It was frightening to think that the Trevor Jones Trust had raised it in fivers and tenners, that this car was the result of four or five major events and a lot of really hard work.

All blown in one vehicle which would rust, fall apart and need replacing like any other car. It was wonderful to have it but it brought home to me that I couldn't expect people to organise events for me for ever.

As Gill drove me down I nursed my usual feelings of apprehension as to whether or not Caryl would be pleased to see me. A mass meeting of born-again Christians was her milieu, her environment, I might well be out of place, she might well feel as awkward with me there as she had when convinced everyone was staring at us at Stoke.

Gill and I stayed nearby in a B & B in Minehead, and he'd drop me off each day at the Butlin's holiday camp. To my relief Caryl did seem to enjoy my presence, she liked showing me around her scene.

It was the most extraordinary gathering I'd ever been to, just far out, man. There was a big catalogue of events going on and you could sign up for whatever took your fancy. For example, lectures on 'Is the Resurrection for Real', stands on faith healing and discussions on gays and lesbians in the Church.

I was taken upstairs for one session. No problems about access. I'd instantly have a million Christians whipping me willingly up the stairs. In the classroom everyone was really into what was going on, there was a slightly stoned atmosphere about the place. They were really praying hard, and I was watching.

'Call out to the Lord to come into our lives . . .' the leader would shout, then one by one they'd stand up and burble unintelligibly. Others would get up, eyes filled with tears of (one assumes) joy. In a bizarre sort of way the whole room started to come alive.

By the end I felt a bit shaken and overwhelmed by it all and wanted to get out. Caryl explained that they had been speaking in tongues: 'That's how God speaks through people.' It was all a bit too much for me, a touch scary, and even Caryl admitted that it had been slightly over the top for her too.

In the evenings there were huge get-togethers, with playlets and skits put on, and singsongs. Everything about the whole experience was happy, uplifting and joyous, good fun.

I had always had a prejudice against born-again Christians, but much of what was happening did succeed in making me feel very comfortable. I was a lost soul, with no real interests remaining, just Caryl and my mother, and I'd have done anything for Caryl.

The Dartmouth Ball had brought home to me how much I loathed my dependency. Jenny enjoyed the social side of the job of looking after me, the getting to know my circle of friends, but rightly or wrongly it made me uncomfortable.

Once I visited a friend called Jill Simpson down at her parents' farm in Somerset. Up until now, against my nature, I had tried to include and accommodate Jenny. After I had confided in Jill how this bothered me, she would say in an unambiguous but friendly way, 'Jenny, give me and my friend a little time together, I haven't seen him for so long,' or send her off on some task.

In fact Jenny resented this, and on the way back from Jill's farm she was so grumpy she wouldn't speak to me. It was the beginning of the end between me and Jenny; if you are dependent on someone you can't be worrying about their moods.

There is a certain amount of give and take but it is not a balanced relationship, because part of the helper's job is to cope with my moods. I now know that balance can't come into it. I pay them, they work for me.

We finally came to the end of the road on a trip up to London to see Charles Wylie, my postal chess partner. I sent her away for a couple of hours while we got on with our meeting and when she came back sent her away again because we still hadn't finished. She flipped because she said I was ordering her about. After an hour she still hadn't returned and indeed didn't return at all.

She was tracked down to Rod's and Angus's (and my) house in Clapham. There was no apology, she wouldn't speak to me, so I said, 'Jenny, I think we should call it a day,' and that was nearly that except that as her belongings were all down in Wales she agreed to work out her notice.

That gave me two weeks to find a replacement. Advertising in the *Nursing Times* and *Lady* magazine is expensive but there was no particularly obvious candidate from the job centre at Llandeilo. When we had recruited Jenny another candidate who'd nearly got the job had been a man called Peter Dade. He was still available. He'd come through an ad we'd placed in the services resettlement bulletin, and although Army not Navy, he was a military man. Having come unstuck with a couple of nurses I thought perhaps an officer's batman type might work better; after all they can do everything from shining a belt buckle to digging a latrine. After I had been looked after by Mum for a few days, he moved in as my new assistant, arriving with all his worldly belongings contained in one holdall.

He wasn't the quickest of learners. Two weeks into the job he still needed to be told the procedure for putting my clothes on and getting me up. None the less he was certainly trying his hardest and had attributes that Jenny lacked such as physical strength, and because we had little in common personality-wise, he didn't ask me questions the whole time, didn't try to integrate himself into other areas of my life. He kept his distance. And he didn't watch *Neighbours*.

On my birthday he bought me a magnificent cake from the baker's – my mother had also brought me a cake, but no matter – and a very expensive-looking Aran sweater. I was embarrassed by this latter, because his wage was not exactly sky high, and in any case in our family we don't give lavish birthday presents, a token something maybe, nothing more than that.

Later he bought me a Volkswagen jacket and baseball cap. I didn't want to upset his feelings but I told him to stop buying me presents and he did.

This strange kind of attentiveness began to get on my nerves, however. I also became conscious that he was on the phone an awful lot. 'Have you been on the phone?' I'd ask and he'd deny it.

I started to lose my temper with him. I was lying in bed waiting for my bowels to move when a man arrived to fit my carphone to the Caravelle. Peter went out to deal with it, despite my having told him that I needed to be there to make sure it was put in a place where I could use it. Why everyone tried to arrange things without consulting me I will never know. It was incredibly annoying. I shouted myself hoarse trying to get his attention, failing all the while because he was outside.

To his credit he didn't answer me back and calmly took my laying into him.

Just before Easter I moved into my mother's house; Frank had insisted that I vacate the holiday cottage in which I lived so that they could be let out for Easter and beyond, so I was living in their sitting room. Peter was given a room upstairs. Now we were under my mother's roof the terms of our relationship and the balance of power altered slightly. At the last moment he asked for the weekend off. I didn't know much about his private life but was aware he was separated from his wife. He had a child too, but I didn't know that then.

When he'd gone my mother said, 'I wouldn't be surprised if we never see him again.' There was something about his arrival with only one small holdall containing all his worldly belongings, and there was also a kind of emotional detachment about him that was slightly strange.

Mum was right, he didn't come back, but on Easter

Tuesday I got my Barclaycard statement which contained a whole host of transactions which had nothing at all to do with me. Not strictly accurate, some did; there was the birthday cake, the Aran sweater and the VW bomber jacket and baseball cap.

Then there was Interflora and a transaction at a jeweller's in Tunbridge Wells. It was most strange, none of the thefts had been for his own benefit. You got the picture of a slightly sad man without proper roots, somewhat lacking the basic skills needed to build a life for himself.

The Llandeilo police were flabbergasted; more excitement than they had seen in a while. I had an address for Peter in Edinburgh, where a blank was drawn, but two days later he was picked up in Tunbridge Wells, which was where his ex-wife and his mother lived. He was brought back for questioning, charged, then bailed.

Welcome to the world of dependency on care. That was four care assistants in four months, and apart from Isaac, I'd had difficulties with all of them. This latest incident struck at my being, was another blow to my self-confidence. I was deeply dependent on others, but couldn't apparently trust them, so I gave in slightly and for the first time since childhood was back to being looked after by Mum.

There was talk of an extension to Mum's house for me, much of this going on out of my earshot. Mum's diary says that Frank was 'stone-walling' plans for it, an appropriate expression.

My mother was a massively competent carer. She ran her holiday cottages, catered for up to twenty a night, gave some private physio clinics and still had more time to help me than most of my helpers before or since.

We got on well most of the time but it must have been very tough for her, not just the physical graft but coping with my constant presence, my every need and every mood. Her understanding of my needs without my having to ask was instinctive but I think at the same time she wanted me to be finding a way to get on with my life.

We had grown exceptionally close through this accident, but my mother more than anyone understood my need for space and some distance. Mothers aren't meant to have to look after their grown-up sons. She had her own needs and her already difficult relationship with Frank was getting no easier.

Mum was protecting me from the outside world too, which is not necessarily a good thing, but at that time was what I probably needed.

In May it was off to RAF Headley Court having finally got a place there more through my own efforts than through those of my Navy rehabilitation officer. Even so I still had problems. 'Can I stay in the accommodation with my care assistant?' This was refused. One of the big frustrations at Stoke Mandeville had been having to wait for a free nurse, to ask even to have the pages of your book turned over, so if at all possible I'd have liked to bring someone with me. 'Can we stay nearby at a local bed and breakfast?' This was refused too.

The officers at Headley Court had a mess with rooms of their own in a large country house, but it was completely wheelchair inaccessible, so I was shunted off to the ward with the men. If I'd been able-bodied I wouldn't have minded, I'd have thought, 'Brilliant, this will be fun.' But I felt that I was being marginalised, dis-integrated from my fellow officers because I was disabled and I resented it.

I was also being treated as ill or sick when I was not – but disabled. The needs are very different but it's easier for everyone else to lump them together. I needed single accommodation and an assistant but they put me in a ward.

Headley Court was a strange mixture. The militarily trained nurses were undoubtedly more professional and happier (there was less stress) than the ones at Stoke Mandeville. On the other hand for a hospital for the rehabilitation of injured servicemen it was strangely lacking. None of the doors were automatic, there were steps everywhere, the beautiful gardens were largely barred to me by thick gravel paths and there were not even any wheelchair-accessible showers. I thought, 'If there is no appreciation of my needs here, what hope is there outside?'

I tried to have issues concerning my basic needs seen to, such as, for example, where to live long term. I knew I didn't want to live isolated in Wales for much longer. The Navy were hopeless. When you are a serving officer or man in the forces they look after you absolutely and completely, but since the accident I'd begun to feel I was being dumped. I can't describe how much this hurt and confused me.

There was no effort to help me with care, for example. I was still in the Navy, still being paid. If they had terminated my employment and left me in the hands of the welfare state I could have understood things better but they were still going through the motions of treating me like a serving officer.

At least while I was a member of the service I thought they could have provided me with some of my new basic needs, care assistance for instance. On my salary how was I supposed to buy food, clothes and pay for a carer and accommodation? And one carer was not really enough either; I needed someone available twenty-four hours and no one human being could cope with that. Mum could take up the slack but that wasn't fair on her and at this particular juncture I'd lost Jenny Ray, Peter Dade had done a runner with my credit cards and as yet we hadn't found another replacement beyond temps from an agency.

In reply to one of my letters, I was told by my superiors that it was my choice to employ assistants. How would he feel waiting for a district nurse every day? Or getting his elderly mum up in the middle of the night?

One useful thing that happened was that they put me in touch with a specialist driving instructor called Arthur Baker. I'd had problems with the Caravelle. It was fine on the motorway and the steering was nice and light, but if I went round a roundabout or steep turn, with no support for my torso I'd topple. The danger inherent in that doesn't need explaining. You can't have a toppled driver. I'd persevered even so, going slowly in such places, but it wasn't terribly satisfactory. We'd tried harnesses and all sorts, but Arthur came up with a system of torso support and that was much better. It took a month to install but at least after that I was safe to be on the road.

He was also of the opinion that it wasn't necessarily the right vehicle for me. I'd be far better off with one I could drive from the wheelchair.

I was thinking that I'd have liked to live in London, near my friends and brothers who shared the house we'd been buying together in Clapham just before my accident. I had already spent a lot of time there, sleeping on a bed in the lounge, but it would be impossible to adapt it further. I contacted Lambeth Council about the possibility of a council house. They explained there was a long waiting list and as I had never lived in the borough my chances were poor. I then contacted every single housing association in central London but the answer was the same: nothing available or long waiting lists.

After much pressure the Navy offered me a quarter in Gosport, having fobbed me off endlessly saying there was nothing available (at a time when masses of servicemen were being made redundant this cannot have been true) or that all they had was upstairs and I would be a fire hazard if the lift broke down. God, how that excuse annoyed me.

The quarter in Gosport, when I went to see it, turned out to have steps up to the front door, which was itself very narrow. The corridor behind it was so cramped that you couldn't manoeuvre a wheelchair into the kitchen and the bedroom was upstairs.

Spinal breaks are quite common in the forces, perhaps a dozen every year, but the appreciation of their needs appear to be zero.

I complained about the treatment I was getting and got a

message back through Charles Wylie saying, 'Wind your neck in mate, make less fuss.' This sent a shiver through me, made me feel even more helpless. Charles has been a very good friend in so many ways but he is a very traditional serviceman used to clicking his heels. It was poor advice and I ignored it.

After I had rejected the quarter at Gosport, the final offer made to me was by the tri-service head of the medical branch – my complaint had finally got to the very top. It was a place at the Star and Garter Home in Richmond. I went there one summer's day with my carer from an agency called Peter's People, entering through a marble atrium into a grand Victorian building.

I met the manager, an ex-Army major and (this is not inter-services rivalry) I took an immediate dislike to him. He referred to the residents as his 'men'. Quite a lot of 'his men' seemed to be the aged veterans of the First World War if not the Crimean. The thought of becoming one of them filled me with horror.

He proudly showed me around, including a large, old-fashioned ward containing a mixture of age groups. It was past midday and yet some of them were still waiting to be got up. There was an all-pervading stench overhanging the place. Some of 'his men' were still being cleaned up. Each bed had its own telly and a bookshelf, but the general feeling was overwhelmingly of a run-down institution.

There I was, a young man, late twenties, most of my life still ahead of me, with lots to offer and this was the encouragement I got from my employers. In the Navy I had learnt to do things to the highest possible standards; everything from how to make a bed properly to flying a very sophisticated machine. And it all led to this ward for disabled ex-servicemen who, even at midday, were still waiting to be got up.

Then I heard a voice I recognised. 'Trev, Trevor Jones, is that you? I don't believe it.' It was Sean Jackman from Stoke Mandeville, the eighteen-stone Black guy who'd bust his neck in a weight-lifting (or rather dropping) accident. 'You're not coming here are you?'

'I'm thinking about it.'

'Whatever you do, don't. It's living hell.' He described the stench, how the staff never did anything you wanted and how lazy they were. Sean was the same age as me and surrounded by people waiting to die.

He was in a more vulnerable position than me. When he'd had his accident he'd been living in a first-floor council flat with his pregnant wife. The baby was born after the accident. While he was at Stoke Mandeville and after the council would do nothing to find him a ground-floor flat to move to, even though he had a wife to help him. She stayed in the flat but there was no choice but to shunt him off to a home and thence to the Star and Garter.

Sean and I had lunch together and he said, 'Trev, it's worse than your worst nightmare.' If a film is ever made of this book he should be played by Lenny Henry with body padding.

I listened to what he had to say and never looked back at the place. It was a seminal experience; I found it difficult to accept that such institutions still existed in our civilisation, even more so that they were thought suitable for a young person with his life ahead of him.

A resettlement programme is offered to everyone when they leave the forces although it was emphasised to me that this was something that was 'offered and not a right'.

The medical resettlement officers from the Navy had a difficult job to do. They were essentially middle men with no clout. Their budget was very small, they were relatively junior, they were overworked and their boss was a doctor, used to making clinical decisions, not human ones. He had also become my boss, which meant I had no one to act on my behalf.

It was for this reason that Captain Craig, my captain at

Portland, had taken me back under his command, an unusual and irregular step. It gave my morale a huge boost.

After Headley Court they had encouraged me to go to a special college for the disabled in Devon. This whole segregation idea really wound me up, I wanted to be part of a life with everyday, normal people. If I was going to retrain I would do it at a college with everyone else. I applied for a six-week 'Business Acquaintance Course' at Central London Polytechnic and a three-week resettlement course with other officers leaving the services.

This created immediate problems for my resettlement people. All the other officers were given a lodging allowance, but they were not prepared to cover the lodging of my care assistant. Again they would not let me stay in a service establishment in London because the lift might break down and I'd be a fire risk. Apparently even all the Army barracks all over London were full. Was that likely to be true? I was being fobbed off.

Eventually I was told that all they could offer was a bed at the King Edward VIII Hospital for Officers. I'd been out of Stoke for seven months and was fed up with finding myself billeted on hospital wards with no privacy and being treated as if I were ill. I wasn't ill and tried to explain that it would rob me of my independence. Finally they found me a private room in which to stay with my helper.

There were still disadvantages to the room. If I wanted to go out I had to summon a porter to put down a ramp to get my chair out over the step. A step is not just a physical barrier, it is a mental one too, because you have to put someone else out to get you down it. It is a hassle to find them, wait until they are free, then ask them, wait again, then line the ramps up, adjust the spacing and carefully reverse down. Such hassle, sometimes you can't be bothered asking and end up doing nothing. You'd think in a hospital they'd have created equal access.

Such considerations apart the six weeks on the business course were fantastic for me. For the first time since leaving

Stoke I was out in the normal world, getting out of bed in the morning with a purpose, finally mixing with my peers. Meanwhile mum was able to go off on her first proper holiday since my accident, a barge holiday in the Bourgogne.

Not long afterwards I was officially discharged from the Navy. I had to go before the medical board down at Gosport. Despite it being bloody uncomfortable I struggled into my uniform, after all it would be for the last time. There were half a dozen men in the waiting room. As I waited my turn I practised saluting but could not raise my arm far enough and thought better of it. Then I was wheeled in before a commodore, two captains, a commander and a lieutenant commander.

'The board has considered your reports and takes the view that you will have to be discharged. Is there anything you would like to say?'

It was my last chance, my only chance to speak up so I did. First of all I complained that the link with my rehabilitation and resettlement officers had been unsatisfactory. They had been unable to meet any of my requests or even tell me how much pension I'd get.

It must have been clear to everyone that the only way to rebuild my life was with a care assistant, yet no help had been offered. I'd had to spend my entire naval salary on care assistants and there had been no attempt to help. Contrast that with what happens if you serve on a ship with substandard accommodation – you get extra pay.

Much of the problem, I conceded, was because the resettlement department for disabled personnel received a paltry budget. Despite the Navy knowing roughly how many people are injured every year there is no insurance, no budget and no support.

Their Lordships had continued to pay me, even though I would have received more on welfare. They had prevented me from taking up a job at Portland Air Station which Captain

Craig had created for me and had left me to the care of my mother or a college for the disabled. At Gosport, I told them, I'd met someone with multiple sclerosis and although he was slowing down they'd found work for him until he was discharged. Why hadn't they allowed me to do any work? Why had they not discharged me sooner? Reintegration with my peers had been actively discouraged.

One of the commanders was taking notes but at this point as I got into my flow he gave up and just listened as my grievances poured out.

I accepted that I had to be discharged but I did feel that although I accepted it, I didn't fully understand the reasons. It was symptomatic of the discrimination against the disabled in our society. If disabled people were ever to have equal rights, as I felt they should, then they should be employed by the police and the Ministry of Defence. Not all Navy personnel need to go to sea, an inability to go to sea should not be a disqualification.

I'd spoken for a long time in a great stream. The officers clearly felt sorry for me. 'We do appreciate the strength of your feeling, what you have said is very interesting and very helpful.' I'm sure they meant it but the system was bigger than they were.

There is a means of redress in the Royal Navy in the form of a service paper detailing the complaint, submitted through your commanding officer. Captain Craig sponsored this process for me so my complaints were submitted officially but I never did see the reply. By the time one was formulated – if it wasn't suppressed – I'd moved on.

One way and another the summer was spent thinking about what the future would hold for me. I knew I did not want to live in Wales. I wanted to live in London near friends of my own age, but should I find accommodation or a job first? It was a Catch-22: I could not go to work without an adapted place to stay, but if I adapted a place to stay, what if I could not then find a job nearby or lost the one I had? Where my priority should lie wasn't clear to me.

After the business course I thought these things out while staying at Georgia's flat in Battersea. She'd had it adapted for wheelchair access with ramps and even a wheel-in shower.

Caryl remained firmly on the scene too. All things considered, my relationship with her had been going pretty well. We'd been on holiday together to Portugal and saw each other a lot. My main escape from spending twenty-four hours of every day with a carer was Caryl and every plan I had for any activity was built around considering whether or not she could be included.

I just wanted to be with her, it was the only time I was completely happy. There was still that tension between us arising from her open and outwardly expressed kind of Christianity and the far more private relationship with God that I had discovered since my accident. Her religion wasn't for me and she was constantly frustrated that I wouldn't declare myself openly for Christ, that I was not the soul mate she sought. She'd gone through one of those full immersion baptisms, for example.

She'd often say, 'I'm praying that you will come to love God as I do.' There was little room for interpretation of the Gospels, she was very literal about what they meant whereas for me they were open to interpretation, they were a guide not a rule book. Neither of us could see this from the other's point of view.

But overall we were getting on well, enjoying each other's company. In the heat of Portugal she'd lost her inhibitions with me to such an extent that she'd sleep with me with no nervousness at all and, with a measure of control, experiment in the joys of the flesh. It became another source of tension between us.

There was this very strong physical attraction between us, both complicated and heightened by the fact that it could not be consummated. On the one hand I filled a sexual need for her. She could sleep with a man who desired her more than anything else in the world but with minimal threat to her virginity. What other man would lie in bed with her, touch her gently and for a period of several years stay exactly where he was told to?

On the other hand, my sexual desire was accentuated precisely because I could not have her. Not because of my own impotence but because she would not let me. For both of us it was the ultimate hunt.

Which isn't to say that religion and sex were the main driving forces of the relationship, not at all. We each satisfied many of the other's needs. Mostly, however, I needed her to enable me. I think she got rewards from doing so and there was no question that we were each other's best friend. So much so that in August I plucked up the courage to ask her to marry me.

It was her birthday and I drove over to meet her at a pub in Amersham. She had been so good to me one way or another, had played such a large part in my psychological recovery.

She too seemed pleased every time she saw me so it was definitely mutual. She was still hoping to convert me into a 'real Christian' but not making a big thing out of it. We'd sometimes go to church together.

When I arrived she helped decant me from the Caravelle into a wheelchair and then we went and sat at a table in the pub's garden. I gave her a beautiful gold bracelet which I'd bought her for her birthday. Then we went inside for something to eat.

I might have asked her as I handed over the bracelet but the courage deserted me. I struggled with my food thinking all the time, 'Better wait till after the pudding.' The pudding having been consumed by Caryl and played with by me, I finally uttered the words that might change the rest of my life: 'Caryl, will you marry me?'

The moment the words were out of my mouth I realised I didn't actually mean it. I was asking her for all the wrong reasons, born out of my own despair. If I could marry Caryl she could help look after me and maybe then I'd be able to cope with things. I was utterly self-absorbed. It's funny how, after thinking about it for so long and, I thought, so deeply, it took the saying of it to make me understand that I didn't really want to marry her at all, I didn't want the hunt to end.

For her part Caryl looked shocked. I don't think she could believe I'd thought about it, still less asked. She went into an instant flap. First she said, 'I don't know . . .' Then she said 'Yes' and then 'No', then 'I don't know', then finally. 'I'll have to think about it.'

I went home to Georgia's flat thinking. 'What have I done? I must be mad,' and hoping she wouldn't say yes. There was no way to unask her – the toothpaste was out of the tube – nor could I say I had just been joking. I hadn't been joking, I'd been serious but once I'd said it I realised that marriage to Caryl was not what I wanted. Not at that moment.

The next day she phoned in tears and said, 'I've got to come over,' which she did that evening, driving down to London after her day's work at Stoke Mandeville.

She was distraught. 'I can't marry you, Trevor. I'm really sorry.' She must have been terrified of the effect her refusal would have on me but I was as relieved as she was upset.

We left it at that and if anything it took a lot of the strain out of the relationship. We weren't 'just good friends' (as the euphemistic saying for lovers goes) but very, very, very good friends, without the stress-inducing question mark about how the thing should progress.

Assisted Reproductive techniques:
Details of this claim are to be found in the report by Dr Frankel.
The Plaintiff will be unable to father a child in the conventional manner and probably have need to have recourse to artificial insemination. There is a chance that artificial insemination will be possible without recourse to more complex procedures, but should attempts fail, the

Plaintiff will have to rely on in-vitro-fertilisation ('IVF'), which costs up to £30,000 for each successful pregnancy. The Plaintiff would like to have two or three children, but claims the cost of only one conception by IVF against the risk that he will be unable to father children without this procedure.

Sixteen

Michael Mavor, who been made headmaster of Gordonstoun (at thirty-one an incredible achievement) when I was Guardian, offered me a job at the school to help the new boys and girls settle in.

It was an inspired idea. It is tough going away to school for the first time, especially for those first weeks. I was absolutely delighted by the offer and despite much apprehension agreed to give it a go. Fortunately Caryl had some holiday and she agreed to drive me up in the Volkswagen Caravelle (staying with friends Bill Johnson and family in Chester and Guy Solleveld, recently married and living north of Glasgow, on the way up). As a vehicle the VW was fine once I was ensconced but the ensconcing was such a palaver.

At Gordonstoun we were billeted in the san. The next day Caryl left me to return to work. I had a care assistant from the agency but soon discovered he was more or less unneccessary, a huge relief for me.

To begin with I was as nervous and unsure as the new boys and girls. The first thing I got involved with was going from house to house introducing myself to parents dropping off their loved ones. Once term got under way I developed a routine of joining in classes and visiting the boarding houses in the evening for brews: coffee and a chat.

The educators were quick to exploit the possibilities of having me there and it was wonderful to feel that I was having a positive effect on those around me.

I remembered the boredom of my first weekend sixteen

years earlier, so on Sunday afternoons I started to organise games of football and refereed them from my Quickie wheelchair with power pack.

This was a revelation for me. In hospital I'd once remarked to Mum that I saw a future in which my value was akin to that of a bag of cement. Since then I had learned that I still had a lot to offer but this was the first opportunity to show it. Taking the initiative in running a game of football, being in a position of authority and respect, contributing to the lives of others made me feel a lot better about myself.

Socially I had always felt the odd one out, the one others had to look out for. Yet here I was, just another member of staff, indoors, outdoors, rushing around doing things for others that I'd organised, the children dependent on me. More than anything, though, I was enjoying myself.

Wednesday afternoons were service days and I got involved with those activities too. The coastguards and mountain rescue service invited me to be a fallen climber with a spinal injury. I was carried to the top of a cliff and put on a stretcher, then lowered over the edge. For them there was the benefit of playing with an authentic real-life victim, while for me there was the thrill of being suspended on a stretcher at a slightly crazy angle one hundred feet up a cliff knowing that I was an integral part of a team exercise.

On another Wednesday the sub-aqua section dressed me up in a wet suit and took me diving in the pool. It was a worthwhile exercise for the kids and it also demonstrated to me another activity possible for wheelchair users. Later this experience formed the basis for a *Challenge Anneka* TV programme.

At first it was hard work conversing with the kids all the time and fighting my inhibitive demons. My self-confidence was still low but then so was theirs. Most of them had never met someone in a wheelchair before so they were hesitant but soon their natural and genuine personalities came through, quite unlike the slightly embarrassed and awkward front I was used to from adults. After a while forcing conversation out of them was not a problem – they would come up to me to chat.

In the evening I'd get the boys and girls together to help break the ice between them. I remembered being terrified of the girls when I arrived at Gordonstoun. As chief ice breaker I had a huge advantage because I was a youngish old boy and not a member of the staff.

The freedom I obtained at Gordonstoun was a revelation too. A rota of kids was organised to help get me up and put me to bed, the nurses at the san did my bowels. The power pack on my Quickie wheelchair meant that I had the run of the grounds. If ever I needed to get in anywhere there would always be someone to help and I was even able to send my care assistant back down south.

I remembered my state of mind before going up to Gordonstoun. I had suffered from this recurring dream. Whenever I went into a room with steps and the door was closed I felt imprisoned, I would sit there in my chair unable to get out as the walls moved closer and closer. As they did so I would get more and more agitated, but the walls continued to move. At the time John McCarthy and Brian Keenan had just been released from prison. I remembered thinking how lucky they were; I would never be released.

Now that I had a genuine and worthwhile role to play I was being empowered. For example, if a child was feeling homesick the housemaster or mistress would bring him or her to me and we could go off on a long walk together around the grounds. I discovered I could, for a moment at least, make them feel better about things. I was the one adult at a busy school who had the time to do this. There were so many unique facets to my situation which qualified me for this pastoral role but whatever the good it did for others it benefited me a hundred times more.

It was so different from living in Wales which felt remote and lonely, or in London where I was a prisoner of the environment but where there was no community to carry me.

*

After two months at Gordonstoun, with the new boys and girls settled, Graham Broad, formerly my tutor there, invited me to stay with him at Rockport Preparatory School in Northern Ireland. He was headmaster.

The great time I had been having at Gordonstoun continued.

I loved being surrounded by the boys and girls and was amazed at how little prep schools had changed since my time at Gayhurst. A thirty-five-minute class would pass in no time at all. All the time, though, my demons were lurking, waiting for a moment to come out.

I hated being dependent on this young, blonde, leggy girl I was employing. I'd sit with the kids in the dining-room and she would come and cut up my food for me. That would remind me how disabled I was.

It made me embarrassed and I thought less of myself. At the same time I was quite happy to let the boys and girls cut up my food and help me into rooms or on and off with my jacket – indeed they'd fight over the job they were so keen to do it for me. It was good for them to be around me helping. There was also a quiet little girl in a chair, disabled from birth; it was good for both of us to know we weren't 'the only one' as perhaps we sometimes thought.

I had to tell my helper not to sit with me, I could not be myself with someone sitting on my shoulder, just waiting to help me, to point out what I could not do.

I was never happier than when with the boys and girls. Possibly when I've got the adventure thing out of my system I'll become a teacher. I enjoy it and I think I would be good at it. To begin with, even thinking about sitting in the gym coaching basketball or organising obstacle races filled me with considerable apprehension. Would they listen to me, what should I say to them, what if this or that happened? Achieving it gave me not only a sense of empowerment but also a growing belief in myself on which I could build.

None the less my moods were lurching between satisfaction and despair. I'd be fine playing chess in the school library in the evening but then would come the reality of being put to bed. Graham's house was down the hill a few hundred yards away. By this time of the year it was very cold. Even the small trip between the school and his house meant putting on the full range of sweaters and rugs. I'd be fine with the boys and then I'd find myself back to slab-of-meat status as the perfectly pleasant and blameless leggy blonde put me to bed.

Just before I went to Northern Ireland I'd received a telephone call from Richard Branson's office inviting me on a trip to Japan to watch the launch of his latest balloon, this time to cross the Pacific Ocean, 'and bring a friend'. I don't think I would have gone without Caryl and thankfully she agreed. However, it would have been a bit tough on her to have sole responsibility for helping me so I asked if I could bring two friends. 'Fine,' came the response and so I invited Bill Carrington as well.

Flying Virgin Upper Class to Tokyo was a great experience and I'm not just saying that because Richard Branson has been good to me. Obviously it helped that I was a bit of a VIP but I had never been spoilt rotten on an aeroplane before, or been as comfortable, plus I had Caryl next to me with a shoulder to lean my head on and a hand to hold. Also on the flight were dozens of journalists, Richard's parents, some friends from Oxford such as his next-door neighbour and his gardener. In the back of the plane was a Royal Marine band.

At Tokyo we had to transfer to a regional flight down to Kyushu, Japan's second biggest island. None of this was that easy, especially as the helper, Bill, who was supposed to supply the lifting power, put his back out.

In Kyushu we were met by the Virgin balloon site manager, Bruce Renny, who shortly afterwards became a governor of the Trevor Jones Trust. That night there was a get-together for which I was too exhausted. Caryl didn't want to go without me but Bill took her anyway. She came back in quite a distressed state and wouldn't explain why, which was quite common in our relationship. It might have been that somebody had come on to her, but I think she felt for me missing a big party at which she had danced and had fun in a way she could not with me.

The next day there was a big reception held in Branson's honour by the mayor of Miyakonojo, the small town where we were staying, with lots of speeches, traditional dance by girls in kimonos and a sumptuous feast, including that disgusting raw fish stuff, sushi, which I didn't take to at all. It looked amazing but did appalling things to my bowels which created much hard work for Caryl.

Altogether we were there for two weeks. We went down to the football pitch to watch them laying out the balloon for inflation (a process which would take six hours) and assembling the capsule. It was slightly bigger than the one I'd rescued and many of the systems had been redesigned. Per and Richard had taken aboard the odd lesson from their previous experience.

We were befriended by a Japanese woman who told us that she was a Christian and a teacher. She invited us to her home, her school and one evening to a restaurant. My face dropped when I entered, everyone was sitting on the floor. I could cope with not being able to use chopsticks but would have felt very left out with everyone sitting on the floor below me. I needn't have worried, they got me a funny seat with no legs in which I was just fine, indeed happy to be released from the wheelchair for a while.

The woman had got the relationship between Caryl and me a bit wrong in describing Caryl as my 'angel specially sent'. It was true to the extent that Caryl was a fantastically liberating and enabling presence for me and the description amused me but I could see that it loaded the pressure on to her and that she didn't like it.

The balloon launch was almost certainly the biggest thing

ever to happen to the small, quiet country town of Miyako-nojo. Everywhere there were banners proclaiming 'Richard Branson, Hero of the World'. In the evenings the place was so deserted you wondered where everyone could have gone. The only signs of activity were at the three or four pachinko parlours, where row upon row of garishly lit pin-ball games were being played by stationary Japanese men staring seemingly blankly at their game.

There was the odd bar, though. When Bill went out on forays in the evening he discovered that if he ever poked his head round the door of a bar he'd be fêted like a hero: 'You barroon pirate.'

'No, no, I'm not Richard Branson, I'm not the pilot,' he'd insist, but they still wanted this rather effete estate agent from Chelsea to sign their T-shirts, so he did.

Once the balloon was laid out on the football pitch there was a huge ceremony sponsored by a company called Pocari Sweat, the makers of a canned 'isotonic' sports drink of the same name. As its name suggests, it replaces the bits you sweat out. Very good for hangovers, I'm told. After the ceremony the balloon was to be filled with air and launched for North America.

On the day of the ceremony it poured with rain but they'd been fantastically thoughtful, even going so far as to hire a limo to take us there and a second one for my wheelchair. On arrival there was a special place reserved for us and I was provided with a kimono-clad Japanese girl whose job was to clutch an umbrella over me while getting soaked herself.

Unfortunately that day it was decided that the winds were wrong to attempt a take-off and so it persisted for the next two weeks, giving us time to kill. Bill and Caryl were invited to go off and make up tennis fours with Richard up at his parents' slightly grander hotel. I persuaded them but it left me sitting it out in the pro's shop trying not to work myself up into a state of frustration.

In one sense I was having the time of my life in Japan, in

another I was still learning how to be a disabled person. When we went on a trip to nearby Nagasaki my frustrations boiled over. It was fine getting on the train, the Japanese did not object to me blocking the aisle and as such were far more helpful than the corresponding British Rail employees would have been. I tried to enjoy myself as we went through the paddy fields past the active volcano, Mount Aso, billowing smoke.

When we arrived I managed to work myself up into a right strop over where we were going to have lunch.

'That looks a nice shop, let's eat there,' said Bill or Caryl.

'No, don't like the look of it.' After a while they lost patience with me and we settled in to have some quite exceptional hand-made noodles which I determinedly failed to enjoy. I had my mind set on a good Japanese restaurant but could not communicate it to the others, I was overwhelmed by my own difficulties, my dependence and their power over me.

I continued to behave gruffly until we got back to the hotel where I said, 'You can't begin to understand what it's like being in a wheelchair.'

'No, I effing can't,' said Bill. 'Neither do I want to because I'm not in an effing wheelchair. Grow up, Trevor.' At which he and Caryl left me on the bed to stew quietly. 'Can't talk any sense into him,' he told her.

The conditions never did come right for a balloon launch and we had to leave because Caryl needed to get back to work. Sadly for Richard the whole enterprise had to be put off for another year when a freak frost (they're not supposed to happen in Kyushu) damaged the fabric of the balloon.

I came back to the prep school and the cold of a British late November exhausted and feeling the reality of my situation more harshly than ever. I developed this idea that the boys and girls would no longer want to see me, that I was just passing through the school and that there was no point to it all.

These feelings were quietly crucifying me. One day as I was

wriggling in my chair to make myself more comfortable, alone in the living-room, I fell forward out of my chair and on to the floor. I lay there feeling my paralysis, the unnaturalness of it all, stuck. It was the final straw. Exhausted from my trip to Japan and from acting through others the whole time, the constant all-over burning started to consume me. I needed an escape and the only place was bed. At least in bed nothing could go wrong.

I didn't want to talk to anyone, I couldn't cope with leaving the room. I got myself into such a state that I didn't even want to call my carer to be turned and made more comfortable, I preferred to suffer. To ask for help would be giving in. If I saw the tall blonde thing, Deborah my carer, she represented to me all that I hated about my dependency and I didn't want to see her.

Eventually, the term came to an end and I decided I would have to go. The Broads had been so kind and generous to me. Theirs was not a large bungalow, they had three children of their own and a dog, plus the chaos of a prep school's comings and goings. On top of that they had had to make house space for me and for my carer.

It was clear to the doctors – but not to me – that I was having a bout of depression. I was getting little things out of proportion and bigger things were becoming utterly unbearable.

The all-over burning sensation on my skin now completely overwhelmed me, playing on my mind and paralysing my thoughts.

I'd been given a series of drugs. They started me out on anti-depressants and then anti-epileptic drugs, which made me feel really unwell, causing a sort of floating sensation inside my head. I thought I was going mad and that made me more agitated. My mouth tasted of chemicals when I woke and then I had to take more drugs to help build a false world inside my head.

It was in this state that I flew from Belfast to Luton where

Caryl met me. I stayed one night on a mattress on her floor and then she took me into the hospital. I went to see Dr Kennedy, the clinical psychologist. It was a meeting that helped to change my life.

I didn't know I was depressed although I did know that I hated being disabled. Dr Kennedy managed to get out of me all the things I hated about my situation. We identified these things and especially the total dependency on care assistants symbolised by the blameless Deborah.

He was an Irishman in his late thirties, with a softly spoken manner in which he took great care to weigh his words, to phrase things carefully and sensitively. Amazingly, he was the first clinical psychologist ever to be employed in any British spinal unit. Incredible when you think that it is an attitude of mind more than anything which is going to help you cope.

Everything he says comes out with great sincerity but you never completely trust him. By which I mean he wants you to leave feeling more positive than when you arrived. He is trying to help you and so has to decide what information he is going to give, and how to deliver it. He is careful not to overwhelm you with stuff which is going to send you into a further tailspin.

Getting started is always difficult. By our very nature, inherent coping skills prevent us from admitting how horrible our situation is. Usually I would talk around the subject making light of everything.

It is not until Dr Kennedy cuts in and somehow says that coping with severe disablement is really hard work, demanding on skill and energy and a very great achievement, that I say to myself, 'Is it?' then think about it briefly, 'Well yes I suppose it is,' and start to open up.

Mainly, though, his approach is a minimalist one; rather than giving advice he tips thoughts off with a few carefully chosen words and gets you to tell him what is bothering you.

I was confused about what was bothering me, there was so much. He started to lead me. The first thing he helped me to identify was how difficult I found it having a care assistant around me twenty-four hours a day.

'Can you give me an example?' he said.

I explained the embarrassment I felt every time I went out, and the hassle involved getting in and out of the Caravelle.

'Is there anything you can do to avoid this?'

'Not unless I could get a vehicle I could drive from the chair.' Once spoken, the solution was blindingly clear. That was what I had to go out and do.

Still on the matter of care, he said, 'It's clear from what you say that you have difficulty asking for help and to get people to do things for you. Let's take a minute to think of things people are doing for you at present that could be got round in some way.'

One simple-sounding thing was getting a drink in bed. One of my agonies was not being able to get a drink in the middle of the night. Nowadays I have a jug of water with three bendy straws coming out of it so that I can suck out a drink. The system took a while to perfect but it works very well.

He made me realise that I had to get my living environment properly adapted. If I wanted to work on my computer it would be so much better if I could avoid having to get it set up each time.

Automatic doors would be a huge boon.

Some things, it was concluded, I would have to make an effort to accept, but for others there were solutions. He asked such simple questions that in retrospect I wonder why I didn't ask them myself, rather as Charles Wylie's game plan of objectives made a year before had been so simple and obvious.

It was the most profitable session I had ever had with any kind of medic. He finished by emphasising his point about coping. 'Trevor, spinal cord injury requires very great coping skills, and already you've done a lot . . . but really what we've talked about today is that when something is not right, and you can feel it is not right, you must identify it, and then do something about it . . .'

It is such good advice, so good that probably you don't need to be spinally injured to benefit from it.

> The Plaintiff needs a period of cognitive behavioural psychotherapy to help him in making further adjustments to the consequences of his disability and in developing effective coping skills.

Actually, I don't think I do any more.

> Such therapy costs between £55 and £95 per hour-long session . . .

> The Plaintiff relied heavily on his mother, Margaret Jones, for care and support. In consequence, she suffered very substantial financial losses, because the extensive care which she provided disrupted both her career as a senior NHS physiotherapist and her independent business activities.

> By January 1988 Margaret Jones was working four days a week as a senior physiotherapist, as well as attending to her holiday cottage rental business. When the Plaintiff was discharged from hospital Margaret Jones offered him one of her holiday cottages, which had previously been converted for use by the disabled. She assumed responsibility for his care, providing seventy hours of care per week. She gave up her job as a physiotherapist, stopped catering for her visitors and employed staff for the weekend change-overs.

Seventeen

Being in Wales I was not in much of a position to make more than fitful contributions to the activities of the Trevor Jones Trust and so I resolved to try and sort my life out. Dr Kennedy had helped me to find a real sense of direction and hope which was big enough to outweigh the major psychological set-back of being robbed by a second care assistant.

Target number one was to tackle mobility. The VW Caravelle I had been driving since March 1989 had been my lifeline to freedom in some ways but in others it added to my dependence. I had to rely on someone to enable me to operate it, either to get me into the driving seat or operate the lift system and lock me into the back as passenger.

By the time I'd been through either process I had almost lost interest in going anywhere especially as arriving at the other end I would have to prevail upon someone to enact the entire process twice more, once to get me out, once to get me back in again.

As a priority, therefore, I began to research the vehicles market in earnest with the intention of getting something that could be driven from the wheelchair. I'd looked at a Ford Transit van conversion a year before but it was no longer possible to make the conversion because it involved lowering a floor and Ford's replacement model had a fuel tank there. Besides, who other than a jobbing builder wants to drive around the place looking like a jobbing builder?

A tetraplegic man in Oxford wanted to sell me a 10-litre American Ford van, making light of the fact that he didn't like it. Me neither. Too big and too fuel-thirsty.

I visited a businessman up north who wanted to sell me a Transit van which he'd adapt and then he'd design a wheelchair to go with it. He had me to stay and made a real fuss of me. Having plied me and my mate with drinks he tried to force a sale on me, offering a significant discount if I agreed there and then.

He himself had made a lot of money out of the disabled – nothing wrong with that – but I didn't like the way he knew what was best for me, or his hard sell. After a disabling accident you are easy prey to sharks who have all the answers. I was glad to escape with the Trust's wallet still intact.

I also got the impression that he was interested in muscling in on the Trevor Jones Trust and its money for disabled sportsmen, and on me because he thought that as I'd been at school with Prince Andrew I might help him get the Queen to open his new factory showroom.

A few weeks later Mum met Vic Henney of the Keep Able Foundation. Vic was an American entrepreneur who had started a business called 'Keep Able Limited' which had a large showroom in Brentford, a sort of Texas Homecare for the disabled.

After my northern businessman I was a bit wary of Vic to begin with but soon warmed to him. His was a genuine fascination with helping the disabled to find solutions. He recognised that people are people and are disabled by the nature of their environment more than anything. For him, finding the right equipment and technology was both a hobby and a crusade.

The most interesting disability going for Vic would be a $C_1/2$ tetraplegic (like Christopher Reeve), a man who cannot even move his head or breathe for himself.

I was immediately hooked on what he told me of developments here and there. He showed me a Permobil wheelchair from Sweden, which he told me was the most advanced wheelchair in the world. I'd never heard of a Permobil.

It had two thick nine-inch drive wheels at the front and a pair of very robust-looking but smaller ones at the back which just followed on the supermarket trolley principle (but far better made).

He demonstrated to me how the joystick control could raise and lower the seat, could lie me down or stand me up. The standing function would be especially useful for keeping the circulation going to help the organs drain, a lot easier than my standing frame, which was now doing service in the garage as a spot for my mother's hens to lay eggs.

Vic would have liked to sell me the Permobil there and then but I already had a wheelchair. What I was really interested in was the right vehicle. I certainly wasn't going to fork out £15,000 on a Permobil. My own wheelchair had cost £1,500 plus another £2,000 for the motor which I found shocking enough. I couldn't believe the prices of specialised equipment. Just before my accident I had lashed out £200 for a bicycle and £60 for a squash racquet. That was what I called extravagance. Well, apart from *Yoldia*, my yacht.

Shortly afterwards he reported that he'd been to the Permobil factory in Sweden and that they had a car which might interest me. I was very excited when I saw the picture of it. For a start it looked like a car. I could not come to terms with having to drive a builder's van just because I was disabled.

The brochure was in Swedish and I could hardly wait to see what it said so Mum got a friend to translate it for me. I discovered that it was a Chrysler Voyager people-mover sort of thing, built in the States and adapted by a firm called Independent Mobility Systems in New Mexico. Permobil's system for integrating it with their wheelchair promised undreamt-of independence, a car which I could drive from the chair without transferring.

I had booked a flight to Sweden within the week and Vic –

who was on business in America – said he'd meet me out there. I decided to save on an extra £500 air ticket by getting care locally from an agency, imagining that they'd be well geared up for that in Sweden.

First I rang up SAS, the Scandinavian Airline. After a little confusion they rang back to say that in Sweden there is no such thing as a nursing agency.

I rang the Swedish Tourist Board and asked the girl there if she could track down the equivalent of our Spinal Injuries Association. Another blank drawn; I was told that there was no such thing as that either.

None the less the girl was very helpful. She said she knew someone in the town I was going to, who in turn got in touch with the local government officer for the disabled. What I was rapidly learning was that there was little need for agencies or a voluntary sector in Sweden. Adequate support is a right, not something you struggle to achieve.

The trip was nearly organised. I set myself a challenge; I would do the whole thing alone and not even let my mother drive me the five miles to the station.

I got on the phone to the local Dial-a-Ride, which was in Cardiff, seventy miles away. They said it would cost £60. Too much. British Rail said that I could catch a train in Llandeilo, but that I would have to travel in the guard's van. I'd phoned BR the day before my departure and the guy had said, 'You're leaving it a bit late, aren't you?'

I lost my temper at this.

'OK, OK,' he said, 'but in future we would like to have a couple of days' notice.'

Already my challenge was under threat. Eventually Mum had to run me down to the station in her Golf. She was in her fifties and, although fit and a trained physio, experienced in lifting techniques and in caring for me, none of what she had had to do for me over the past year had been easy. Just dismantling the Quickie wheelchair, then reassembling it at the station and putting the motor back on was a big enough job.

I had abandoned the idea of a transfer from Reading to Heathrow, which as crows fly would have made better sense because the airport coach is utterly inaccessible. Instead I went on to Paddington, from where I had prebooked a wheelchair taxi.

At Paddington no one came to help me. Soon there was no one left, just me, sitting in an empty carriage.

Then the cleaner came. She hadn't spotted me when I addressed her. She nearly jumped with fright. 'I'm only the cleaner,' she said, looking as if she'd seen a ghost or a pervert and scuttled off. I was left abandoned again, thinking that I might well be forgotten until someone came across my skeleton a decade later in some railway siding.

Then a businessman came in looking for a briefcase he'd left behind. I asked him to find a guard. Five minutes later he returned alone saying that the platform was deserted. Under my direction he fetched a ramp, helped me off and carried my bags for me down to the taxi rank. (NB Europe's most prestigious and new train, Eurostar, is not independently accessible by wheelchair.)

My taxi-driver was waiting for me but mightily disgruntled. 'I've been waiting twenty minutes,' he said.

'So have I.'

'You can get out of that thing, can't you?' he said.

'Well, no, actually.'

'Should have called a disabled taxi.'

'I did.'

He got in his taxi and without a word drove off.

Well bloody hell, thanks mate, I thought, and asked another driver if he could summon me a wheelchair taxi on his radio. In those days only about fifteen per cent of taxis were wheelchair accessible, whereas nowadays all new ones have to be.

But just then my original taxi driver returned with one of his mates in an adapted one. All was forgiven.

At Heathrow I asked a redcoat to take my bags. He said, 'Oh, we've got special people to help you.' He left me while he went off to seek out a 'special person'.

At check-in the electric motor was taken apart and put in a box. They tried to transfer me to another wheelchair but I resisted. There was no sound reason for not being able to stay in my own chair until the aeroplane. Using an airport chair is like asking someone to wear high-heeled shoes two sizes too small. Not very comfortable and you feel a prat.

Then I was wheeled off by my special person, destination the aircraft. *En route* I got to see all the parts of Heathrow only special people ever reach. I was wheeled through Arrivals where every so often someone would come up and ask my pusher directions to somewhere and I'd have to sit around while he gave an answer. Then it was deep into the bowels of the place, through long corridors with air-conditioning ducts and important- but random-looking wiring. As we went through double doors he'd have to barge through them backwards and they'd come crashing back in on me.

Eventually we ended up outdoors and I was parked for a while among the dustbins while we waited for transport out to the plane. By this time I was both cold and pissed off. An ambulance pulled up.

'Why do you have to humiliate me every time by putting me in an ambulance? I'm not bloody ill.'

I was transferred to an ambulance chair, which was very small and precarious, then carried up the steps to the plane. The chair was not designed for this and bits of me like my feet kept slithering off it and shooting into spasm.

As all this was happening our in-flight meals were being loaded by one of those telescopic lift systems on the back of a lorry. The meals were getting a far more dignified entry into the plane than I was.

The flight was a pleasant relief – the hostesses were charming – and I soon recovered my sense of humour.

On arrival in Stockholm the door of the aircraft was opened. Instant culture shock. A clean-cut young man came on board and in perfect English said to me, 'We've got your wheelchair waiting for you, sir, just let everybody pass. And do please let me know how we can help you.'

There was none of this 'Here, you grab that bit' kind of attitude. They were well trained and well organised right from the start. First he asked me how I'd like to be lifted, then he and a steward did it. I was put in my own chair at the door of the aircraft, then wheeled through a succession of (automatic) doors to the transit lounge.

'You have a thirty-minute wait, Mr Jones. Can I get you a newspaper, a coffee, perhaps some duty-free goods?' I couldn't believe my ears.

The transfer to the next plane was equally smooth. I kept expecting them to wheel me out into the cold and leave me by some dustbins, but they never did.

At Sundsvall, my destination, I was left waiting in the Arrivals area for a short time. Then the automatic doors opened and a man came towards me in what I recognised to be a Permobil wheelchair.

'My name is Anders Vickberg. I've come to take you to your hotel,' he said.

What, you? I thought but didn't say. I waited for his assistant to appear but none did.

I followed him out in my Quickie wheelchair with electric power pack on the back to what I recognised as a Chrysler Voyager as seen in the photos. I wasn't sure what Anders had done but the side door slid open and a ramp came down like something out of *Thunderbirds*. He guided his chair into the vehicle, manoeuvring it behind the steering wheel until it locked into place to become the driver's seat. I steered in behind him, the ramp went up, the door closed and we set off.

Apart from a man carrying my bags we'd had no help from anyone at all.

It was unbelievable and I'd seen enough. I could easily have got straight back on the plane and returned to England. Job done. This car with this wheelchair. I had to have them. They were fantastic.

It was good to see Vic at the hotel. We had dinner with the MD of Permobil. It is run as a business but is in fact a foundation. Once salaries have been paid all profits go back into the company and not out to shareholders.

The factory had the feel of a high-tech weapons research laboratory, like Q's laboratory in the James Bond films with different rooms for different gadgetry. There was a room for improving electric motor efficiency, another for miniaturised gear boxes, a computer room where they were working on both soft- and hardware, such as voice-recognition technology. They had a room in which they were developing a chair for blind quadraplegics which responded to magnetic strips laid on the floor so that even the unsighted could have some independence at home.

They told me that they built the best wheelchair in the world, and had done so for twenty-five years. As far as I was concerned it was obviously true. I had to have one of these chairs. And the car.

Apparently there were none in the UK, which I found amazing until they explained that their market reasearch had revealed too few people in the UK who could afford one, so they had not tried to market them there.

They demonstrated the chair and explained how they had researched the most compatible car to go with their system. The Chrysler Voyager conversion by Independent Mobility Systems (IMS) of New Mexico was the best. Most driving systems for the disabled have a Heath Robinson feel and look to them but here the engineering was superb. The hand control was built to match the car and unlike those I had seen in the UK it was beautifully designed and engineered. The look and the feel make a big difference to how you regard yourself.

Additionally they assured me that everything was crash tested, fully integrated and completely automatic. They invited me to have a go so we went for a drive around the snowy streets of Sundsvall. I discovered I could drive it without any special modifications for me at all.

I spent just under a week in Sundsvall getting a feel for what was available. The whole experience was an eye opener. All the buildings in the town were wheelchair accessible, all you needed was a Permobil. The disabled people I met working there were an example of what was possible. In Britain few tetraplegics make it back into the world of work. In many cases another member of the family, usually the mother, has to drop her employment to look after him. A severe spinal injury thus means the loss of two incomes – a vicious circle from which few families escape.

In Sweden, I discovered, every effort is made to reintegrate tetraplegics into the world of work. It may be that they have to live in sheltered accommodation or in annexes to their homes, but the attitude is that their welfare state supports each individual on the basis of his needs and wishes and not on the basis of 'This is what's available now, sod off'.

As soon as I got back to Wales I put in an order for a chair and a car, to be funded partly by the Trust and partly by a £20,000 bank loan raised by Mum. I should also mention that Richard Branson sent me a letter in which he'd said something like 'I thought the best way to help you was to give you this money directly.' With the letter was a cheque for £10,000.

The Chrysler Voyager would take about four months to arrive and then I'd have the best vehicle and chair combination of any tetraplegic outside Scandinavia. Four months. I could barely contain myself.

For my part, 1990 had started well. After my varied experiences of the year before which included my interview with Dr Kennedy, I had a much clearer sense of purpose. This was to be the year in which I began to sort out my future. By April I felt I'd cracked my mobility problem and just could not wait until the summer when I'd have a vehicle into which I could roll, say goodbye to my care assistant and be off.

On return from Sweden I moved the three short yards from the living-room, my base for the past year, into the cleverly designed annexe. Half built into the old smithy and half new, it had the most staggering views down the valley. When I sat at my desk it felt as if I were part of the field the room had been cut out of. I was almost looking up at the recently born lambs jumping around just feet away. Mum had brought her refined and practical talents to creating a warm and cosy atmosphere, everything had been thought of. She even had a table built which I could spin round, so nothing was out of my reach.

There was an open-plan living–dining–kitchen area, a large wheel-in shower room, my bedroom had a low-beamed ceiling and wash basin. A wall separated it from a similar bedroom for the carer. Care continued to be a problem, stemming in part from my not being able to match the market price. As Charles Wylie once put it, 'You pay peanuts you get monkeys.'

My naval pension was sufficient to disqualify me from most of the means-tested grants available to help pay for care but not sufficient to pay for an adequate system on its own. Under the guidance of the Spinal Injuries Association and from the security of my new surroundings I set about lobbying my local authority's Social Services Director and other funding agencies. My letter explained the problem and suggested a solution:

Under the threat of being institutionalised I have experimented with various sytems of care, including recruiting assistants independently or from agencies, relying entirely on my mother, or my mother and volunteers, or my brothers and friends with occasional help from district nurses, or entirely on my friends.

227

My capital is already exhausted, service pension insufficient, the drain on my mother unacceptable. The government directly contributes £46.05 a week towards my care. They have accepted the principle of Care in the Community, but in reality the cheapest option – for me to have full-time care – would require a grant of £350 per week . . .

It took several months of persistent badgering, meetings, phone calls and letters before I secured an extra £50 a week from the council and £50 from the Independent Living Fund, a government charity. About a third of what I was aiming for, not enough to employ two assistants but it did allow me to pay the going rate for one.

Over the same couple of months I spent some time helping to organise a 'Helicopter Air Day' at Moyns Park, George Milford-Haven's country home.

George had a helicopter business at the time and had even offered me a job helping to run it, but it was too early for me. He also had a Gazelle of his own which we went flying in a couple of times.

We flew down to Culdrose to meet the Sharks, the Navy's helicopter display team. He flew in to pick me up in Wales, gave me the map and I had much pleasure in steering him down to my old base. I felt quite melancholic as the controller asked, 'Are you familiar with the airfield?'

We were late and parked in front of the squadron building. George's black stretch Gazelle (the helicopter equivalent of a stretch limo) dominated the scene, a picture of the extravagance of the 1980s.

The Sharks agreed to be the focus of what was to be the largest meeting of Gazelles on UK soil to date.

George was in charge of inviting those with civilian markings, while it was to be my job to try and get one from each of the services. Meanwhile Sarah Slight took on organising the party lunch, a band and a marquee.

The day itself was the highlight of the summer for me. Moyns Park is a fantastic setting. The grounds were buzzing with activity, two or three hundred guests and about thirty-five helicopters pitched up.

Sean Parry Jones was selling art and Vic Henney had a Keep Able Foundation stall showing off his robotic arm developed from *Spitting Image* puppet technology and a dental plate used for controlling a wheelchair with the tongue, for those with no use of arms whatsoever, and of course the Permobil.

At the start of the day Sarah Slight came back from the docks with my new Chrysler Voyager and when Vic later arrived with the chair they were officially handed over to me on behalf of the Trust.

I was lifted into the Permobil – an incredibly exciting moment and instantly, I mean instantly, liberating. Up until that point I'd been in the grounds of the house in my lightweight Quickie wheelchair with power pack which still required a helping push from someone to cope with the grass. Suddenly I was free. I could motor out to one of the helicopters and chat with the pilot. If I saw an old friend I wanted to chat with I just headed off in that direction confident that by the time I got there he wouldn't already have moved off.

Now all I needed was for the car to go off to the adapters and be customised to me. Then I'd be really free.

I had a temporary carer who was a local school leaver, and obviously I was very excited about my new Permobil (the car was still with the adapters) and so one exceptionally hot summer's day while the girl was having a snooze in another room and Mum was out, I decided to go for a wander. The chair offered me new freedom and I could not wait to escape from the confinement of my Mum's plot, my prison for so long. I imagined myself racing along the ridge road at the top of the drive. Without a moment's thought I was out of there.

The drive is quite long and steep and it is not the easiest to mount in a wheelchair – even a Permobil – but after a bit of slithering about I got to the top. Then there was nothing between me and the open road and the wind in my hair.

Nothing except a cattle grid.

I eyed it. Uncharted territory. The front wheels would be no problem, but the trailing wheels were about the same size and idea, if chunkier, as a supermarket trolley's. Ideal for falling into cattle grids.

But I had my freedom, and I was going to enjoy it, there was no way I was going back. I shaped up for the grid and decided to go for it. At top speed I'd get across. I was successful to begin with. About half-way across I could feel the back wheels get caught and the wheelchair sink. I tried reversing, turning, going forward, but I was absolutely stuck, anchored in the middle of the grid.

It was one of those days that you get only once every decade in Wales, the temperature in the nineties if not the hundreds. I had no shoes and no shirt and very white hospital skin. It was a completely still day; the wind in my hair had been a mistaken idea as well.

Unable to sweat like a normal person, my body thermostat broken, I began to get hotter and hotter. After a while I could feel myself going faint and knew I was in trouble. I had to keep conscious.

I could lower my head backwards because the Permobil will go flat and this helped get the blood to my head. I could lift my feet with the chair too, but I had to be careful about getting pressure sores on my heels. The footplate is hard and my feet were bare.

Shouting was out of the question; Dan y Cefn is miles from anywhere and I was a hundred yards from the house round a bend in the drive. No one was going to hear. I carried on trying to remain conscious.

I think I had been there for about an hour when a car pulled into the start of the drive about fifteen feet away. Saved, I thought as a feeling of relief swept through me. It was an elderly man and his wife in their 1953 Morris Minor. I leant on my horn, and waved my hands. I tried to shout but my throat was too dry, no sound came out.

When the man saw me he clearly thought I was some kind of nutter because he slammed his car into gear and drove off.

So it was back to a routine of five minutes of head down, feet up, then a return to the sitting position while my throat got drier and drier. I carried on with this until my brain began to get so addled I could no longer work out the wheelchair controls. I could feel the panic rising as I tried to remain calm and collected. It reminded me of decompression chamber training in the Navy when the brain cannot control or co-ordinate for lack of oxygen.

And then another car pulled into the drive. It was my helper's parents. When the girl had woken from her snooze and found me gone, she'd searched high and low (but not up the drive) and in terror and confusion at my disappearance had rung up her parents.

They helped me, by now nearly unconscious, back into the house and started the standard process for cooling me down, using lots of wet towels and fans blowing air across me.

The only good thing to report from this episode is that although sunburnt, I couldn't feel it. And we now have two metal tracks for wheelchair access across the cattle grid.

In the summer it was decided to seek to have the Trust run professionally. An ad was placed in *The Times* and another in a forces resettlement magazine. A problem was that I was doing one thing but quite often Bill Carrington entirely another. Bill, Mark Dowie and I selected Priscilla Rawlins following a series of interviews held at Bill's office. It was all done very quickly, before the forces resettlement magazine applications had come in. She visited me in Wales to learn the scene and a new lease was taken out on offices in Kensington.

As elements of my life fell into place, I embarked on a project of my own. The Llandeilo Round Table had invited me to give a talk on the Navy. The idea of giving a talk terrified me, but I'd gritted my teeth and done it, helped by Mark Dowie who'd come up from Dartmouth with a whole lot of slides of helicopters and ships. The talk was far less entertaining than what happened afterwards at the dinner. It was a beautiful roast which I asked the waiter to cut up for me. He took it away and brought it back having put the whole lot through the blender.

We fell to talking about the difficulties of integrating when using a wheelchair. Llandeilo is built on a hill but given my new mobility it seemed a shame that access was blocked to the bar at the rugby club, the local hotel and indeed most of the shops.

This was the birth of the Llandeilo Access Group. Many towns have access groups, but my idea was different: actively to raise the money and awareness to make it into the first fully accessible town in Britain, a model of what could be achieved.

With the help of Round Tablers, Nigel Brick, chairman of the Chamber of Commerce and the town clerk, Craig Jones, who also worked in the planning department, we set up a committee. In an attempt to get the whole town behind the idea we invited representatives of all the local clubs, including Rotary, the Heritage Society, the Victuallers Association, the Disabled Driver's Association, for example. I went to give my Navy talk for them and enlisted their support.

We organised public meetings and engineered several stories for the local press and TV, trying to generate awareness for the problem and support for the solution. With the help of Mum and my care assistant I got photos of the entrance to every public building and wrote to its owner.

It was hard going. Few replied and those that did protested poverty (even though my letter said I planned to raise the money and it would cost nothing).

The postmaster came up with the most original excuse when I went to see him. 'I'm canvassing for your support,' I said. 'If I got the work funded would you agree to have your step turned into a gradual slope, using the same materials as are there already? It would make it easier for prams, chairs, old ladies with arthritic hips . . .'

'Dunno, to be honest. If I didn't have a step all the dust would blow off the street into the post office.' I tried to explain that shops without steps were no dustier but to no avail.

The local architect told me, 'Trevor, I've lived here all my life and yours is practically the only wheelchair I've ever seen in Llandeilo.' He obviously didn't ever stop to wonder why.

I wasn't going to need him anyway. An architect called Gordon Popplewell from Bath, who had polio, saw me explaining my plans on TV and volunteered to do the work free.

Most strange, perhaps, was the refusal of the banks and building societies to co-operate, even though I was offering to raise the money. These are big national PLCs who could easily afford to make their properties accessible. The Principality, the Midland, Lloyds and Barclays have no excuse.

My personal circumstances were to change before the fund-raising ever got off the ground but local awareness had been raised. A couple of shop owners took the point when they were doing refurbishments, the local council adapted the entrance to the job centre and when the National Trust bought the local stately home in Dinewyr Park, they took the subject of equal access very seriously and even built a half-mile-long boardwalk into a swampy forest of outstanding natural beauty.

My recent experiences continued to bring home to me the hideous cost of everything – not just sophisticated Permobil wheelchairs – but low-tech things like a ramp into a shop.

Marc Koska took me along to a presentation by a network marketing company called NSA given by a guy called David Hunt, brother of the late racing driver James.

Many of the people at the presentation seemed to be on a kind of high, drunk with the thought of how much money they were going to make selling these water filters. The dream was defined as 'the Beach Scenario'. This meant that the people below you in the network were achieving so much income that your share of it meant you no longer needed to work. You could spend your life on the beach.

Where the dream breaks down is that you've got to sell the bloody water filters but fortunately Marc wasn't after me for that, all he wanted was introductions to Trevor Jones Trust supporters. The spin-off for me would be that the Trust would get a proportion of the earnings in the network.

I attended several of David Hunt's meetings. Their aim was to get you thoroughly fired up to go off and sell. We were given lots of statistics about how the sales of bottled water are showing double-digit growth year in year out. A bottle of mineral water costs at least sixty-five pence retail, but the same amount of water from the filter costs ten. So even though the filter might seem expensive at two hundred quid or so, in the long run they were an unbeatable can't-say-no bargain.

They had professional motivational speakers, many from America, complemented by members of the network standing up to give two-minute testimonials. The experts talked for up to thirty minutes, whipping the audience into a frenzy of the kind you would normally associate with Billy Graham or a Nuremberg rally.

The message was: 'All you have to do is pick up that phone. You can do it' and by the end you'd believe you could do anything.

For somebody whose self-esteem was so low that giving a talk to the Llandeilo Round Table on the Navy filled me with fear, I'd have to say that my involvement with NSA network marketing was something else which helped me to change my life. It taught me to put niggling doubts aside, to make the difficult telephone calls of the day first, to go for what you want in life.

David Hunt invited me to address one of the meetings. It was the major motivational slot, thirty minutes in which to tell my story to an audience of four or five hundred.

It was relatively easy speaking about oneself but nevertheless

I was nervous. My way of dealing with the nerves and self-doubt in that situation was to say to myself: 'Well, you're living in constant pain, what could possibly be worse?' Then somehow it became easy.

I spoke about my accident, the part my friends played in helping me to rebuild my life, the importance of setting goals and working to achieve them, and finally about the work of the Trevor Jones Trust, inviting them to complete a direct debit form which had been distributed earlier.

The Chrysler was ready to collect from the adapters during the second week of August. It had been a frustrating wait. I'd like to have taken one back from Sweden under my arm.

I couldn't use the Permobil with the Volkswagen so when I went to Mark Dowie's wedding I took the Quickie. His eighty-seven-year-old great aunt was chatting to me politely when she brushed against the joystick sending me lurching forwards. The frail old lady was lucky not to be crushed to an untimely death (she had a good ten years left in her) because if I'd been in the Permobil – which weighs twenty stone – she would have been. That is if she hadn't landed in my lap.

Despite the danger to old ladies I was thrilled to be finally getting hold of my Chrysler and Permobil combination.

I had to move up to London and stay with Stuart and Angus in Clapham, then commute daily to the adapters in Wembley for fittings to ensure that they didn't make a mess of the adjustments.

In comparison with what I had seen in Sweden the workmanship was disappointing. It was functional but little attention had been paid to its appearance. If it worked it was OK, was the attitude. It annoyed me that standards were so low and that they seemed either not to listen to me or to ignore my instructions.

The longed-for day came when I could pick it up. It was already a bit later than expected mainly because the adapters had taken so long to install the locking plate for the chair, somehow taking eight hours over a job that should have taken less than one.

Angus drove me across to Wembley in the VW along with Fiona Stark, a school friend who was working for me at the time. On the way back, Fiona drove the VW, while Angus joined me in the new Chrysler. It was a Friday afternoon and very hot as we threaded our way back through traffic trying to get away for the weekend. I have to admit that I didn't feel entirely in control.

We stopped for petrol. Angus went to fill it up while I waited inside with the air-conditioning on and the windows closed. As I sat there I felt a sinking feeling. 'Oh, no,' I thought, 'the air suspension is failing.' The car sat on air rather than springs. But no, I must have brushed the control on the wheelchair. It was quietly elevating me, trapping my arms, which were resting on my lap, under the steering wheel. I panicked. If it carried on I thought it might snap my legs. I yelled for Angus, but he couldn't hear because the window was closed. Besides he was preoccupied working out why the petrol nozzle wouldn't go in (the car uses unleaded and he was trying to fill it from the leaded nozzle which is fatter).

By the time he came to the window to get my wallet I was beside myself. 'What the f--- is going on Trevor?' he asked sympathetically. I couldn't explain but he worked it out, released me and went to pay the bill.

We were both a bit shaken when we set off again. Also, we'd had a bit of hanging around to do at the converters and the traffic was appalling, as was the heat. Both our senses of humour were fragile so it was a relief when we finally turned into Angus's road. Quite what happened I don't know but I over-steered, lost control and drove straight into the side of a parked van. I hit it quite hard and left a big dent in the side. Just at that moment a police car was passing. They didn't get out of the car and as Angus spoke to them I heard coming out over their radio, 'Car registered in Wales owned by disabled driver Trevor Jones.'

They seemed to find this too funny for words and drove off, which suddenly made us laugh too. Angus left a note on the van's windscreen – it was pretty beaten up and the owners never got in touch. The whole incident gave us a bit of a buzz and we arrived home strangely happier.

Having got the car, I went almost immediately to Gordonstoun, driving up on my own. I was going to visit Angus Buchanan whose wife had just had their first daughter. I was on my way to their house outside Glasgow when I suddenly thought, I haven't got them anything. As I was cursing myself, I drove past a gift shop and it dawned on me that I could stop, get myself out of the car and into the shop (I'd noticed that there was no step) and go and buy something. It was the most alien experience imaginable to be in a shop on my own, not having to deal with a shopkeeper talking to my assistant rather than me. Alien but oh so liberating, after all that time, to be able to do something like that without having planned it in advance and asked someone else. Shopping on impulse was not somethiong I had thought I'd ever be able to do again.

I was keen to tell others about my car and chair and also bring attention to the Trust and the way that new technology could enhance the lives of the more seriously disabled. I called up *Tomorrow's World* and persuaded them to do a feature on all my new equipment. They came down to Wales and although unwilling to plug the Trust, they picked up on the issue of wheelchair access, filming me at meetings of the Llandeilo access group and demonstrating the unprecedented freedom the chair and car gave.

The day after the programme was shown I found myself stuck at the bottom of the hill in Llandeilo with a flat battery on the Permobil and the Chrysler parked at the top. I was rescued by a couple of policemen who pushed me all the way back up again, no mean feat because the chair weighs twenty stone and the hill is steep. They laughed the whole way. As it happened they'd both seen the programme the night before.

*

What about my love life during this year of consolidation? Caryl and I were going wobbly rather than steady, but going none the less.

She took me to see the evangelist Billy Graham at Earl's Court, just before I went to Gordonstoun to see in the new boys and girls for the second time.

The atmosphere at the Billy Graham meeting was an experience much like the NSA water-filter-selling rally in tone. 'I can feel people out there wondering if it's the right thing to do, to make that commitment, that's why you're here tonight, this is your opportunity.'

He was speaking to people like me, the waverers. I was sitting near the back in an area for wheelchair users. 'You know who you are. Come down to the front, come down from where you are sitting, make that commitment here and now, before the Lord.'

Billy Graham was bloody convincing, he had all the right words and I could just sense Caryl willing me to go down to the front.

All about me other people, including some in wheelchairs, poured out towards the stage. I was left feeling uncomfortable, sitting there thinking I'd quite like to have done it for Caryl, but, No, this just is not me. My religion is a private thing. I never did make my way down to the front of Billy Graham's stage.

A distance had been developing between me and Caryl. The fact is that the stronger I became the more we drifted apart. I was more sure of myself in every aspect of my life. She was naturally a shy and reserved person and I don't think was ever very comfortable in the presence of my more self-confident friends such as Georgia – although I saw little of Georgia herself because her bank had posted her to Tokyo.

None the less Caryl and I continued to see each other when we could and I managed to persuade her to take some of her holiday with me to visit the châteaux of the Loire.

I set out from Dan-y-Cefn a bit concerned that the device

that locked my chair into place in the car was damaged and drove off to meet Caryl at a hotel in Bournemouth selected with the RADAR (Royal Association for Disability and Rehabilitation) book on accessible accommodation.

The place was more OAP home than hotel, which explained the facilities. When we arrived they were just clearing away the dinner tables to set up a whist evening for the old ladies. It wasn't a good start to the holiday.

The rooms were small, the beds uncomfortable, Caryl had a horrible cold and I was worried about the car.

The ferry trip was hard work because the vessel was largely inaccessible for the electric chair – even the cabin was not big enough to get me and the chair into – and then we stayed in a slightly soulless Campanile hotel in France where Caryl read her bible well into the night rather than talk to me. The atmosphere between us became that little bit worse.

In the châteaux region of the Loire we stayed in a very nice hotel. It was quite expensive, which was against Caryl's Christian ethos, whereas I love good food and good wine. The fact that I couldn't share my enjoyment took us down further.

Touring Loire châteaux might not seem an obvious holiday for a tetraplegic, but I was becoming increasingly self-confident and sure that although the turrets and sweeping staircases would be out of bounds to me I'd still be able to soak up the architecture and see some of the rooms.

The difference in my mental attitude to that of eighteen months before, when I'd been diagnosed clinically depressed, was enormous. I was no longer afraid to go up to young tourists and ask for help, whereas Caryl, being by nature shy, still found the whole thing slightly embarrassing.

'Go and ask those two blokes to help,' I'd say to her and she'd be reluctant. By the time she'd plucked up the courage they'd be gone and the next lot of tourists would be a bunch of elderly widows.

She felt exposed and self-conscious. Also she wasn't that interested in the châteaux. She'd come back from the bits I'd not been able to see with a peremptory description which revealed that she'd been pretty bored by it all. Historical monuments were not her scene.

So we'd both be frustrated. She was bored and I hadn't seen the bits I wanted to see. It all came to a head at about the fourth château where she'd expressed reluctance to ask someone to help get me in but had then relented. We had a row about it. 'OK, she said, 'I'll help you get in.'

'No, it's all right, I don't mind.'

'No, I said I'd help you.'

'No, that's OK, I'll go round the gardens in my chair instead.'

'I don't want to look at the gardens, I'd prefer to sit in the car than go round the gardens.'

'Right, I'll go and look at the gardens alone,' I said and off I went. Once in a leafy arbour I realised that things between me and Caryl must have got really bad because without her I started to enjoy myself. It was a lovely mature garden with the château as backdrop, I could go almost wherever I liked in my Permobil and above all, once I was alone, there was none of that ill-defined tension making us both uncomfortable.

The best night of the trip was when we fell into conversation with some English tourists at the next table. Caryl didn't really participate but I had a good time talking to them. It beat the rather awkward silence between the two of us.

The final straw was when one of the motors on the chair went. It has one motor for each front wheel and one of them began to misbehave, then recover again. It finally packed up in a château forecourt; I found that all I could do with the chair was drive it in a circle, quietly digging a hole in the gravel.

One of the gardeners spent a couple of hours trying to fix it. He had no English and my O-level French was little help. Finally Caryl had no choice but to get the car and drive into the grounds of the beautiful château which she found incredibly embarrassing in front of a fair old crowd of tourists.

She loaded me up and we drove straight back to England more or less in silence.

Caryl and I broke up. Since we'd started to go out with each other I'd moved on such a lot that the natural differences between our personalities grew. She'd moved on too. I hope she feels for the better, she was certainly a much more confident, less shy, more mature person.

In the three years we'd known each other we'd journeyed far together in every sense. Physically we'd done two trips to Portugal, one to Japan, two to Italy, four to Scotland, one to France. We'd been to shows, concerts, plays, weddings. Without her I'd have done a quarter of all that and if I'd had to do these things with a care assistant I'd have had a fraction of the fun and the fulfilment.

Then there was the emotional, spiritual and sexual part of the journeys. That hadn't been easy, but the tension had been half of the fun, what made the experiences rich. All my feelings of love for her had been accentuated by the near-masochistic pleasure of a physical closeness which could never be satisfied.

Caryl and I were very different personalities and given all the things that stood in our way it is amazing that we stayed together so long. I shall be grateful to her for the rest of my life and I thank God for all she gave me.

Eighteen

Bruce Rennie, whom I'd met as Richard Branson's balloon site manager in Japan, had become a governor of the Trust. He'd had various madcap ideas for raising funds and consciousness about disability. It started with Bill Carrington, fresh from the pub, suggesting at one committee meeting that I be put in a canoe and paddled down the Amazon. A back-up team and documentary crew would come too and the resulting film sold for hundreds of thousands.

Bruce was the only one to take this idea seriously and went to visit the expeditions officer at the Royal Geographical Society. He had a mind-set different from most, after all he'd helped launch a balloon across the Pacific (Branson had been successful second time around).

The expeditions officer Shane Winsor soon put him straight – the Amazon would be tough enough for an able-bodied person. She wasn't completely dismissive, however, and together they looked at all the expeditions coming hither and thither. One was crossing Canada by microlight aircraft. The idea of these miniature flimsy aircraft rang some bells and the upshot was that he came back to the next trustees' meeting saying, 'Amazon's off, but Trevor is going to fly a microlight across the Nullarbor Plain, a desert in Australia, never been done before.'

Several months on and Bruce had had no luck whatsoever with this plan. The whole flying idea had died a death until one day I met someone in the local Llandeilo wine bar – despite my campaign, still the only wheelchair-accessible hostelry. He was the boyfriend of the owner Jillie England, a guy called Paul McNichol.

I was chatting to him about the Llandeilo access group and plans for the Trust, and he'd seen me on *Tomorrow's World*. I explained how our microlighting plans had come to nothing.

He was a bit like Bruce Rennie and before he'd even got through a second bottle of wine the idea of me flying a microlight seemed to have captured his imagination.

'Forget all this stuff about the Nullarbor Desert and the Amazon. What about the English Channel?'

He was a journalist and within a week he had dug up all the press cuttings from around the time of my accident about Branson and Prince Andrew. Even better, he had organised not one but two documentaries.

The first was for HTV Wales about the Trevor Jones Trust, its work and my ambition to fly. This would be screened locally and cover much the same ground as the *Tomorrow's World* item, but in greater detail over thirty minutes rather than five. The second was to be a follow-up documentary by an independent company for S4C (Welsh Channel 4) tracking my efforts over the next year to find a suitable aircraft and, it was hoped, filming my flight across the Channel.

The S4C one started filming a month later at the Noel Edmonds helifest at Duxford where I was filmed meeting old colleagues and beginning to pick brains on the feasibility of finding an aircraft.

While this was going on, the big excitement was in finally moving from Wales to London. I'd had the spectacular offer of accommodation from the Rufford Foundation and after a year's search and six months of adaptions it was finally ready. It was a ground-floor flat in a mansion block in leafy Fulham, fully adapted for me with automatic doors, a shower room big enough for my chair, taps with handles on I could turn, electric switches I could use – a place I could call my own, work from, entertain from. There was a bedroom at the back separated from mine by the kitchen, offering a valuable space between me and my care assistant. Basically I could live as near as damn it alone and independently. The aim 'to achieve maximum independance ASAP' had at last been achieved.

I was incredibly lucky in my neighbours Charlie and Fi Turner. They soon invited me to dinner, one of their first dinner parties since getting married and all their best stuff was out. One of their guests was pouring me a glass of wine when his jacket caught the joystick. As the chair lurched powerfully forwards the joystick became trapped under the table, pushing it and three of the guests and pinning them up against the opposing wall. The Permobil has two strong motors and non-slip tyres. As the table hit the wall opposite me it began to tip upwards, and the food and the wine to slip down with the beautiful white tablecloth. I managed to wrestle my chair under control while those guests without table in their stomachs grabbed whatever lead crystal they could. Nothing was broken and I have been invited to dinner many times since. More recently, they have moved to Wandsworth and chosen a house with so many steps that my ramps aren't long enough to get me up.

There were not a few problems facing me before I could get flying again.

We needed:

1. Funding: This was not going to be cheap.
2. A suitable aircraft.
3. Somebody suitable to adapt the suitable aircraft.
4. Certification of the adapted suitable aircraft.
5. Certification of my health from a doctor.
6. A private pilot's licence.

The biggest obstacle was probably going to be the CAA (Civil Aviation Authority) rule that the pilot must be able to get himself into and out of the aircraft unaided.

In November 1991 the Trust held a big fund-raising lunch at

244

the Café Royal with various important guests such as the Duke of York. Another was Ashley Mayer, the managing director of Lillywhites, the sports store. After I had addressed the assembled company and announced my plans for a cross-channel flight it was Mayer who proved the more significant. He came up to me and offered to lend a secretary to help with administration such as getting letters out to potential sponsors. It was the most wonderful offer you could imagine.

The final sequence of the HTV documentary was made at the Midlands Microlight School where Bruce introduced me to Gordon Faulkner and the school's owner, Mark Amu, people he'd already consulted when still on the idea of the Nullarbor Plain.

Gordon took me up. It was my first flight in a microlight and quite a new experience to fly with the wind in my face and look straight down at the ground, especially as that day the wind was blowing well over the official limits for the aircraft, a Thruster, and the rest of the day's flying had already been cancelled.

Flying is like the old cliché of riding a bicycle – you never forget – so when Gordon let me have a go I found that I was able to take the Thruster off, to control it in the air (although never quite sure of his input from the back) and indeed, with the slightest of inputs from his rudder pedals in the rear I was able to fly an approach and land it too. Or so I thought.

Flushed with this success I lost my own scepticism and Mark Amu too became fired up with the idea, and agreed to help me find the right machine.

We visited a factory called Main Air where a new aircraft, something called a Spectrum, imported from America, was being constructed. We met the engineer who said he felt quite sure that he'd be able to incorporate the right modifications for me. I was less sure. The guy was a bit vague about what these mods might be and I remembered the difficulties there had been in converting the VW Caravelle and the Voyager for my use. Especially the problem of balance given that I have no muscle control below the shoulders.

It was a lovely-looking aircraft but plenty of people warned that it was the first of a type and that it could take a couple of years to establish the reputation of any aircraft in operating conditions.

In December Mark invited me to the AGM of the British Microlighting Aircraft Association at Duxford which was combined with a microlight trade fair. The Spectrum was there, now nearly completely built, but one look told me that there was something wrong about it for me. The instruments and controls were too far away and it was awkward for me to be lifted in.

Still, this was a trade fair and there was the opportunity to try out every aircraft type there, from the Flexwing (engine and seat suspended beneath a hang glider wing) to sophisticated motor gliders. Each was very different in terms of cockpit layout and access. It was far from easy getting into most of them and involved press-ganging a team of willing lifters each pulling on a different part of me or holding something clear on the machine.

It was an exhausting business. After about twenty aircraft we'd had enough and decided to leave. I was slightly disappointed as I was far from clear which was the best option and had resolved to extend my research further. 'What about that one?' I said to Mark on our way out. It was about the only aircraft I hadn't sat in.

'That's the Shadow, but the cockpit is so small you wouldn't fit,' he said. He was a big fellow himself. I asked to try it out even so.

We got some guys together to lift me in and within seconds of being in the cockpit I knew instinctively that the Shadow was the one. It was like Cinderella's slipper and fitted me perfectly. The very fact that it was small and cramped made it good: I felt just as if I was wearing it. Support for my torso was inherent.

A couple of other features also gave it potential. The joystick was on the right (not in the middle) and the throttle was on the left which meant that I'd be able to rest my elbows along the sides of the cockpit coning giving my body added stability. Because of the crampedness my arms wouldn't slip off, neither would a map placed on my knees disappear without trace on to the floor whence my paralysed fingers could never retrieve it. It also had a perspex canopy offering some protection from the elements.

The main modifications would have to be to those controls operated by the feet. I hoped it might be possible to fix the rudder to the throttle control on a dual-axis stick, so that movements back and forwards would control the throttle, sideways the rudder.

Another control that would need a bit of close attention and clever design was the braking system, currently heel operated.

Overall, even on that first sitting at Duxford, I could operate almost everything including the three switches. I had a great feeling that the Shadow offered me my best chance of getting airborne again.

That there would be no pilot more paralysed than me in the world seemed certain. Having seen what looked like a suitable aircraft I made enquiries worldwide to see if there was anyone whose experience I could borrow.

I found no record in Europe of any tetraplegic having piloted an aircraft. From America I got press cuttings about a tetraplegic who'd converted a microlight in the days before there were any regulations governing them, but his break was much lower than mine. In Israel a paraplegic had successfully converted a microlight, but he had full use of his arms, and in neither case was the aircraft as sophisticated as a Shadow. In the course of my enquiries I spoke to many sceptics, doubting that it would be possible under the current regulations and in the time available. It made me more determined.

The first thing to do was secure a little bit of funding to help get the project off the ground (literally). On my way back to

London I rang up Richard Branson from the car. He said he was a bit short of funds at the time, but that I should try him again later in the year.

Shortly afterwards I arranged to visit the factory in Leiston, Suffolk, where Shadows were made. It was a long journey for me. I got my cousin, Danny Bruton, to drive me in the Voyager because I'd have found the three-hour trip exhausting and I wanted to appear on tip-top form without showing signs of fatigue when we arrived. Five miles short Danny switched the seat over and I did the last bit.

We met the designer of the Shadow, David Cook, a prominent figure in the world of microlighting, who we hoped would agree to do the conversion. He was, among other achievements, the first man to fly a microlight across the Channel (if you don't include Louis Bleriot's effort in something which can't have been far outide today's microlight classification).

He was small, fortyish, definitely a talker not a listener. He told stories about his aircraft from the minute we arrived until we left – he was in no doubt that the Shadow was the finest available – and all the things people had done in them. They'd broken altitude records and distance records, two had flown to Australia and so on. He must have told each of these stories a million times before and yet he spoke as if it was the first time.

Although prepared to talk to me he didn't spare my feelings when it came to assessing the chances of doing my own Channel crossing. Some time before he'd been visited by Philip Scott, a tetraplegic with aviation ambitions whom I had visited when I came out of Stoke.

He'd taken Philip up, at one point giving him control, but found that he didn't have the strength to keep it out of a dive. Naturally he feared I'd be much the same. The unstated message seemed to be, I respect your enthusiasm but I'm not prepared to let you kill yourself, especially in one of my aeroplanes.

When we came to leave he accompanied us to my car

which he hadn't seen until that point. I zapped the automatic doors, the ramp came down smoothly. You could see that the engineer in him was both instantly impressed then surprised when I wheeled in and slotted myself in front of the steering wheel and everything closed up again. I think he'd assumed that Danny was going to be driving and yet Danny hadn't done so much as open a door for me.

I let the window down for a final chat and found that his entire attitude had changed. He mumbled something to the effect of 'Impressive piece of kit. Look, with the proviso that I think you won't be able to do it, it's a fantastic project. I'll think about it over Christmas and maybe we'll see about a test flight in January.'

He'd been right about Danny driving me, though. The day had worn me out. At the very first lay-by I pulled over. I was all in. 'Danny, you drive.'

David Cook thought about it and clearly came to the conclusion that it would be OK to offer me a flight – with luck it might dissuade me – so in January I went back to Leiston.

David had even made a hand grip for the joystick similar to the one he'd seen on my car's steering wheel in which I could lock my wrist. After a short display in which David demonstrated the remarkable handling characteristics of his invention, including a short landing on the village cricket pitch, I was strapped into the front. He was in the back when we took off. I was very nervous that his doubts would prove correct, that I wouldn't have the strength to fly the thing but as far as I could tell from the short flight the Shadow was the aircraft for me. It has a long wing-span and I was pleasantly surprised at how little input it needed from me to control it.

David seemed converted and won over, fired up even, and agreed to start work on adapting an aircraft immediately, although he still insisted he'd only be involved in the conversion and not in helping me learn to fly it. To watch this flight he'd brought along a couple of colleagues, both microlighting enthusiasts, who might help with designing modifications. There was Keith Garnett, who was in the electronics business, and a guy called Rex Garrod, whom he described as 'a special effects wizard'. If he had been born in the twelfth century he would have carried a wand and worn a pointed hat.

Rex had done a lot of clever work for TV commercials and designed some of the more innovative displays in the Science Museum. Sometimes he worked with his brother, a stuntman. The brother would drive the cars, he would blow them up.

The next day we visited his house in Mickfield. The first thing you see is a school of rubber dolphins with rusting metal insides. The doorbell is another indication of his character. You press it, then out of a box pops a bird which runs up a bicycle chain above the door releasing a toy train which runs along the window frame releasing a scoop of water which pours into a trough and somehow sets off a loud klaxon within the house.

He sized up what I could and could not do and I took him for a spin in the car so he could see how its systems worked and get some ideas. Rex cast his expert's eye over all the gadgetry on my chair, instantly recognising a lot of the standard components which Permobil use and charge a fortune for. Like everyone who sees them, he was very impressed by the combination of car and chair; he couldn't believe I could actually drive.

Like David, Rex was an enthusiast, a bearded boffin, never happier than when explaining his gadgets to you, something for which he has a gift. He could talk you round the inside of an egg cup and make it sound interesting. From his workshop he produced a giant biro which he'd made to demonstrate how they work. You got the impression that designing a braking system for a tetraplegic flier would be no trouble at all, or if it was, he'd have a lovely time solving the problems.

I felt confident that between David, Rex and Keith they would come up with something suitable.

The producer of the S4C documentary, John Watkin, already had quite a lot of film in the can and, fearful that if there was no aircraft there'd be no programme, he offered to pay the £2,000 deposit required to get work under way.

I took up the offer of a secretary sponsored by Lillywhites, recruiting Isobel Bircher. Another company, Laing Management, seconded to me a personnel manager called Jill English to help with the project. Her salary was being paid for by the Rufford Foundation, the owners of my adapted flat.

If I was to fly in the summer there was little time to lose.

The aircraft would have to be paid for by sponsors and then at the same time a fund-raising effort would be made on behalf of the Trust which would then be able to go out and buy equipment for those whose injuries resulted from sporting accidents. I'd been the major beneficiary of the Trust but now the effort was to be concentrated on helping others.

We'd been able to help one or two people, such as Owen Lowery, British Junior Judo Champion, who'd broken his neck. His National Health chair could carry a ventilator or a motor, not both. His school had raised £8,000 and so the Trust chipped in with the remaining £6,000 to buy him a Permobil.

The Trust had also lent my Volkswagen Caravelle to a young chap who'd broken his neck falling off a horse. That had been a less happy experience. We got word of it being used in Ireland by his mother to tow her horse-boxes around three-day events. Bill Carrington nipped off one weekend and nicked it back to give to somebody else.

Just as important as raising money was raising consciousness of how a severe disability could be overcome with the right equipment, enabling integration and participation on more equal terms than had ever been thought possible before.

So these were the aims of the project. Meanwhile funds had to be raised, the aircraft adapted and then I had to get enough hours on it and convince the powers that be to grant me a licence to go solo.

*

Another time constraint was that in February I was off to Miami.

Dad had heard about an excellent charity called 'Shake a Leg', a sailing school set up by a paraplegic my age called Harry Horgan, using adapted 22-foot day boats called Freedom 22s.

As it happened Mum's new Canadian boyfriend Dick had ninety-year-old parents living in Florida and she and he planned to meet out there in February.

I say 'new boyfriend'. It's rather a sweet story. Thirty years before, when Mum qualified as a physio, she went to Canada to work for a while where she dated a guy called Dick. By complete and utter chance she met him again recently while visiting old friends in Canada. This was the same Dick who she'd turned down thirty years earlier when he'd proposed to her (before my father did).

When they met again fires were rekindled and the upshot of it was that Dick came to live at Dan-y-Cefn with Mum. There's a bit in Mum's diary which says, '. . . really, and at my age too . . .'

He's a great improvement on Frank. She and Frank had been having difficulties with their relationship even before my accident, and when it happened he never really rose to his responsibilities to support her. On the contrary, he resented her looking after her son. Dick, however, is a top man. A professional pilot, too, who has flown most things from DC–3s through to my microlight.

So Mum was well positioned to find out about Shake a Leg in Florida. Her researches indicated that apart from the sailing there was a lot happening. At the nearby University of Miami there was a major initiative called the Miami Project where they were researching a cure for spinal cord injury and not far away there was a really good private physio clinic dedicated to spinal injuries.

I spoke to Shake a Leg on the phone, and described what I

could move. They sounded confident that I'd be able to sail their boats. I had my doubts but the thought of even being near the tiller of a dinghy again (especially in the Florida sun) meant that I weighed up the possibility of not going for about five minutes.

I decided to give Richard Branson another call. I caught him just as he was leaving the house for a family holiday. He said I should ring up Anne Leach of the Health Care Foundation, a body of which he was a trustee. 'You've got my vote and if you can get hers and that of one more trustee we'll make you an award.' £5,000 was the upshot of that conversation.

While I was away it was important that the microlight fund-raising effort didn't grind to a halt. I needed someone to continue the work in my absence and after meetings with various professional fund-raisers I finally settled on one firm and put what money I had towards hiring them.

They didn't inspire complete confidence – they seemed more concerned about the terms of their contract than anything else – but a decision had to be made. They were retained for ten hours a week, which totted up to £2,000 a month – not cheap, but then they promised to be very good.

I couldn't wait to get to Miami. What with the success of the Chrysler Voyager and the realistic possibility of flying again I had become slightly obsessed with finding out just how independent it was possible to become. I wanted to push my limits as far as they would go. I also wanted the world to know what was possible and to use a bit of publicity to help push down a few barriers.

With this in mind I suggested to John Watkin that he bring his cameras to Miami and film what I discovered, especially those activities not available in Britain. There would also be the opportunity to compare access to buildings and public transport with that in Britain.

I would demonstrate how a dependent quadraplegic could

cross the Atlantic alone – I wasn't going to take an assistant – buying in the services I needed along the way.

I got on the blower and started to arrange it. The first thing was to get a Chrysler identical to mine. The adapters, IMS, agreed to lend one but that fell through because no one would insure me for a month.

Persevering further I found a rental company with a drive-from-the-wheelchair Chrysler similar to mine available (only in the States) and arranged for it to meet me off the plane.

Care was less of a problem, quite the opposite of Sweden in terms of choice. It was just a question of deciding how much I wanted to pay. For $300 a day you get a qualified spinal nurse complete with medical back-up, for $50 you get a Cuban immigrant with no English and no training. I decided to pay $25 for a West Indian girl with nearly incomprehensible Island English just to put me to bed, sleep on the sofa and get me up.

Nineteen

I left for Miami courtesy of Virgin Atlantic. The film crew were to follow on a week later, also courtesy of Virgin.

On the plane out I had the good fortune to strike up a conversation with a pretty and vivacious blonde called Anneka Rice. I was able to say, 'Hi, Anneka, I've been shopping with your mum,' which was true. Her mum, an interior designer, had done some work with a friend of one of my brothers. Anneka's mum is – if you can believe it – even more exhaustingly energetic than her daughter. She had taken me around several fabric shops in Fulham and Chelsea, sweeping through the entire shop and selecting half a dozen fabrics for my consideration before I'd had the chance to get out of the car. I'd hardly have begun to think about the first bit of cloth before we were off to the next shop.

Anneka and I chatted for a couple of hours. I told her all about my planned filming with Channel 4 and about the sailing, the water skiing and scuba diving I was hoping to do in Florida, plus I told her all about the microlight challenge and its aims of promoting the disabled and the work of the Trust. During the conversation she suggested that on my return I talk to her producer about the possibility of doing a *Challenge Anneka* TV programme. 'The trouble with Channel 4,' she said, 'is that no one watches it.' The kind of jocular statement that only someone with a prime-time slot on BBC 1 can get away with.

Quite apart from meeting Anneka the flight was fantastic.

CAA regulations apparently prevent cabin crew from emptying leg bags, so the airline assigned me my own personal hostess. When she was not spoiling me she told me dirty jokes.

I was allowed to stay in my Permobil right up to the aircraft, in fact jumbos are wide enough for me to go all the way in, which makes a huge difference to morale. The problem arises when it comes to getting the heavy Permobil from the jetty down into the aircraft hold. Generally there is no lift which means taking the chair back through the departure lounge.

I always have a fight over how near the aircraft they will let me go before transferring me to a small, uncomfortable chair. On TAP to Portugal once the flight was delayed an hour and a half while the pilot insisted it was dug out of the hold and its batteries disconnected. I tried to tell him it was a dry battery and thus no fire danger but he wouldn't have it.

British Airways once dropped it and ended up paying me £3,000 for the damage their baggage handlers caused, although their letter was careful to point out that the small print showed that they had no liability to do so.

I have had a special steel box made for it, on which are written such helpful things as 'This Way Up' and 'Fragile' but few baggage handlers at any airport seem to take much notice. So it is always tense wondering if I am going to have my wheels when I arrive. As I was a guest of 'the Boss' Virgin had made a special effort to get my chair straight up from the hold and waiting for me.

The car company – 'Wheelers', run by a tetraplegic – delivered my car to the airport for me. Mum and Dick were there to meet me, of course, which made things easier, but they were on holiday and I was determined I should not make any extra demands on them.

The car was the same Voyager as my own although not an IMS one, and the conversion not quite as good. The door was not automatic, the hand control different, the power steering not as light, but I could drive it. Not bad for a vehicle arranged over the phone from England.

I settled into the hotel and with the help of my twenty-five-buck Island girl, who slept on the sofa, I had a restful night. In the morning she helped me up again before disappearing.

Outside I quickly discovered that I could be my own master. Miami's public transport system was moving towards a hundred per cent disabled access. There was a fleet of wheelchair taxis and around twenty per cent of the buses were accessible. The Americans don't put up buildings that aren't fully accessible, and those that haven't been are adapted. Even the City Hall, with a hundred steps up to its front entrance, had a ramp so that wheelchair users could go in by the same entrance as everyone else. I could go anywhere and better still, it was T-shirt weather.

I went on a bus just for the thrill of it, I hadn't been on a bus for so long.

'Where do want to go?' said the driver, after I'd got on.

'I don't know, just drop me at the next metro station.' The metro system was fully accessible too. You could roll yourself from platform to train with no help. Imagine it.

'This bus doesn't go near the metro . . .'

'Another accessible bus route then.'

'None on this route.'

We'd gone just a hundred yards and he had to pull over and get the lifting system out to get me off again. He was a bit hacked off, didn't quite embrace the advantages of accessibility as I did.

During the first week I got into my physio at the private clinic run by Robin Smith. I was doing a couple of hours in the morning four days a week. They were real pros, giving one-to-one treatment with every bit of equipment imaginable.

We established my goal, to transfer from the wheelchair to the plinth alone without using a sliding board. Something I still haven't managed, it remains a goal.

In the afternoon I went sailing. The boats could take six people, with two moulded seats for disabled sailors. A cunning design involving a counterweight under the cockpit allowed you to change sides by swinging the seat over. The obvious problem with sailing for disabled people is that the average boat could capsize in a strong wind. This had been overcome by the addition of extra lead and concrete to the bottom of the keel.

I spent the first week developing my technique and getting my ticket. I found it best to strap my left wrist to the tiller extension with a sail tie while I put my right arm behind the seat to aid my stability.

What a great feeling it was being back at the tiller of a dinghy as we sailed around Biscayne Bay under the warm winter sun.

In the second week I was joined by a girlfriend, Louise Husband, which enabled me to dispense with the $25 helper. Together we researched the possibilities for John Watkin's documentary.

I was very excited about this documentary because the presenter was going to be the greatest scrum half of all time, my schoolboy hero, Gareth Edwards. His autobiography was the first biography I had ever read.

Shake a Leg was only involved in sailing, but through their contacts and through Robin we tracked down other filming possibilities. Scuba I'd done at Gordonstoun, so we got that arranged, then there was swimming with dolphins and deep-sea fishing. I could have gone hang-gliding from behind a speedboat too but Robin talked me out of it.

When John and Gareth arrived with the crew they filmed me apparently arriving too. A bit of a set-up, but never mind, that's show business.

We all got on famously, I think Gareth might be one of the funniest people I have ever met. Some of his British Lions stories had me crying and choking with laughter.

For the sailing sequences Gareth and I went out on a race which Shake a Leg organised twice a week, along with a gorgeous paraplegic girl called Maureen Rung, who was also good fun.

I had my hand tied to the tiller and a strap round my chest to keep me in place. From the other seat Maureen had the jib and main sheet. Gareth was our safety number. Still, I kept him busy issuing commands as I used to order my brothers around on the Merlin dinghy we sailed as children. He may have been one of the all-time rugby greats but he didn't know much about sailing, in fact the water generally was not his element.

Mostly it was a pleasant and gentle breeze, enough to make it exhilarating for me but not frightening (for Gareth) – sun cream and T-shirts, perfect sailing weather. I was loving it. It had been four years since I last sailed.

I could see some trouble brewing in the shape of a large black cloud which was coming our way. Under it would be some pretty squalls, I thought. I ordered Gareth to reef the mainsail. Half-way through the operation I decided that the approaching squall would need two reefs not one, but despite great aptitude he had not a clue and it took him longer than I'd hoped. Then the squall hit us and the boat was tipped right on to its side.

I wasn't worried, even though water was pouring in. The cockpit was self-draining and the keel very heavy, the boat could never capsize.

The problem was that I was looking up at Maureen while she stared at the sea, hanging in her straps. Gareth had one hand for himself, one for her to stop her falling.

I suppose it was a bit of a mishap. While Gareth and Maureen had been reefing I'd been in charge of the main sheet. It was stuck in the cleet and I couldn't get it out. Normally Maureen was on the sheet but she'd given it to me while she helped Gareth put in a reef.

I couldn't get a grip on the it – one end between my teeth – and knock it out of the cleet to spill the wind.

Eventually I got the boat into wind and upright. Bloody exciting. So much so that the race was called off.

We had a further mishap with the cigarette boat carrying

the cameras. John wanted me to pass close by. On the third run in the guy driving the launch thought I was going to hit him – I wasn't, I'm a good helmsman – panicked and slammed the thing into reverse which made us crash, taking a slice of paint off his launch. The driver was beside himself with fury, blaming me, which is where Welshmen come into their own.

Gareth and John eat that sort of pressure with charm. Anyway, we got some great footage.

And so it went on. In the Florida Keys we went to swim with the dolphins. Gareth is not happy in water but had to go in for the sake of the film. For me the trick with the dolphins was to crook my arm while the trainer tried to persuade one to nuzzle in under it and give me a ride. Gareth just grabbed hold of a passing fin and was whisked about thirty yards away. There was something very comical about this great athlete disappearing up the lagoon on the back of a graceful dolphin, then struggling to swim back – he is a rotten swimmer, especially in a life jacket too big for him, but he had to come back because he was supposed to be looking after me. It took him ages to splash towards me. Meanwhile a dolphin had finally got the message about my crooked arm and carried me off to where Gareth had just come from.

We also went deep-sea fishing on one of those Earnest Hemingway boats which is where we hoped Gareth would come into his own. He broadcasts on fishing and knows a lot about it. Somehow, although we could see huge tuna fish leaping out of the water – a very spectacular sight – and he saw one nick the bait off his line we didn't get a bite, not, that is, until the very last cast when we caught a small barracuda.

The film crew and Gareth went, and I had a final week alone. All in all the whole experience of living in Miami had been one of such independence that it was as if I'd been cured. My disability was almost an irrelevance, everything was so easy in Miami. Well, nearly everything.

I'd been on one of my little trips, getting off at a metro

station about a fifteen-minute trundle from Robin's. I set off along the sidewalk. Half-way there I came across a huge crater – a couple of feet deep, six feet across – blocking my path.

The sidewalk had four-inch kerbs all along, so I was faced with a ten-minute trip back to the station. Or, going down into it and hoping to come back up the other side. It goes without saying which I did. I went down into the crater and of course I got stuck, wheels spinning. Shades of the cattle grid at Dan-y-Cefn.

The pavement was now at waist level. I shouted at passing cars, but no one took any notice. Then a truck stopped and a Black guy as wide as he was tall got out.

He was quite aggressive. 'What are you doing down there?' he asked. 'That's a dumb place to be, you shouldn't even be in this street.'

I didn't appreciate this lecture. 'Give us a hand out.'

He called his mate and they tried to lift me. 'No, no, push,' I said.

They got me out and then the big bloke said, 'Hey guy, I've got some advice. If you see a crater like this again, don't go in it . . .'

When I got to Robin's his jaw dropped. 'Have you heard where Trev's been?' he said to a colleague. 'You were lucky to come out of there with your wheelchair. I never stop my car for anything when I go through there.'

He told a story of another client who one night had his chair nicked and was left lying on the pavement. Apparently I'd traversed one of the roughest parts of town, the sort of place where an annual crop of stray foreign tourists meets their end.

The best thing that happened to me was when I was in downtown Miami. Being on my own and using public transport, I would get to meet all sorts of people.

A tramp came up and asked me for fifty cents. After relying on charity myself for four or five years this gave me a fantastic buzz and did my self-esteem no end of good. The spiel was,

'I've got two dollars, if you give me fifty cents more I can get a beer.'

I gave him the fifty cents but was puzzled. 'Why do you ask for fifty cents when you could ask for more?'

We fell to talking. He explained that he would say exactly the same thing to the next guy, it was the best technique. Not a stupid bloke; he'd been a civil engineer, things had gone wrong, his marriage had fallen apart, he'd decided to become a tramp. The Lord provided him with what he needed.

And if he was was going to become a tramp, then Miami was the place.

I got back to England to find that not a great deal of fund-raising had happened while I was away. The firm I'd hired had so far succeeded in raising only a £25 voucher from Sainsbury's and some free photocopying from Kallkwik.

David Cook wanted the next instalment and had stopped work. Essentially we had a project in crisis so Jill English, Isobel Bircher and I sat down to decide what to do next. Isobel was a lovely girl, bright, good fun, energetic, a joy to have round at the flat helping me but with two major drawbacks as a secretary. She was awful at typing and quite severely dyslexic. My spelling isn't the world's best either, so as a team made up of a dyslexic and a one-fingered typist our efforts at writing compelling letters to the kind of people who might give the project money were not dynamite.

Jill, though, was efficiency itself and it was decided she would concentrate on organising the event and the launch. My job, helped by Isobel, was to get the aircraft built and sponsored.

We got a lot of support from the Shadow owners' club and its secretary, Barry Burchill. One of David Cook's stories about Shadows was that Barry, who had been diagnosed as having terminal and inoperable cancer, bought a Shadow as a final fling, since when he had had not a day's illness.

First Barry persuaded one of the club's better-off owners,

James Edmunds, to put £5,000 into the project in the form of commercial sponsorship for one of his companies. This enabled us to pay David Cook to continue his adaptation design work.

The other idea the Shadow owners' club came up with was to get loads of aircraft to fly together across the Channel with me. The departure and arrival sites had to be arranged and everyone we spoke to suggested that the ideal place for the former would be Headcorn, a grass strip in Kent. It is a busy place with light aircraft, microlights, gliders, parachutists, ballooning and model aircraft flying. I went to meet the owner, Chris Freeman, who offered to make his airfield the base for the crossing which was to become, in Barry's words, 'the biggest Channel crossing since the Battle of Britain', and that was what Jill went away to organise.

All this meant that the Challenge could go ahead in so far as paying for the aircraft was concerned. The date set was 5 September. We were still way short of the initial plan of raising £100,000 to fund a national appeal and so decided to curb the ambitous plans for this.

I was a bit upset that the fund-raising firm had the gall to invoice us £6,000 for the almost totally unproductive three months' work, ten hours a week. Eventually our respective solicitors had to sort that out. We settled at paying half, which I still thought added up to an expensive Sainsbury's voucher.

Twenty

On the 5th I visited David Cook's factory and saw the nearly completed Shadow minus its paint job which would include the Trust's logo. Rex had given a lot of thought to the brakes but as yet had nothing to show. He was in favour of a pneumatic system with a little compressor and an air reservoir and promised he'd do it soon.

I sat in the tiny cockpit and tried all the switches and controls for manageability, all the time spotting little things which needed adapting.

On the right side remained the joystick, no modification necessary beyond a grip designed to lock my wrist. It looked as though there would be a solution to most problems, but the one big worry was whether I'd have the strength to work the rudder. There would be no way of knowing until I flew it.

On the left was the throttle which was now mounted on a dual-axis stick so that sideways movements could be used to control the rudder.

All the changes to the aircraft had to be certified by the Civil Aviation Authority and the paperwork for this, huge volumes of it, was being done by the British Microlight Aircraft Association's chief technical officer, Paul Owen. To some extent this is the sort of work the BMAA exists to do but he went far beyond what membership entitled anyone to and yet never charged for his work.

You got the impression that more time was spent doing sums, stress tests and paperwork than building the thing.

Having done all the hard work, he had to submit his report to an engineer at the CAA for approval.

On 29 May I visited the factory again and saw it newly painted red and white. The engine was fired for the first time with Breakfast Television in attendance. Jill had got the company used by Laing Management to design an identity for the campaign and a logo with which to emblazon the aircraft and any posters or promotional material we produced. We used the slogan 'A Question of Support', which had come out of an earlier idea to recruit sports heroes Bill Beaumont and Ian Botham as patrons of the Trust.

Rex had finally come up with an ingenious pneumatic solution for replacing the heel-operated braking system. Fire extinguishers are filled with foam but the foam is propelled by compressed air from a bottle in the middle. He'd borrowed the compressed-air bottle from an extinguisher and placed it in the wing root. This gave a reservoir which was topped up by a small compressor. Should the compressor fail there would still be enough air for a landing. The clever thing was – I say 'the clever thing', everything about it was clever – that I would release the compressed air into the system by pressing my head back on a pad.

If you are taxiing at speed you can steer using the rudder but at low speed you have to use the brakes.

Pushing back with my head released compressed air into the braking system. This air would then be distributed to the left or right wheel also by selecting the rudder stick left or right.

Thus the brakes, rudder and throttle were all interconnected but did not need to interfere with each other. Further, the system had to marry with conventional controls for any able-bodied pilot sitting in the back.

Part of the solution was a series of microswitches attached to the rudder/throttle stick in the front cockpit. If you had any throttle on, you couldn't embarrass yourself by applying both brakes by mistake, say on take-off.

*

A further pleasurable but time-consuming distraction in the middle of all this was the *Challenge Anneka* programme. I'd rung Anneka's producer as she suggested and she asked me to come up with suggestions for a challenge.

On screen it all happens with fabulous spontaneity, but in real life it takes a lot of planning. They didn't like my first suggestion for a challenge which was to take a tetraplegic straight out of hospital and equip him and his new house, showing all that is involved. I think they felt that it would be focusing too much effort on one person and cost too much. A couple of years later, though, they did completely adapt a house for wheelchair users as a half-way house for former patients of Stanmore hospital. The programme achieved a lot in raising awareness.

My next idea, to build an English version of Shake a Leg, bit the dust because it would have been impossible to get the boats donated.

Finally the focus shifted towards taking a bunch of wheelchair users scuba diving. The programme makers narrowed it to paraplegics with a concession to allow two tetraplegics, me (it had been my idea) and one other, my mate Sean Parry Jones. The location was sorted fairly quickly, Eilat on the Red Sea. The Israeli national tourist board was keen to help in return for a bit of free publicity.

Once the idea had been agreed upon there was a massive amount of ringing around to find suitable participants. I wanted to challenge the viewers' stereotypes and strived to get a group mixed in race, sex, age, weight and social background. Then it was virtually non-stop filming for four days, at my flat, then at the travel agency, apparently struggling to find seats on a flight out – though I don't suppose too many viewers bought that. There followed a weekend of medicals and learning how to scuba dive at the St Paul's school swimming pool and then on the Monday off we went to Eilat where the challenge came to fruition.

On our trip there was one woman called Joanna who'd

never been in the sea before and a bloke called Lorn who was so excited by the whole thing that he didn't go to bed for four days, preferring to stay in the bar in case he missed something.

It brought home to me the importance of the work done by groups like Back-Up, the Jubilee Sailing Trust, Sailability, the wheelchair basketball associations, disabled fishing clubs and all the million little groups that bring people together whether disabled or able-bodied.

Learning to scuba dive with a bunch of people similarly injured is much more rewarding than it would have been with the able-bodied, because you can share the experience more, feeding off each other. Disabled sport generally is a fantastic medium of learning and sharing, though I must admit I am as reluctant as most others to volunteer to join in with a group of disabled people. It takes someone to encourage you along.

It was certainly rewarding for me to get our group together. We had a lot of fun and they made a very positive and entertaining programme of which we were all very proud. I for one fell in love with Annie. I had hopes that when her marriage broke up she might marry me – still I live in hope.

Earlyish one morning as I still lay in bed I got a phone call from the CAA's medic, Dr Tony Evans. Immediately my hackles rose and I told him, quite unprovoked, that I was fed up with being told what I could and couldn't do. Most people who fly microlights don't require medicals, a letter from a GP will do. My own GP, Dr James, had already signed a letter to say that I was medically fit.

At first I said I wouldn't submit to a medical but when he said, 'You wouldn't want to spoil it for anyone else in your position in future, would you?' I relented.

He assured me that he only wanted to help but made me understand that I would have to have a medical check-up if I was to be given a licence. Reluctantly I agreed to visit him at Gatwick. My attitude was trenchant; discrimination by the CAA was not going to stop me flying, legal or not.

I got myself down there in the Voyager. I was convinced that the doctor would take one look at me and squash the whole thing so just before I got out of the car I took a double dose of Baclofen to steady the spasming in my legs and had a good stretch. I had to present myself as being as fit as possible, just had to hope and pray that I did not have a spasming fit in Dr Evans's presence.

The medical proceeded in the normal way: blood pressure, temperature, pulse, no communicable diseases, eyesight (20/20), hearing fine, no history of mental illness. My knee reflexes were normal. Urine sample? No problem, I have it on tap in my leg bag.

He put the question I dreaded; 'I have to ask you this, Trevor. Can you get in and out of that chair unaided?'

I thought, You bastard. You've been going through the motions, humouring me, knowing full well there was no chance I could pass this medical.

I said, 'You know I can't get out of this chair.'

'If you pass the flying exams and prove you can meet the criteria the CAA just might relax the getting-in-and-out rule for microlight aeroplanes. I'm afraid you'd still be expected to fly a medical flight test with an examiner of the CAA's choice. And of course you'll be expected to do your pre-flight checks just like anybody else, check fuel contents, control surfaces.'

That made me angry. 'That's ridiculous. How am I meant to reach the wing or get the fuel cap off? Look, I'll always have someone with me to put the aircraft together and to get me in. I'll supervise, they can do the checks. The checks will get done, it won't make any difference.'

He was trying to avoid a confrontation with me and just repeated that I would be expected to carry out all the checks as laid down in the pilot's notes.

Although Dr Evans had clearly been making efforts to be kind, to appear to take me seriously and to be careful not to condescend, the vibe I was getting was, You must be joking . . .

But I'd got my man wrong. At the end of the interview he surprised me by saying, 'I will pass you fit to fly, but you must carry a qualified pilot on your solo flights until you are licensed.'

Still I was suspicious; I had a mixed impression of Dr Evans. On the one hand I could see he wanted to help me in any way he could, on the other I got the impression that issuing a medical certificate was a risk-free gesture from his point of view. He thought I would never pass all the tests.

He walked with me to the car where he saw the door slide open, the ramp swing down and me slot in to drive off, all without effort. Then, just as had happened with David Cook, his whole manner changed. It's amazing the way that car changes attitudes. Over the years it has been the best ambassador going for persuading people what is possible.

Dr Evans is a good man and when it came to the medical side of getting me a licence my impression was that – without letting me know – he fought quite hard on my behalf against some pretty sceptical people.

During the whole time of the Microlight Challenge my carer was an Australian called Tanya. She was a lovely girl, perhaps the loveliest girl I have ever met and certainly the best care assistant I've ever had.

She was happy all the time and would breeze in and lift my spirits. She was very sensitive to my needs, anticipating them, sensing my moods and adapting to them, no small achievement given that I have never completely come to terms with needing full-time care and perhaps never will.

Once when she was putting me to bed I had what the doctors would call a reflex erection. I couldn't help it, wasn't aware of it even, it happens from time to time. She covered me with a blanket and said, 'I think I'll come back a little later,' in a way which made me laugh rather than be embarrassed.

When I go to see friends, if it can possibly be avoided I

really don't want a carer present. Partly you want to treat a carer in the same way as you would treat any employee; with respect, at times with affection, but always with some distance.

My perfect carer is like a butler who is always there but never there, they know instinctively when to retreat and never impose. It's a bit different from a Jeeves figure; Jeeves doesn't have to be a car or aircraft mechanic or secretary. Also, I like it if my carer looks right by which I don't necessarily mean a stunning female. Some of my best carers have been gay men. The job is far better described by the term personal assistant, facilitator or enabler.

The right person has to be massively competent in all sorts of departments; caring is about equal in importance with being a good mechanic.

If you visit a friend with your personal assistant you feel pressure to integrate them, often coming from the friend. I find it the most awkward time. Even if my PA has become a friend it is one from whom I need space, especially when we go out together.

Many of them are Australians who, gregarious by nature, find it difficult to be left out, but Tanya was very popular with my friends. You couldn't fail to like her. If she came with me on some social occasion she would always keep a distance. She would start a quiet conversation with someone else, allowing me to let my hair down unselfconsciously with my friends, knowing she wasn't attempting to listen in.

Often PAs unwittingly draw attention to me in a way I don't like. They ask me over-solicitously if I need something, cut my food up; straighten my collar. Tanya would completely ignore me which was brilliant.

She had the ability to socialise, the intelligence to converse if need be. Sometimes a PA draws attention to himself by sitting in a corner reading a book looking bored and left out, and then a friend feels he or she should go over and talk to him. Somehow Tanya could even read a book right.

That I should find someone to work for me with whose presence I could feel comfortable was a landmark in progress for me and could not have come at a better time.

At first Tanya was quite nervous about the microlight and obviously I was dependent on her to use it. She was anxious about hooking up the thirty-foot trailer and driving it but was massively practical and competent. We would assemble the microlight together, but once she'd got the hang of where things went she didn't need telling again and took a great deal of pride in looking after it. When she once had to drive the trailer through the night the experience didn't seem to faze her at all.

Competence was her trade mark in every department; a good cook – maybe that's the most important department of all – always well dressed and never late. I like my PAs to bugger off and leave me to myself. What they get up to in their quarters is their business, but if I call them I don't want them to look as if they have just woken up, or to appear resentful because I seem to have caught them in the middle of something more important.

By July the aircraft's modifications were ready to be inspected by the Civil Aviation Authority. The date for the challenge had been set at 5 September and Jill English's plans for a mass crossing of microlights were well advanced. In the two months remaining the Shadow would have to pass all its technical tests and I'd have to get in twenty-five hours of flying, including solo hours, in addition to passing ground exams. The exams would be a basic version of those I'd done in the Navy, so there should be no problem there, but having this finished aircraft and waiting for CAA approval was frustrating.

Before the inspector arrived David said, 'I wonder if they'll notice there's no fuel cut-off. I bet they don't.' It was a CAA regulation that there be a fuel cut-off in case of an engine fire. David and Rex had left it out because:

1. There was no room.

2. I'd never be able to grasp the ball-shaped handle on the lever to operate it.

3. It was argued that turning off the magnetos was just as effective.

4. There has never been an engine fire reported in a Shadow.

Of course the guy noticed and insisted that one be installed. The inspector was a bit puzzled and concerned by an apparent lack of brakes, but when the head-pad system was explained to him he was happy about that.

The aircraft passed the inspection with the proviso that a few minor details were attended to and a fuel cut-off installed in time for the test flight a week later, another challenge for Rex.

David flew it for the first time before the test pilot came.

He would not let anyone fly something he had not thoroughly tested out for himself. He was impressed with Rex's brakes and even remarked that the system worked better than his own.

The final minor panic was Rex's fuel cut-off; he improvised an electrical cut-off using a motor taken from a household appliance and a solenoid, don't ask me how. The key thing is that he did it the night before the CAA's test pilot came and it was ready to be tried.

The test pilot, a former RAF pilot, was a dandy and a perfect charmer, a complete refugee from a Biggles story. He'd flown everything under the sun and I felt a pilot's empathy with him. 'The braking may take a bit of getting used to,' he said, 'but you won't have too much trouble with this will you, Trevor?'

And neither did he. He took it up, putting it through all the manoeuvres on his list and on landing pronounced himself satisfied.

This left me the month of August – just four weeks – to rack up my twenty-five hours, to pass my exams and to satisfy the medical pilot from the CAA that I was safe to fly.

I rented a cottage near Mark Amu's flying school in Lichfield and went and stayed there with Tanya.

It must have been one of the wettest and windiest Augusts on record. Incredibly it was the 29th before my first flight. With the Challenge set for 5 September I was up against it.

I had Simon Baker sitting in the back. Simon is a top aviator, winner of several world and national titles in microlight competitions. It was nerve-racking for me knowing that my instructor would pick up the slightest sign of weakness. I may have had more flying hours than most of the people teaching me but I was desperately worried that I didn't have the strength to fly this aircraft we'd spent over a year finding and adapting.

He was a very personable, precise kind of pilot and a very good instructor. I felt he'd have made an outstanding pilot in the forces and was surprised he'd chosen the microlight world, but not that he was one of the best pilots in it.

That first flight was relatively straightforward in that the input on the controls was mainly Simon's as he showed me around the local area. We landed safely an hour later and Simon, all smiles, congratulated me. My euphoria and excitement were still tempered with doubt. During the flight I'd achieved everything Simon had asked me to do, but it had been too early to test my limits, the point beyond which I would no longer be able to recover the aircraft into controlled flight.

The only limit I was sure of was that one hour was enough for me that day. Tanya took me back to the cottage and put me to bed in mid-afternoon, whacked. The next morning I was still utterly exhausted when she came to wake me and tell me it was time to get up and go flying again. I could barely open my eyes, I had never slept so soundly or for so long. She dressed me and pulled me into the sitting position on the side of the bed. I was utterly exhausted, every muscle paralysed with fatigue, my brain had maxed out.

The Challenge was looking increasingly difficult. One thing was certain, there was nothing like enough time left to get the hours. To fly would be out of the question until I felt fully refreshed. If I went to the airfield now I would never be able to disguise my state from them. Concentration, physical strength, I'd have had none. Doubts about my ability, possibly fatal to my plans, would be sown in the minds of my supporters.

Tanya pulled back the curtain and my heart lifted a bit as I looked out and saw the trees bending violently in the wind. Just at that moment the phone went. It was Simon Baker. 'Bad news I'm afraid, Trevor, the wind's got up and it's pouring with rain. Can't fly today.' I did my best to sound disappointed. Thank God. I smiled at Tanya and subsided back into my bed.

My attempts at racking up the hours were repeatedly beaten back by the weather so Jill postponed the event from 5 to 12 September.

I lost my instructor, Simon, who had to go off to the world championships. An older guy called Graham Nock took over. He had been a Crab years before. I christened him 'Grumpy' because he was such a miserable old sod. A good instructor like Andy Barnwell (from Navy fixed-wing days) wills his pupil on. To be fair to Grumpy he seemed to want to get me through the course but I could almost feel this conflict within him when confronted with me and my disability. His head would be telling him I had been a Navy pilot while his heart told him that I was a smashed-up young cripple. He was wrestling with years of accumulated prejudice. Occasionally he would let his doubts about my capabilities slip out. As a result I did not enjoy flying with him, he made me nervous that he was just waiting to catch me out.

None the less I began to explore my limits, after all I needed to know what they were if I was to fly within them. Take-offs worried me. As the Shadow gathered speed down the bumpy old runway I felt I lacked control over direction, that I didn't have the strength to control the rudder. The Shadow would begin to veer left. I remembered my first ever solo flight in the Chipmunk when I'd gone careering off the runway. I had the same feeling of a lack of control now.

I learnt not to be afraid of this apparent weakness on the runway. The Shadow leapt into the air pretty quickly, before the veering left became too noticeable to Grumpy in the back. Once in the air it was easier to apply the right amount of pressure to the rudder and correct the fault.

I did have one major wobble in the air when I was up with Grumpy one day. I was banking steeply to the right during a forced landing practice when I didn't trust my weak right arm to have the strength to level the wings. Instinctively my left hand abandoned the throttle and rudder control to go across and reinforce it. The aircraft seemed to lurch as I sent my left hand back to its proper spot, paralysed fingers wrapped round the stick, wrist held in place between two padded rods. I saw myself being grounded as unsafe but when we landed Grumpy didn't appear to have noticed. Phew.

It was very soon apparent that I wasn't going to get the hours in time. The weather in September remained as wretched as in August and even when it was good enough to fly my stamina levels were such that I could rarely manage more than an hour a day. As 12 September came round I was still fourteen hours short.

It would not have been fair on the others to postpone the crossing yet again so it was with a heavy heart therefore that Tanya and I decamped from Lichfield and headed for Headcorn and the Kent coast from where the massed microlights were to take off. A year of preparation and I was going to miss it. Many of the fliers had sponsors of their own to satisfy and the event would have to go ahead without me. I was bitterly disappointed.

Many, including David Cook, thought I should fly in the

back of somebody else's aircraft; just being a passenger would surely be achievement enough.

Not for me, I decided. I would go as pilot or not at all. The word went round the Shadow world that I was letting everyone down. I didn't think so; flying as a passenger had not been my challenge, that would have been the antithesis of what I was trying to prove, namely that disabled though I was, I was still able. Not a passenger to be carried or looked after by others, but able to do things that people said I couldn't or shouldn't. 'Well done, Trevor, sitting in the back of a microlight as it flew across the Channel.' Get lost.

There had been a bit of needle from the Shadow world. I think David thought I should have been doing my training with Fiona Luckhurst who ran a microlight school specialising in his aircraft, but I preferred to work with Mark Amu and Simon Baker.

On Saturday 12 September I was at Headcorn to watch the massed microlights being assembled for their flight and to wish them well.

The departure was delayed because fog shrouded Headcorn airfield. It wasn't possible to see more than half-way across the runway. More disappointment was on its way; it wasn't just my participation which was no longer possible, the whole event was now threatened. The forecast remained for fog the next day too, so sure enough the whole thing was called off.

I'm certain a lot of people were bitterly disappointed. Secretly I was delighted. We quickly realised that here was another chance to put the whole thing back. Jill seized the opportunity to put the event off not just for a week but for over a month until 17 October. I'd get my hours.

I returned to Lichfield with Tanya and carried on racking up hours at Mark Amu's flying school with old Grumpy in the back. I had begun to understand my limits, to counteract in time the tendency to veer off left on take-off, how to overcome the many ongoing challenges in the cockpit, posed by my disability.

Lack of strength, stamina and dexterity were the most obvious challenges but in a way the psychological strain caused by a slight increase in the phantom pain was the most difficult.

The Shadow carries a lot of wing for an aircraft of its weight and is sensitive to small movements from the pilot. It doesn't require too much strength to fly. I never once regretted my choice of aircraft, in every respect she has proved the perfect choice.

We had one moment of drama when Rex's compressed-air system caught fire on landing one day, ironic given that part of it was adapted from a fire extinguisher. I thought it was the engine and cut it off, which at least proved that Rex's other system worked. We sent the parts back for him to fix and carried on getting my hours while Grumpy braked from the back with his feet.

Everything looked fine. I was conquering my self-doubt and, almost as important, the doubts of others. When Grumpy Graham Nock was unavailable another pilot, Nick Barnett, took over and I got on very well with him. On one memorable day I managed to put in five hours. Feeling that the man sitting in the back believed in you made all the difference. I knew he wanted me to succeed. Grumpy did too, it was just that somehow he was less good at transmitting the fact.

Then, out of the blue, I got this bizarre fax from David Cook signed by everyone working with him at Leiston. It said that he and all his staff thought that what I was attempting to do was foolish, irresponsible and dangerous. He urged me to abandon my idea of flying the Channel.

We were incredulous. The guy had been involved almost from the start. He'd put a huge amount of effort into the enterprise, gone to great lengths to help me. What a strange time to express doubts in such strong terms. He'd left it a bit late, hadn't he? Together we'd proved nearly everything that needed proving. Had the whole thing been a charade, an exercise in humouring me?

I read it, laughed and threw it in the bin, trying to hide how upset I was. Mark, Grumpy and Nick were furious.

I telephoned David to see what was eating him he said the same things to me as he'd expressed on his fax. 'If it were up to me, I wouldn't let you fly out of sight of the airfield boundary.'

There was no shifting him. Grumpy came into his own at this point. He penned a long and indignant reply in my defence and faxed it off.

We left it at that. They wouldn't budge, their view was entrenched, but in the final analysis it shouldn't matter what they thought. After all, I had the aircraft and it was paid for. I didn't yet have a licence, though, and I was terrified that word would get out that the designer and adapter of the aircraft I planned to fly across the Channel thought the whole enterprise foolhardy. Suppose the CAA got to hear? It could scarcely help.

I got my hours, this time with plenty of time before the new date. Simon Baker had returned from the World Championships and put me through a one-and-a-half hour Final Air Test (FAT), including engine failure and forced landing routines, all of which I had practised many times with Grumpy Graham and Nick. With the generous words, 'You can handle the Shadow better than I could', he told me I had passed.

More tense was the test the next day when Dr Evans of the CAA brought up the chief examiner, Julian Doswell, chairman of the BMAA examining panel – himself an airline pilot – to check whether, medically speaking, I was up to it. It started with my pre-flight checks when, with Dr Evans looking on, I got somebody else to check the control surfaces and remove the petrol cap.

I was also performing for the television cameras. A friend of a friend was marketing manager of Sega, the computer games company. They had sponsored some PR through their account with the well-known Lynn Franks Agency. They had arranged various televion interests in addition to radio, magazines and the newspapers.

John Watkin, who'd come to Miami with me and Gareth Edwards, was not there. He had no English-language broadcaster so he had agreed to share some of his footage with Peter Williams, who was making a programme for the series *The Human Factor* which goes out on a Sunday morning religious slot through TVS.

Midlands Television filmed as I was taken up by the examiner and put through various tests, mainly to see exactly how much strength I had. He would put the aircraft into various attitudes, increase the stick force and ask me to recover to straight and level flight.

We landed safely, everything looked as though it was going to be fine. Dr Evans checked out Rex's modifications from an aviation doctor's point of view and the chief examiner pronounced that so far as he was concerned he could detect nothing that might interfere with my ability to handle the aircaft.

Hey presto, a licence.

Not quite. There was paperwork to be signed and countersigned and sent off to Flight Crew Licensing. Apparently my application had now to be considered by a committee.

When I rang the authority to ask when I might expect an answer the guy I spoke to had just seen me on the local news. He warned me to count on no favours. 'Don't expect us to make an exception for you. Your application has to be considered in the normal way. We usually respond within three weeks.'

I said I wanted no favours, just a licence, 'but within two weeks, please. My challenge is in two weeks.'

There was nothing inately obstructive about the guy. He promised to do his best.

The next two weeks were the most nail-biting of all. O-levels, driving licence, Naval training, I had never been as apprehensive in all my life. I'd done my hours, passed my tests, the aircraft was fully adapted and approved, the Channel, or rather its far coast, was beckoning.

There were many pilots getting ready to fly with me, the press campaign was geared up, especially TV. It all hung, as we had known it would all along, on the CAA and their final decision.

Tanya and I settled into a hotel in Maidstone near Headcorn. Two days before the Challenge and still no word from the CAA about a licence. John Watkin was also down to film the final part of his Welsh documentary on 16 October when what looked like the crucial letter arrived.

I felt like an Oscar nominee as John opened the envelope and handed it to me to read first.

I must have pulled a face because he said, 'What, don't say they've turned you down, Trevor.'

'No, they haven't, they've granted the licence, but they've put two restrictions on me. I'm not allowed to carry a passenger and I have to have written permission in advance from the owner of every landing site I use. Can you imagine doing that each time?'

'Is that all they've restricted you?'

'Yes, but why can't they let me fly like anybody else?'

Within the hour I was up for my first solo flight since my accident. I can't remember if I got Chris Freeman's written permission to land on his airfield.

Probably not.

Twenty-One

The day of the Challenge, 17 October, arrived. Microlighters had started streaming in from the day before, and there would be around forty for the flight. Dr Evans was there too, having arranged to fly across in somebody else's aircraft. By complete chance this friend turned out to be the father of my great friend from the Navy, Simon Kemp.

Dr Evans told me that the licensing committee had been divided down the centre when it came to the question of my licence, some were against it altogether. Finally a narrow majority emerged in my favour. I was pretty sure I had Dr Evans to thank for that although he didn't say as much.

Following that famous fax there was not a great turn-out from the Shadow world. There was the secretary of the Shadow owners' club, Barry Burchill, David Gore and James Edmunds, one of my most generous sponsors.

Given that the event had been postponed twice I hadn't felt I could invite many friends and supporters but even so, many came, some making the effort to come down from Scotland.

My brother Stu was there with my young nephew Willow, and there were many friends from Gordonstoun such as the Knatchbulls and Alex Howard. Anneka Rice was there and Gareth Edwards plus the kids from St Mary's School Putney, my local primary school. I'd spent a couple of days there and they'd raised money for the Trust, but better still they'd done a brilliant survey of the new Putney Exchange shopping centre. It was full of wonderfully natural observations of the kind that only children can make; they'd tested everything. 'Doors to entrance too heavy for wheelchair users.' A dozen of them came down to watch the start of the flight.

It was a beautiful day, with clear skies and not a breath of wind. Peter Williams of *The Human Factor* had arranged for Caryl to come down and watch the event. He wanted a bit of love interest for his film. Caryl had refused – she certainly didn't want to be on telly – but Peter, had somewhat craftily promised her that the programme was a Christian one and this would be her big chance to spread the word of God.

It didn't work terribly well. As we met again for the first time since we broke up in the Loire I said to her, 'Give us a kiss then,' but she certainly wouldn't do anything like that on camera and dived for cover. Still, it was great to see her.

Navy friends had planned to be there in force, including several helicopters but FONA (Flag Officer Naval Aviation) had put out a cryptic edict, not referring directly to my flight but saying that 'No naval aircraft are to be used in fund-raising flights'.

In the event only a Lynx came from Portland piloted by an old friend, Mike Burroughs. He had with him a diver and a winchman. It had been kept quiet from FONA; officially they were doing Search and Rescue drills in the Channel.

My departure was held up by all the press. There were half a dozen different TV crews, as well as a dozen photographers and assorted reporters, all crowding my aircraft and asking me how it felt to be taking to the air again.

I was enjoying all the attention but by the time I took off I was twenty minutes behind the rest which was to have serious consequences, principally that the Lynx was with me and the rest had no rescue cover.

My flight was exquisite. It was only the second time I'd ever been completely alone in the plane and the first time had just been a short circuit. I felt a fantastic sense of occasion. There had been a great turn-out, far better than expected. This was the culmination of a year's work and five years of dreaming.

It was a crystal-clear autumn day of the kind that makes

England such a beautiful country. Everything was green and still, crisp and fresh. The sky was completely blue, there was a wisp of cloud at most.

When I took off I had the Lynx to one side of me and to the other a Queen Bee (a souped-up Tiger Moth). It had a television cameraman in the back as did the Cessna which was above me.

With this escort I turned 180 degrees towards Folkestone. There were twenty mintues of flying before edging out across the expanse of cold water stretching towards France. Coasting out was very exciting. From here on if I suffered engine failure the chances of surviving, even with the Lynx, were slim and there was that thought of going abroad.

I climbed as high as I could, but despite all the clothes I was wearing I got colder. At 1,500 feet I could only just bear it, so I levelled off, then in mid-Channel as I got colder still I had to come down to 1,000.

From about mid-Channel there was a lot of radio chat, much of it in French and I didn't pay a great deal of attention. All the way across I didn't see a single one of the other microlights.

In the Navy I'd spent a lot of time over the sea. I'd forgotten how much I'd come to enjoy that environment, I had a sense of coming home. It was staggeringly beautiful. The sun glistened off the sea, ships plied peacefully, there was almost no turbulence, it was just perfect.

On one side the Queen Bee, the antique biplane and symbol of the history of flight; on the other the Lynx, symbol of my past life. To be between the two I found quite moving.

I felt comfortable despite the cold in my perspex bubble. You get little sense of movement over the sea, even less in a slow microlight. Gradually the French coast came up and as I came within gliding range I started to relax. Make a big effort for the landing, I thought, conscious of the cameras. There was no turbulence as I came down the glide slope to land on the huge runway at Calais–Dunkerque, touching down just in front of the piano keys. Without question it had been the best flight of my life in any aircraft ever and I was ecstatic.

I taxied up to the waiting press. Gareth was the first to greet me and I was just trying to articulate what I was feeling when Jill English passed on a message she'd just heard. Peter Keel, flying another aircraft, had crashed in the Channel. His aircraft had sunk, no body had been found, he had almost certainly drowned.

Later it emerged that another aircraft had circled for a while and a fishing boat had come across and run over his sail sinking his craft – possibly that was what killed him.

I flew back in a sort of daze. More than a year's work had ended in the death of Keel. I'd never met him but I felt I bore some responsibility for it and, worse, I found that I couldn't bear that responsibility.

His body never was found, which was hard for his family. Some months later a memorial service was held which I didn't attend. Peter Keel's father wrote to me, disappointed at the lack of a Trust representative at the service. This shook me out of my moral laziness and I went to visit his widow and children to offer my condolences properly.

It had been slightly strange behaviour on my part. I'd never written to Tim Knatchbull when his brother was blown up and had been so moved when he took the trouble to visit me in hospital. Prince Andrew had got round to writing me a very comforting post-accident letter after a *Sunday Express* article. You'd think after all I'd been through I might have learnt.

After so much nerve-racking suspense I had finally achieved my challenge, certainly at the personal level. I'd become the country's and possibly the world's first tetraplegic pilot and flown the English Channel. The Trust had not benefited on the scale hoped for but the project did end up with a £10,000 surplus.

For some weeks afterwards I disappeared back into my shell to some extent, shocked by the death of Peter Keel. One of the things that got me going again was a fax from James Edmunds congratulating me on my achievement and saying how pleased he had been to have flown with me. 'What do you think,' it asked me, 'about getting together a squadron of adapted aircraft?'

After the Channel flight and following a fabulous week's holiday with Tanya at the Cyprus home of my dad's oldest friends, I turned my attention to the Trust. It was in crisis with just £12,000 in the bank and the same amount owing to my mother. There was no sign of any gifts and Priscilla had nothing in particular organised. My living arrangements had been fully adapted, in every sense I was as independent as it was possible to be. My lawsuit was progressing well, the indications were that it would yield sufficient to cover my care and equipment costs. What I now needed more than anything was a job.

I was appointed Trust manager and Priscilla was made redundant. We closed down the office in Kensington and the Trust moved into my front room. I was unpaid and apart from the phone absorbed most of the running costs myself.

If it hadn't have been for a couple of large donations that year, one from Sir Donald Gosling of National Car Parks and another from the Butlin family (who had kids at Gordonstoun) we'd not have made any grants to tetraplegics at all. Salary and rent were eating up the money made at parties, which created a lot of goodwill and gave great PR, but never raised a large amount of money. The £10,000 surplus from the microlight challenge was the first event in two years which made the Trust a net profit.

I had a new personal assistant, a Canadian called Linda, another human dynamo and the best possible replacement for Tanya, although I missed Tanya a lot when she'd gone, still do.

With Linda's help over the course of the next year I did more work than I'd ever done before. She slightly became a victim of her own efficiency; she was so competent and hard-working I gave her more and more to do.

I was also helped by Ross Westgate, a friend of Stuart's, and together we set out to raise £80,000 – enough to cover the set-up and first year's running costs of a charity which would then be professionally run.

A meeting was organised of the Trust's key supporters at which we announced the target and our subsequent intention of recruiting a top fund-raiser and administrator to start a new charity registered in England and Wales. The old Scottish entity, the Trevor Jones Trust of which I had been the named beneficiary, would be dissolved and replaced by an English one, more generally for sports-injured tetraplegics in need, later called the Trevor Jones Tetraplegic Trust.

One of the first things I did after that was to go and see James Edmunds, not entirely about his idea for a squadron of microlights. He'd just sold his businesses and was seeking new challenges, and I secretly hoped I'd be able to recruit him to run the Trust, since administration is absolutely not my strong point. He declined the job offer, but before I went took out a cheque-book and wrote a cheque for £30,000, enough to buy two mobile homes from which to operate the new flying school for disabled people.

At the time I was seeing rather a lot of round-the-world walker Ffyona Campbell. I had written to her as a possible Trust supporter. Her father, I read in the newspaper, had been at Gordonstoun and was also a helicopter pilot. In addition, she was starting the South African leg of her walk on 20 March, my birthday. I wrote to her suggesting that she could walk for people who can't walk. She called me, we had lunch, got on well and kept in touch.

When her walk was temporarily blocked somewhere in Central Africa because of a war she came back to the UK and occasionally stayed in my back room.

'Trevor, you were an inspiration. Every time I flagged I thought of you,' she said. This may be true, but I doubt it. My power to inspire was certainly not mentioned in any of her books.

Another thing she said while she was staying with me was that she had been having 'trouble with her sexuality' and that she had rediscovered it through me. This is another fact that she hasn't referred to in print. Rather disappointing.

She had a fascination with some of the difficulties facing me and decided that if she was going to walk for those who could not walk, she wanted to know what it was like having to use a wheelchair. So much so that she insisted one day on getting into my spare chair and going out to lunch.

We got into the restaurant with some difficulty. The management were marvellous, moving heaven and earth – or chairs and tables – to get us in. We got stuck into our meal and were having a good feed when she announced that she needed to go for a pee.

I said, 'Ffyona, don't forget you're in a wheelchair.'

But no, she was desperate and would not be swayed from her course. She simply stood up, got out of her chair and walked to the loo.

I was to be upset again, but not entirely surprised, some time later when at the last minute she changed her mind about walking for the Trust and teamed up with Raleigh International.

Throughout the summer I visited clubs and schools up and down the country, talking about the Trust and receiving cheques. Michael Mavor, now headmaster of Rugby, invited me to address his students in chapel one Sunday. On the way back I was going along the pavement to the San where I was staying and wheeled through a puddle disguising the kerb. I found myself falling through the air, ending up face down in six inches of water. The boys rescued me and lifted me back into the chair. Then as we arrived inside it was pointed out that I, or rather the chair was on fire. Smoke was pouring from the motors evidently short-circuited by the water.

I also put in a visit to my old prep school Gayhurst, where the headmaster, Ron Eglin, who had taken over from Mr Stafford was going into retirement. After my visit and hearing what I had to say to the boys he volunteered his time to help with the Trust and over the course of the next year we visited each of the country's twelve spinal units, making contact with patients and staff and forming links on behalf of the Trust.

The Trust benefited from all sorts of supporters who came forward with contributions. An old school friend, Rory England, worked as a broker for the City firm Tullett and Tokyo. He sat next to England rugby star Peter Winterbottom and persuaded him to nominate the TJT as joint beneficiary in his benefit year.

Any opportunity to get the microlight out was leapt upon. I used it to collect several cheques, one from Blackpool Pleasure Beach, one from a Winterbottom dinner in Leeds, another from a field outside Derby. Possibly my most memorable flight was down to the naval air station at Yeovilton.

John Beattie, who'd been my senior pilot when learning to fly the gazelle and more recently had flown the Channel with me, was now CO of the Navy's historic flight. He invited me to fly into the annual Yeovilton Air Day. 'We'll get the crowd going, do a pitch for the Trevor Jones Trust and the lads can take the bucket round.'

I was told to arrive at 13.30 exactly. Five minutes after the Phantoms, five before the Migs.

Dad was over from the States. He had never seen me fly and helped get me ready at my base, White Waltham airfield near Maidenhead. He then set off in the Voyager with the trailer and Permobil, to meet me at the other end.

It was ninety miles to Yeovilton, flying time about one and a half hours. The weather was great and everything was going fine as I picked out various landmarks such as Stonehenge on my way down. Then I noticed that my fuel gauge was showing empty. I wasn't too bothered by this because the gauge is not that accurate; I knew exactly how much I'd put in, how much the engine consumed and how long I'd been up.

So far on this flight I'd flown for an hour and twenty minutes. I could see the runway five miles or so ahead and was about to get ready for my part in the air display when my engine stopped. Automatically I started to go through my actions, first bringing the speed back to fifty knots, trimming her out and issuing a 'Mayday' call, all the time looking for a suitable field to put down in.

I chose a large field of yellow rape beneath me and started a 360-degree turn towards it to end up into wind. Half-way round I found that I was lower than I'd thought. I was over a rise before the descent into the Vale of Yeovil and unlike a practice when the propellor is ticking over, now it was stopped, creating extra drag. I was coming down quicker than anticipated and well short of the yellow rape field.

The field chose me, a lightly ploughed one. I couldn't tell what was in it or how deep the furrows were. All the fields around were small, sloping and enclosed with dry-stone walls. Basically I had decided to give it my best shot but for an instant could not help thinking that I might die.

I came as low as I dared over the hedge, hoping to give myself as much of the field as possible to stop in. Having just cleared it I saw that the furrows were not too deep and that the field was full of cabbages.

I was going faster than expected, downwind now, and the lines of cabbages sloped off downhill. I was not that pleased by the surface the cabbages offered but then half-way along the field turned to grass just as I got the wheels down. 'I've done it!' I thought and pressed my head against the brake pad.

Nothing. 'Shit, I'm sure I turned it on.' The compressor interferes with the radio so I often turned it off until ten minutes before landing. The compressed air bottle used to leak a bit too. I tried again. Nothing.

Ahead of me a stone wall loomed as I careered downhill. I had a tiny bit of steerage from the rudder but not nearly enough to turn. I was going to thunder into it, then a gap emerged with barbed wire stretched across. More by chance than judgement I went into that instead. It worked exactly on the principal of an arrestor wire on an aircraft carrier, snagging the Shadow on the perspex cockpit. I was lucky there was a canopy otherwise I'd have been decapitated. It was dented but did not shatter.

I looked for my radio but the map must have knocked the channel selector. When I got back on frequency all I could hear was a helicopter pilot saying, 'Found him, I think he's OK. He's in the hedge surrounded by a herd of cows.'

The cows were very curious and it was very frightening as they pressed against the aircraft, licking it, more excitement than they'd seen in a while. I told them to 'Shooooo off', but they took no notice.

A Sea King landed, scattering the cows, thank goodness, and a first-aid crew climbed out followed by John Beattie. John was one of the older pilots in the Navy and normally had one of these healthy, ruddy complexions which comes either from years at sea or years in the bar. He was as white as a sheet which made me laugh. Bloody hell, I thought, he doesn't know if I'm alive or dead. The good news is that I'll be able to tell him I'm alive.

He lifted the canopy. He is a very experienced pilot and no stranger to crashing himself, having recently found a field in a Seafury from the Historic Flight, after engine failure and losing a wing on a tree, but surviving by sheer skill. He said something very reassuring to me: 'Well done, you got it down in good shape, we'll get you out and I'll fly it back.'

I was decanted on to a stretcher and carried into the helicopter where I found myself staring up at all these parachutists in leotards who'd been waiting to jump in the display (after me and the Migs, presumably). There was a doctor who came and asked, 'You OK?'

'Yup.'

'Better do a few checks,' and he prodded me, asked me if I felt any pain, to which of course I said 'no'.

'Everything seems fine,' he said. 'You can get up off that stretcher now and go and sit with the others, if you want.'

I still hadn't found a suitable person to run the Trust. We'd been sent various candidates and I had interviewed them with the help of the chairman of the Cranfield Trust, an offshoot of the business school.

The Rufford Foundation meanwhile offered me an experienced charity director free. I lunched with the candidate, taking along Ffyona Campbell for a second opinion. Her view was that I should turn the guy down. It had seemed to her that he'd spent the whole lunch either moaning or talking about himself. 'You can't possibly employ him,' she said.

'But he's free.'

'Do you really want to work with that bloke?'

I decided in a moment of personal vanity that I could do better finding someone myself. I turned down the foundation's offer. It is one of the worst decisions I have ever made.

By the summer Ross Westgate and I were comfortably on our way towards our £80,000 target when I was sent a guy to interview called Jim Goddard. Right from the first he seemed to challenge my reasons for wanting to run the Trust.

But he had a good CV and strong references. He was a youngish sixty with no family and a military intelligence background. It turned out that his speciality was turning the enemy round – on to our side. At least he was Army – Pongos are not quite as bad as the Crabs. I offered him the job.

I was happy to concede the running of the trust to Jim and he administrated the creation of the new Trevor Jones Tetraplegic Trust very efficiently.

A new board of trustees was invited with my postal chess partner from Stoke, Charles Wylie, as chairman.

In order to be absolutely squeaky clean with the Charity

Commissioners, a special dispensation had to be sought for me to be both employee and trustee of the new Trust. My job was one I was uniquely qualified for so it should not have been a problem.

I was all geared up to attend the first trustees' meeting, collecting a pen and my jacket, when Jim said to me, 'Where do you think you're going?'

'I'm going to the trustees' meeting.'

'But you're not a trustee.'

I looked at him unbelieving.

'Didn't Charles explain?' he asked.

'No.'

'The trustees have decided that, in the best interests of the Trust, it would be better if you were not a trustee.'

I was absolutely devastated. The Trust was what I wanted to dedicate my life to. I had benefited massively from the charity of friends and supporters. I hadn't enjoyed being the subject of charity run by well-meaning, able-bodied people, but it had given me something to live for. Besides, I had commissioned the new charity.

Jim employed a secretary for himself and in addition a professional fund-raiser called Nicola Plummer. He confided in Nicola that the Trevor Jones Trust was in a dreadful state and included a character study of me which described how impossible I was to work with.

When she arrived on her first day, Jim showed her around our lovely office in Mayfair (sponsored by Cluttons the estate agents), introducing her to Jane, the secretary, who told her lots of positive things about the working environment and how well we worked as a team. Only when he'd done that did he bring her over to me.

Tensions rose between me and Jim and soon a kind of guerrilla war developed. Nicola didn't like him much either. She was an outgoing, chatty kind of person but if ever she struck up a conversation with me Jim would tap the glass of his cubicle to shut us up.

The problem lay in his very rigid style of going about things which probably wouldn't even work in the Army. For example, my desk was too low for me to squeeze my legs underneath when I was in my Permobil wheelchair, so I got the girls to raise the legs with telephone directories. When Jim saw what had been done he stormed that he had not programmed this bit of work. Every task had to be on his 'programme' and we were not supposed to do anything unless it was. The girls were made to take the telephone directories out and wait until raising the table found a slot.

Sometimes guests would come into the office but Jim often didn't introduce them to me. I disagreed with him on almost every issue. When I argued with him he'd threaten to leave.

'If either of us leave, it would be the end of the Trust,' he'd say. It was true that the Trust had been in a bad state and I believed him. Ross and I had raised that £80,000, we had a duty to make sure it didn't go to waste.

The whole thing was gettting me down but on the other hand, for the first time since my accident, I was wheeling out of my home, up my ramp into my own car, driving to work in an office, doing something constructive. Even if it was only designing an application form for a grant, I was doing this – not yet every day, but three days a week. For me it was the pinnacle of my achievement post accident, I had never felt better in terms of the underlying feeling of self-worth it gave me.

A further side effect was that it had the unexpected benefit of easing the relationship with my personal assistant. Gone was the feeling of being on each other's back twenty-four hours of the day.

Also I cared passionately about the future of the Trust. Without being a trustee I knew that my influence over its direction was irrecoverable. It emerged that Jim was pressing for a 'faceless organisation', raising funds more from grant-giving trusts than the public, and the trustees had bought the idea. It was the antithesis of my own trail-blazing, 'hang it from the rafters' approach but for the sake of the Trust I decided to stick with it for just one year before doing something different.

Jim was dead against James Edmunds's microlight project. James had even offered to fund it, it was going to cost the Trust nothing beyond giving some administrative support. Surely this was the purpose of the Trust? Jim instructed me to say 'no' to Edmunds. He was adamant that microlights were not what the Trevor Jones Tetraplegic Trust should be involved with. 'Expensive microlights are incompatible with a grant-giving trust for individuals in need,' he said.

It was not the way I saw it – all the people who sponsored me across the Channel were given to understand that I intended to teach others once I'd shown it was possible. We had another huge argument.

Then one day the crunch came. I'd gone to lunch with Nicola. We had had a laugh, quite likely about Jim Goddard. When we returned he invited her into his office and I could see (but not hear) him administering some kind of bollocking to her. She came out and went straight to her desk, eyes front, not looking at me.

As soon as Jim was out of the room she told me what he'd said: 'Nicola, I don't want to see you taking sides in this. I cannot emphasise enough how much I do not want you to spend your lunch hours with Trevor.'

I'd had it. I got my jacket. The irony is that I had to ask Jim Goddard to put it on for me. And then, in so far as one can storm out of an office in an electric wheelchair, I stormed out and never went back.

In December, Charles Wylie came round to see me, to tell me that a decision had been made to change the name of the Trevor Jones Tetraplegic Trust to the National Sports Trust, and in fact now it's called REGAIN. I was thoroughly disillusioned by the whole thing. When Charles asked if I would help the new entity I said I wouldn't, I'd had enough. It had been a strained meeting – he didn't take his jacket off and sit down, or accept a beer. When I said I wouldn't help he walked out.

Disappointed by my abortive involvement in the Trust, I resolved that 1994 would be a year of fun and consolidation. The two aims were interchangeable. I embarked on some serious physio under Sue Edwards at the National Hospital in London. I went to Miami again and to Sweden where I got back on skis while finishing off the documentary with Gareth Edwards. I'd thought it was going to be like tobogganing but it turned out to be quite skilful and much more like normal skiing than I had imagined.

The interesting thing is that I went skiing with a broken leg. Not many people have done that. I'd broken it when my leg went into spasm while driving, at least I think that's what happened, I didn't notice at the time.

I was helped enormously in March when John Cahill, my solicitor at Stewarts, got the Ministry of Defence to concede fifty per cent liability for my accident. The other fifty per cent had been my fault. John rated that as a pretty good result, having warned me not to expect them to agree to more than forty per cent liabilty. At last, with the principle of liability conceded, the legal battleground could shift to the all-important question of 'How much?' After six years of legal battling, we were nearly there.

Interim payments started, which meant I could at last afford to employ two PAs to share the workload and I could afford to take the lease on the flat upstairs for them to live in.

The case was to rumble on for another two years, though, while we sought to justify a huge claim. It had been an extraordinary fight already. After struggling to get legal aid there was a further fight to get hold of the MoD's official accident report. A Court of Appeal ruling in another case run by Stewarts had opened the way to get that and rightly; the cause of my accident could scarcely be considered a national secret.

Subsequently no investigative stone had been left unturned. Stewarts had taken testimony off Navy people, even former British ski champions Martin Bell and Konrad Bartelski, to help in their argument that supervision had been inadequate. Then finally they had manufactured a model of the hillside itself which helped establish that the trainer could not have seen the part of the hill on which I had my accident.

The microlights had been handed over to a new charity called APT (Aviation for Paraplegics and Tetraplegics) set up by James Edmunds. He bought the original one from the Trust and gave it to me. What a man. It meant I still had my wings.

As a member of International Wheelchair Aviators I was in touch with like-minded people all over the world and an invitation came from Germany for me to attend an event called the Rolli Fly-in run by Martin Schultz of Die Rolli Flieger. I needed to cross the Channel again and to get permission to land in Belgium, France and Germany.

The Belgian fax was brisk and efficient, saying simply, 'You are granted permission for Belgian Airspace under the rules and regulations of your current licence.'

The Germans had hitherto refused permission for all German wheelchair users to fly, so my request had to go to the Minister of Transport in Bonn. The reply came after many phone calls. It was nothing like as brisk as the Belgian one, being ten pages long. It listed all the rules, in classic German style, of what I could and couldn't do, the only trouble with it being that the whole thing was in German and I couldn't understand a word.

With the French I faxed off my request and when I got no answer followed it up with a phone call, but I couldn't get hold of anyone. '*Monsieur Dupont est en vacances,*' I was told but eventually I managed to get hold of somebody who told me I had to do this and that. I did my level best at this and that, but eventually nothing happened and I decided it would be more straightforward to fly across France without permission and without landing.

My PA at the time was an Aussie called Emma. She was new on the scene. I'd recently got her through an agency but we'd never quite hit it off, and I had already told the agency to look for someone new when I got back.

Emma had said that the car and trailer would be no problem, but I could tell she was nervous about it and about driving on the wrong side of the road in Europe.

I had misgivings about going with her, but there was no time to fix me up with a new PA to my somewhat exacting specifications and I was desperate to get to this mass meet of disabled pilots, only the second one ever held.

I set off for Germany, forgetting my troubles the moment I was in the air. Emma had her own ferry ticket for the Channel and I had booked a hotel where we were going to meet.

After a short stop at Headcorn where Chris and Jamie Freeman lent me a life jacket and filed my flight plan, I headed off across the Channel, nice and high. It was such a lovely day I hit 6,000 feet.

Chris Freeman sent his twin-engined Islander, complete with parachutist all ready to jump if I ditched, to follow me to the coast of France where it waggled its wings in farewell. I headed up the beach at 1,000 feet towards Ostend.

I landed on the huge runway and taxied in. They were expecting me and sent out an ambulance to lead me in. Nobody spoke any English as I tried to explain in my hopeless French (in Ostend they speak Flemish) that I had no need for an ambulance but just wanted to clear customs and get refuelled. They had no interest at all in my papers and certificates or any of the things I'd taken so much trouble to get, but were fascinated by the aircraft and how it worked.

I stayed in the plane while they brought a man across who spoke fluent English, that is to say a man who was English.

Given this, it was amazing how our communications broke down.

'Yeah, we've got to mix the oil with the petrol,' I said, 'and then pour it in the tank.'

He didn't quite get the hang of the methodology I was suggesting and poured the oil straight into the tank and then of course there wasn't enough room for the correct amount of petrol. So they had to siphon it all out again while I sat roasting on the tarmac. He then mixed it in a can before putting it back in my tank now in the correct ratio. I don't want to sound ungrateful, but he was a bit of a plonker.

Meanwhile the wind had got up, it must have been blowing about 20 to 30 knots so I had to ask them if they would walk me out to the runway holding the wings so that the Shadow wouldn't be flipped over. I ended up with this long procession behind me: ahead was a Land Rover with flashing light and each wing had a walker, including one fat Belgian who was struggling to keep up. There was nothing I could do about that; you can't run the engine at low enough revs to satisfy the walking pace of a very large man, so he was soon puffing and sweating. We were followed by the ambulance, two fire engines and a car for the fat wing walker to be driven back in. I said my thank yous, revved up and headed south over Belgium.

I was very tired when I found my destination, Namur, having already been in the cockpit for about six hours. There was still quite a wind so I was careful not to get flipped over as I turned off the runway towards the buildings. There was no sign of life and no answer to my radio calls, none at all.

I taxied as close as I could to a building with the intention of shouting but no one was available. The sun was setting and just as I was wondering what to do, I spotted an aircraft starting its propellor. I taxied across and parked my aircraft in front of it, blocking its passage until its pilot was forced to climb out and investigate.

He disappeared into the building and emerged with a

completely charming young man, a Sabena trainee pilot who couldn't do enough. Before long he had my aircraft in a hangar tucked up safely for the night, knocked together my Quickie wheelchair and put me in a taxi on my way to the hotel I'd booked from England and at which I would meet Emma when she arrived later.

The Hotel Château de Namur was beautiful. The porters paid my taxi – I had no francs – checked me in and deposited me on my bed, knackered.

The dining-room was full of Japanese tourists so they decided to serve me dinner in the room. When they came to take my order there was a knock on the door, then a long wait and then followed lots of subdued muttering and fiddling with the door handle. It became apparent that they were locked out and could not find a spare key. The original lay on the table by my bed. I had no idea what floor I was on, but after a while I heard scraping at the window and a well-dressed but slightly scuffed waiter fell head first into my room having presumably climbed up the drainpipe outside.

The door was opened to smiles and apologies. He straightened out his clothes, dusted himself down and took my order for dinner. The food was French cuisine and delicious. I ordered a good wine which was served with my halibut by two elegant waiters who stayed with me chatting in Franglais and answering my every whim but all the time refusing to sit.

And then Emma arrived. It was clear from her general demeanour that she had had a difficult trip and blamed it on me. She had a drink and a bath, and then I asked her if she could get my Permobil out for me. I'd been feeling a bit trapped in my room even though the waiters had looked after me well.

She said, 'So you want your wheelchair now?'

'Yes.'

'It's so much effort for everyone, why don't you just wait until the morning?'

'Well, I'm always willing to listen to your opinion on things,

Emma, but I would really like my wheelchair now and then we can get away first thing.' I had various things on my mind. Tomorrow was a bowel day, then I had to get to the airfield early for my next flight and I needed to be independent from the word go. We ended up having a row about the whole thing.

I didn't want to wait until the morning. Being able to do something how I want, when I want, is the key. That's why I own a wheelchair costing £17,000 and employ full-time assistants at £65 a day.

She moaned and groaned and said she wanted to go and get the trailer which she'd left somewhere in the town, so I said, 'OK look, just get the wheelchair out of the car, leave it in the car park, and I'll sort myself out.'

By this time most of the staff in the hotel had left for the night, but I managed to get two to transfer me to the electric chair and help me to phone Martin.

'Look, things are not good with Emma, is there any chance of finding somebody else when I am down there?'

He said, 'Leave it to me.'

The next morning's bowel movement didn't go well. I had taken my laxatives the night before but Emma was being bloody awkward and didn't attend to things properly. The result was that I had an accident so we had to go back to the hotel to get me cleaned up and change my trousers which I think she just threw away. She also threw away the cover to my Jay cushion (a special cushion filled with gel, which prevents pressure sores).

We got slightly lost on the way to the airfield, which didn't help matters, and by the time we arrived were even more at daggers drawn than before.

She just went off and sat in the sun sulking while I got a bevy of helpful people from around the place to get my Shadow out, fuel it and put in the little wheelchair. I planned my route and filed my flight plan, all with help from people on the airfield who just happened to be in my way. You couldn't have asked for a kinder bunch.

As I was flying to Germany I had to plan the flight and needed help with all this, and all the maps were a bit strange. It was new territory and, forgetting the cow, I was very excited.

By this stage I was refuelled and ready to go but Emma still hadn't lifted a finger beyond getting me up. We were to meet at the hotel near my day's target, a place called Egglesbach. She had directions and the phone number.

My flight was the longest I'd ever done on one tank (since Yeovilton I'd had a larger one installed) – two and a half hours, mostly over forest. In fact I was a little unsure of my position when I found the Mosel and decided to fly down it until I could identify a railway bridge.

From there I headed for the Rhine which more or less took me to Egglesbach aerodrome, chosen because I had been told I could clear German customs there.

I was beginning to get the fact that nearly nothing on this journey was going to be completely straightforward. I couldn't understand a word of what they were saying about my landing, as a result of which I landed the wrong way up the runway, which didn't matter too much as there was no wind and little traffic.

They were expecting me, knew I was a wheelchair case, assembled the Quickie out of the back and were positively unteutonic in not wanting to see my passport or papers. I was greeted only with a statement that to my almost non-existent German sounded like 'Nichts microleichts', or words to that effect. I could not understand why they were so upset until someone later told me that landing a microlight there was an offence in Germany for which they could remove your licence.

They popped me in a taxi driven by a law student who interpreted for me until I was settled at the hotel, where I knew they spoke no English. They put me by a table in the courtyard where I had a beer or two and a Wiener Schnitzel, and there I waited for Emma.

In vain. It began to get late and I was collapsing with fatigue so I asked the proprietor, 'Kann Sie in die bed helfen?'

* * *

So there I was, the world's most paralysed pilot, stuck in the middle of Germany, with nowhere to stay, no one to help me to bed.

I managed to recruit various helpers around the aerodrome, but then decided that it was getting too late and the whole thing had become too tight to handle. The guy who was mixing my fuel wasn't German but a Black Gambian. He'd lived in England for a while before coming to Germany to study to be a mechanic. He'd failed to get a job and was now working as a petrol pump attendant.

After I recounted my tale he said, 'My God man, I don't believe it,' and promptly offered to drive me down to Erbach with his girlfriend.

'That's really kind of you, but I think my immediate problem is how to get to bed tonight.' I didn't feel I could really go back to the same hotel. There was no way I could have continued my journey in the car, it would have been five or six hours. It was very hot and I was absolutely exhausted physically and emotionally, and just wanted somehow to overcome this rather unexpected problem.

Completely unprompted he said, 'Don't worry, I finish here at ten. I'll book you into a hotel near my home and then come along at eleven and put you to bed, get you up the next morning, you don't worry.'

I went to the hotel he booked for me, but there was no wheelchair access. It was too hot to sit outside even, but eventually they improvised some ramps and got me in. I had a delicious Wiener Schnitzel, then I got the porter to hump me on to the bed.

I'm sure he would have put me to bed too, but the whole

business of getting people to put me to bed had grown so enormous in my mind that I waited for the kind Gambian called Manx and his girlfriend who arrived promptly as promised.

The next day they got me up again too. I showed him how to change the driver's seat across so that he could look after the car while I flew off down to the Rolli Fly-in at Erbach which is near Ulm.

The pair of them were great. They seemed thoroughly enthused by the whole adventure they'd found themselves accidentally embroiled in. When we went back to the airfield Manx reluctantly hijacked a couple of student pilots to help lift me in. It takes quite a while to get ready for a flight but at last I was in, with a line on my map, and all systems apparently go.

The last check I did was a radio check with the tower. Something was wrong and at first I couldn't figure out what. It soon became clear that my battery was flat and that the spare one I had left on charge overnight hadn't charged up either.

I asked if I could leave without a radio but they said no. It was a very hot day, 35 degrees in the shade and God knows how hot in the sun where my plane was parked, and I had quietly begun to roast. They got me out of the aircraft and back into my Permobil. There was not a breath of wind as I wheeled into the shade of a hangar and drank and doused myself in water to cool down. I was so hot and exhausted I couldn't talk.

The problem to be overcome was how to charge my battery. After quite a lot of delving, my growing team of mechanics found the culprit – a loose wire.

We had to solder it back on, but because it was a Saturday everything was locked up. Eventually a soldering iron was found but with no plug, so they plugged the wires straight into the socket. Unfortunately that didn't seem to work either.

They were all very positive about my problems, which was remarkable because by this time they had every right to throw up their arms in despair and insist that I give up and drive the final leg by car.

Various avenues were tried to get the soldering iron ironing. A plug was taken off my Permobil's charger and put on the soldering iron, and then this was plugged through the German/English adapter. That worked but then no solder could be found – there wasn't enough residue left from the original join where the wire had come loose to work with either.

After an extensive search some solder was found. My trickle charger which charges batteries slowly overnight was dis- carded in favour of a big booster charger which was found lying around in the hangar. Finally this was connected up to the radio battery with another dollop of solder, because of course there were no compatible plugs between my equipment and theirs.

We reckoned half an hour would be enough to get my battery going sufficiently for the final two-hour flight and the couple of radio calls I'd perhaps need to make. Just as it started to charge my Permobil conked out, its battery obviously had not charged up overnight eithar. The plug was transferred back on to my wheelchair charger and I was left on my own, immobile, plugged into the wall (a safety interlock disconnects the motors while the chair charges).

I had plenty of water to drink and pour over myself, but while they were away the smell of gently combusting battery began to hit my nostrils, so I screamed until somebody arrived to disconnect it.

I think I eventually got airborne at about five in the evening. It was a particularly beautiful flight down through the valleys towards Erbach. Because I was enjoying the scenery so much I did most of it at low level.

Finally, perched on the banks of the Danube, my destina- tion came into view. During my approach something hap- pened which had never happened to me before in the microlight. The ground hit me at least ten feet before I was expecting it. It was quite the worst approach and hardest landing I have ever done and I couldn't understand how I'd done it so badly.

I taxied in over the beautiful grass strip towards a brand-new clubhouse, built in varnished wood, which must have cost a fortune. There were microlights, gliders, paragliders and aircraft lined up, and lots of people in wheelchairs drinking beer and eating. A band was playing.

I was looking for where it might be appropriate to park close enough so that they could lift me out, when I drove into the tail fin of an antique Sterman. Again it was the kind of error I just don't make, I know how long the wings of my Shadow are and have a good sense of how much distance to leave. I turned off my engine, and sat there in a heap of embarrassment.

I'd just flown across Europe to go to this meeting. Against odds which seemed to get steeper each day I had finally arrived and after an appalling landing driven straight into someone's proudest possession, a veteran Sterman.

My hosts began to make their way across to me. When I was lifted out of my cockpit everyone was cheering and clapping and the band played 'God Save the Queen'. I thought they were taking the piss because I'd driven into the Sterman, but in fact there had been an announcement over the loudspeaker that this tetraplegic pilot had just flown in from England.

I was lifted out and put in my Quickie wheelchair, and then I realised what the problem was with my landing. I was completely and utterly dehydrated and exhausted, spent. Until that moment the adrenalin and excitement of the occasion had kept me going, but once in the chair I could no longer sit up straight and flopped from side to side as people came up to talk – really I could do nothing beyond smiling and murmuring incoherently.

Then Martin Schult introduced himself, this man with whom I had spent so much time communicating by fax and telephone arranging the whole bloody trip. It had seemed as though I'd been on to Martin virtually every evening about getting permission for this or that.

It was an emotional moment. I was dying of thirst, over heating and exuberant at the same time, and we just sort of fell into each other's arms.

Epilogue

About two years after leaving Stoke Mandeville, I got a call from a friend. It was just as I was moving into my new adapted flat in Fulham. 'Trev, I met a friend of yours, Sean Jackman, visit him, he's very depressed.'

Sean had left the Star and Garter Home in Richmond. Meeting him there had been a turning point in my life, post accident, perhaps *the* turning point. He'd saved me from the misery of an institution and I owed him one.

Now he was living in a Cheshire Home. It was infinitely better than the Star and Garter – he had his own room and his own bathroom – but he still didn't want to be there and who could blame him? He wanted to be living with his lovely wife who'd stuck by him, and his daughter, now two years old.

Financially it made no sense for him to be there either. His local authority were paying a lot for his place, money which could have been far better spent on personal assistants and adaptations to a council house. For some people a Cheshire Home might be the answer, but not for a young man like Sean.

I called up his social worker. She explained to me his problem in much the same way that he had done. Sean was caught between two councils and neither would take responsibility for him. The social worker felt sorry for him, angry for him even, but wasn't exactly going to take up the cudgels on his behalf.

I couldn't believe that his social worker was so accepting of this situation. 'Perhaps you should get a bit of publicity for this guy,' I suggested, but could tell by the way she said 'That's a good idea' that it was a non-starter with her.

Tim Knatchbull, I remembered, was now working for the Esther Rantzen programme. I spoke to his producer and recounted the tale of Sean Jackman. 'Can't something be done?'

He didn't sound very hopeful. 'We get thousands of calls a week, there is only a tiny proportion that we can follow up.' None the less a programme did get made.

Such is the power of TV that even before it had gone out the council had found Sean a suitable house and a care package which would enable him to live at home with his wife and baby.

My case against the Ministry of Defence came to a head in the spring of 1996, two years after they'd conceded fifty per cent liability.

We arrived outside a court room in the Royal Courts of Justice where my barrister, Christopher Wilson-Smith QC, began a negotiation with the opposing barrister which resulted in a settlement of £2.5 million, so the £1.25 million I received makes me a millionaire. It sounds a lot, but it basically amounts to enough to buy a house, pay for care and a new car once every five years.

The settlement is structured to protect me against inflation and to guarantee a standard of living for life so at least now I know I will never be dependent on my mother for care.

I see Mum less these days. My independence has freed her and we've gone back to the normal relationship between mother and grown-up son. She's there if I need her and she's rediscovered real happiness knowing that I'm fine.

Of course if she needs me, I'm there for her too. The other day she visited the vet to administer some jabs to Plodge the cat. 'It won't take long, Mrs Jones, Plodge won't feel a thing,' he said as Plodge went limp.

'What's happening?' asked Mum, slightly alarmed.

'But I thought you . . . Oh, my goodness, I'm sorry, I've got the wrong Mrs Jones.'

It is one of the penalties of living in Wales and being called Jones. Plodge had been put down by mistake.

Obviously when your mother suffers a major bereavement like that, her eldest son shoulders responsibility and comes into his own. I got her a kitten very similar to Plodge which we have called Splodge.

The microlight is still getting the hours in and during the summer keeps me in or out of trouble, depending how you look at it. I returned to Germany in 1994 with marginally less drama and the year after took part in 'The Great Adventure', a microlight race from Madrid to London, arriving back the day after prize-giving, having being forced to sit out the tail of a hurricane in a French chateau. The CAA are considering my request to carry passengers and cease having to get written permission from everyone. APT (Aviation for Paraplegics & Tetraplegics) in Salisbury is well equipped to accommodate most disabled people who would like to be pilots. Phone Jack Simpson on 01722 410744 for further information. There are a few more flying tales that might be worth telling one rainy day, so if this one goes well, who knows, there could be a sequel.

Charity-wise I do what work I can for the Spinal Injuries Association. We have a Christmas Ball at the Dorchester which is excellent fun. After the last one Stu, Angus, assorted friends and I carried on to the Dorchester Club downstairs. That was a hassle, it took them about half an hour to work out a route to the club down a lift and through the kitchens. Once we were there I was told to keep out of the main room and sit in the back 'because you are a fire hazard'. It was a long time since I'd been called a fire hazard but we refused to move while the man sought a higher authority, and parked by the bar. He wasn't happy about that, but tough. I hope the disabled contingent didn't put the Arabs off their classy call girls.

I take the care assistant recruiting process far more seriously than I used to. I no longer make the assumption that I will have the personal skills to get the best out of whoever works for me as I did in the past. That just doesn't work. I've got this brilliant bloke called Jeremy at the moment who is fantastically thoughtful and competent (he even thought up the title for this book). It is not an easy job and not something that just anyone can do.

The indefinable is the most important thing and that's still difficult to pick out at an interview; the male PA before Jeremy left one day having fallen out with the other assistant. She came back to a note and all her bras stuffed down the loo.

What next? I would like to get married and have kids. I am constantly interviewing candidates for the job of Mrs Jones but at the time of writing there is no front runner.

Sadly, I've lost touch with Caryl who she has found and married her Christian prince. I was sorry not to be at to her wedding.

The real 'what next?' though, is something called The Next Challenge Ltd, a project far more ambitious than the microlight challenge, at least on paper, but I think it will be easier to pull off. People believe now that I can achieve mad goals.

I am going to sail a yacht around the world.

I've already found the yacht. It is a fifty-four-foot trimaran with very wide decks made by Walker Wingsail. Mr Walker is another David Cook, a maverick inventor. He has spent twenty years designing his revolutionary yacht. It doesn't have a canvas sail but an array of three wings pointing upwards, giving propulsion on the same basis as an aircraft wing gives lift, so there will be no flapping canvas and ropes to cope with. The boat is controlled from the cabin by a joystick and the angle of the wingsails is calculated automatically by computer.

The boat has already sailed the Atlantic and survived being caught in a hurricane so I am confident of its seaworthiness.

Having found the yacht I'm looking for the major sponsor and for smaller ones too. I have calculated that I need £400,000 and I've only just started, so there are plenty of opportunities available, including slots for crew. If you'd like to know more please get in touch. The address is at the back of the book.

Once the vessel has been adapted for me I plan to use it as a hospitality platform for things like Cowes Week and then enter a series of European offshore races in 1998. After that it will be put to work introducing other severely disabled people to hands-on yachting in 1999 and in the year 2000 I plan to circumnavigate the globe, raising funds for spinal injuries charities, taking in the Olympic Games in Sydney and the Americas Cup race in New Zealand.

Mad?

Impossible?

You just watch me.

If you would like to know more about how you can support The Next Challenge or simply want to make a donation, please contact:

Trevor Jones
The Next Challenge Ltd
38 Bishops Park Road
London SW6 6DZ

Tel: 0171 731 8403   Fax: 0171 731 4597

Homepage: http://members.aol.com/nxtchall/index.htm
email:nxtchall@aol.com

"People like you are a real inspiration to me!"